St. Louis Community College

Forest Park
Florissant Valley
Meramec

Instructional Resources
St. Louis, Missouri

GAYLORD

CAMPAIGN
COMEDY

Humor in Life and Letters Series

A complete listing of the books in this series can be found at the back of this volume.

Also by Gerald Gardner

All the Presidents' Wits

The Censorship Papers

Robert Kennedy in New York

Who's in Charge Here?

The Watergate Follies

The Shining Moments

The Quotable Mr. Kennedy

News Reals

The Actor

The Back of the Incubator

Is That Seat Taken?

Miss Caroline (with Frank Johnson)

No One's in Charge Anymore

The Tara Treasury (with Harriet Modell Gardner)

The Way I Was (with Marvin Hamlisch)

Speech is Golden

I Coulda Been a Contender

CAMPAIGN
COMEDY

Political Humor from Clinton to Kennedy

GERALD GARDNER

WAYNE STATE UNIVERSITY PRESS   Detroit

Library of Congress Cataloging-in-Publication Data
Gardner, Gerald C.
   Campaign comedy : political humor from Clinton to Kennedy / Gerald Gardner.
     p.   cm. — (Humor in life and letters series)
   Rev. ed. of: The mocking of the president. 1989.
   ISBN 0–8143–2504–1 (alk. paper)
   1. Political satire, American—History—20th century. 2. Presidents—United
States—Election—History—20th century. 3. United States—Politics and
government—1945–1989. 4. United States—Politics and government—1989–
5. Electioneering—United States—History—20th century. I. Gardner, Gerald C.
Mocking of the president. II. Title. III. Series: Humor in life and letters.
E839.5.G323   1994
324.973′092′0207—dc20   93–33349

Designer: Elizabeth Pilon

For Harriet

Contents

Introduction

The men and women who make their living from mocking presidential candidates found an embarrassment of riches in 1992. Every election year seems to lend itself to political humor, but 1992 offered world-class opportunities. The primary season went over the top for both parties. For the Republicans there was Pat Buchanan; as satirists sought the humorous vein, he found the jugular. For the Democrats, Jerry Brown floated somewhere near Pluto while Paul Tsongas swam laps.

1992 also offered something special—a billionaire with big ears and a funny haircut who started his own party. There was also the ever-appealing George Bush and his teenage running mate, providing a reliable target for whimsy or malice. And best of all, there was a Democrat who, unbelievably, showed signs of *winning*. For a long period, Bill Clinton thoughtfully provided the voters with a scandal a week involving those perennial favorites: sex, dope, and the draft.

Small wonder that America's wits repaid their leaders with an outpouring of humor that lit the political landscape like, well, a thousand points of light.

But then, Americans have always had reason to be thankful to their political humorists when election year rolled around. What would we do without these gadflies who provide a rush of levity and wit to our quadrennial marathons?

Americans should be especially thankful for Art Buchwald, Mark Russell, Jay Leno, Garry Trudeau, Jules Feiffer, and Mort Sahl; for editorial cartoonists like Paul Conrad, Pat Oliphant, Mike Peters, and Herb Block; for the *National Review, National Lampoon, Spy,* and *Mad*; for Bob Hope, Johnny Carson, and the actors and writers of "Saturday Night Live." And with a nostalgic look over our shoulders, we should all thank our lucky stars for the creators of "Laugh-In," "The Smothers Brothers Comedy Hour," and "That Was the Week That Was."

Thanks to them, and to the journalists and entertainers who illuminate the electoral scene, Americans needn't always look at their politicians, parties, and political struggles with a sober, solemn, self-serious air.

Thanks to the satiric insights into the pretensions and posturings of our leaders, we are able to keep a sense of perspective about our presidential candidates.

Thanks to the humorists who brighten our election campaigns in the bright glare of their ironies, we can maintain our sanity, even when those who seek our votes seem most crazed with their quest for power. We can keep our sense of humor when the candidates' frailties, follies, and frauds seem most manifest.

Bromidic as it may sound, humor is arguably the most essential element in a democracy. Curiously, the one ingredient that totalitarian societies seem to share is a lack of humor. In a dictatorship, the practice of satire is a jeopardous pastime. This is doubtless because no public figure willingly subjects himself to the barbs of the satirist if there is a way to dispose of the troublesome fellow. There were few cartoons mocking the Führer in the Nazi press or Saddam Hussein in the *Baghdad Gazette.*

As our planet becomes more autocratic, rulers tend to become more hostile to humorous reproach. This is not altogether surprising. Humor can be a wounding weapon, and a persuasive one. The witty plays of George Bernard Shaw proselytized more theatergoers than the grim narratives of Henrik Ibsen. So humor is considered subversive by the powers that be, who often pay it the ultimate compliment of suppression.

Humor is necessary in a democracy for reasons other than serving as a device for mocking fools and knaves. In a free society, every few years the populace engages in a wrenching struggle for power. Humor lets us take the issues seriously without taking *ourselves* too seriously.

And Americans certainly take their politics seriously— especially once the World Series is behind them. A presidential campaign could be a most divisive exercise and one that leaves wounds that are slow to heal. Yet, it is essential that once the votes are counted and nearly half the electorate finds their savior has been denied (in 1992 more than half), the struggle cannot end in bile and bitterness, regardless of the depths of our differences. Humor helps this bonding process. If we can laugh at the failure of our fallen hero or the feet of clay of the victor, some of the pressure is released. It is a consummation preferable to storming the palace.

If humor is precious to the voter, it is doubly so to the candidate. For the president or challenger on the campaign trail, he and his staff are beset by a never-ending series of problems. Acrimonious charges, malignant editorials, insidious rumors, dipping polls, rallies where the microphone unaccountably goes dead, others where the faithful do not appear in the expected numbers, a substantive speech that the press ignores and the public scorns—all of these are enough to sap the spirit of the candidate. As S. J. Perelman advised: "Go into politics—earn big acrimony." Humor lends a healing balm for this campaign travail.

Absolute power corrupts absolutely, as does the prospect of absolute power. So humor has the added merit of preventing the presidential candidate from developing messianic delusions. No man is a hero to his butler, and no man is a hero to the cartoonists and journalists who follow his campaign odyssey. To find yourself the target of these witty men and women is to be both humbled and freed of self-delusion. Every politician is his own best defense attorney. Each judges his opponent by his actions and himself by his motives. A heroic face looks back at him from his motel mirror. The candidate is further insulated against unpleasant truths by obsequious aides who have their eyes on a White House office. But when a presidential candidate becomes the object of the rapier wit of columnists, cartoonists, and comedians—a Jay Leno or a Mark

Russell—he is less ready to ignore his own deficiencies. To err is human, to forgive supine. And humorists do not readily forgive the errors of presidential candidates.

The dissection of humor is not a promising enterprise. It is not unlike the dissection of a frog in a high school science lab. The student is permitted to take a close look at the innards of the frog, but what has he really learned? Dissecting political humor is equally unproductive, and so this book will not attempt it.

However, it is useful to examine humor in the context of the presidential campaign that generated it, and this we will undertake to do. For the issues of a political battle and the personalities of the participants are magnets for the humor of observers, and they are illuminated by it. (Indeed, they often provide far more illumination than the candidate might have wished.)

The humor of presidential campaigns is seldom bland. Too much is at stake, and emotions run high. When Senator Edmund Muskie was moved to tears in a New Hampshire snowstorm because a newspaper editorial had pilloried his wife, it was not long before bumper stickers appeared reading: VOTE FOR MUSKIE OR HE'LL CRY. Candidates can survive laughter but not snickers, and so it was not long before Muskie withdrew from the race. Similar visceral humor was aimed at Richard Nixon, John F. Kenedy, and Hubert Humphrey. The targets, respectively, were venality, religion, and verbosity.

Campaign humor is frequently caustic. Perhaps it must be strident to pierce the growing apathy of the voter. "Humor is anarchistic," said Malcolm Muggeridge, the irascible one-time editor of *Punch*, and anyone familiar with the mordant humor of Mort Sahl knows Muggeridge was right.

Be it mordant or antic, this book explores the sweep of presidential campaign humor and examines the relationship to the issues and personalities of the campaign. Humor is, after all, a basic form of communication through which the press, entertainers, and the candidates themselves convey their skepticism, anger, and arguments. There are many issues that are best joined with humor, and many subjects that are best discussed with it. And given the unrelenting pressure of presidential campaigning, humor is a wonderful outlet for frustration. It is a release for the insiders, who are ravaged by exhaustion, and for the outsiders, who are enraged by obfuscations.

There is irony in the fact that the people who create our most delicious campaign humor—columnists, cartoonists, and comedians—often have a serious conflict of interest. Editorial cartoonist Jeff MacNelly of the *Chicago Tribune* expressed it well when he said that he is often torn between "what is good for my country and what is good for my business." It might be observed that Richard Nixon's fiercest foes in the comedic community would have been denied a promising target had Nixon lost the 1972 election to George McGovern. And where would America's humorists be if Ronald Reagan had lost to Walter Mondale in 1984? The mind boggles, along with the funny bone. If each man kills the thing he loves, as Oscar Wilde said, then each humorist loves the thing he kills.

But frequently, given the vagaries of the public will, comedians find that they have lost a wonderful target for wit. A Dan Quayle gets voted out of office to be replaced by a wooden Al Gore; a George Bush with all his syntactical flaws and curious body language is replaced by a Bill Clinton with nothing but a saxophone and a libido that has been beaten into the ground. What to do?

But sing no sad songs for the satirists. Though they will briefly miss the easy targets of Bush's words and Quayle's vacuities, one can be sure they will find rich fodder in the new First Family. Said political satirist Harry Shearer, "I recall people asking me 'Aren't you going to miss Ronald Reagan? Bush isn't funny at all!' Well, Bush was hilarious and Clinton already offers more prospects than Bush did."

Inevitably, the satirist's eye focuses on the people with the most power, and in the next few years that will mean Bill and Hillary. Satirists feel no reverence for the presidency. Their aim is irreverence. And, as political humorists like to remind us, "We don't create the news. We just react to it." And should a little blood flow, well, that's part of the game.

Actually, it appears a somewhat daunting job for the comedy writers to find a fresh vein of humor for each new president. But never underestimate the inventiveness of these cut-ups. America's wits always seem to develop some sort of amusing caricature. The chapters of this book reveal the characteristics of the presidents (and their challengers) that funnymen have seized on through the years. Only rarely have they failed to find the right button.

Whatever respect or fear of reprisal that may have inhibited humorists in the earlier years of the republic have gone the way of the buggy whip. It may also be that at one time the public's moral standards and reverence for the presidency left little room for such derision. But today, the mocking of the president is a cottage industry and a thriving one.

Campaign humor can also be viewed as a public service.

As a sometime participant in national political struggle, I am drawn to the unmistakable conclusion that it is impossible to endure the stresses of the campaign trail without a well-developed sense of humor and the wisecracks of witty people. Ronald Reagan loved to swap jokes with anyone within earshot. Gerry Ford thrived on funny lines. Jack Kennedy swapped jokes daily with the reporters who covered him. Most incumbents and challengers need this steady infusion of humor.

Given the antic nature of our media and professional humorists, they are not likely to ever be without it.

Chapter 1

Campaign 1992
The Comeback Kid

Bill Clinton smoked marijuana and didn't inhale.
And they call Dan Quayle stupid.
—JAY LENO

Mark Russell said that for political humorists 1992 was "the gift that kept on giving," and so it did. As the battle raged, Russell was asked if this was the dirtiest campaign he had ever seen, but he wasn't sure. "Ferdinand Marcos is dead and can't defend himself," he replied.

Because sex is such a staple for everyone from standup comics to Hollywood screenwriters, Bill Clinton's affair with Gennifer Flowers attracted the eager attention of the wags. Though there was an occasional whisper of reproach aimed at Miss Flowers—one comic said "Who can trust anyone who spells Jennifer with a 'G'?"—for the most part, the japes were leveled at the candidate.

When Dan Quayle said that the three words Bill Clinton feared most were "telling the truth," Jay Leno corrected him, observing that the three words Clinton feared most were "Hi, 'member me?" Leno said that Clinton was having trouble with his voice and quoted the doctor's diagnosis that Clinton's voice was hoarse from overuse. In that case, Leno cracked, he should also be suffering from a groin pull.

Comedian Gary Shandling explained that the reason

Shandling wasn't running for president was that he feared no woman would come forward and announce she had had sex with him. And in the 1992 edition of my quadrennial captioned photo book, *Who's In Charge Here?*, I showed a picture of Bill Clinton playing his saxophone, with an off-camera voice saying: "Do you know 'The Lady is a Tramp?'" Dennis Miller, the sardonic late-night talk show host, observed that scientists had made new discoveries of the Big Bang Theory. He reflected that "this should help the Clinton campaign." Miller added caustically that Clinton had "promised to get a circumcision as soon as his erection subsides." Noting Clinton's performance on MTV, editorial cartoonist Summers in the *Orlando Sentinel* showed a record album picturing the candidate wearing dark glasses and playing the sax. The headline on the LP album: "G.I. Blues in Stereo and High Infidelity."

With the departure of Johnny Carson from television's "The Tonight Show" earlier in the year, Jay Leno arguably had become the successor to the satiric tradition of Carson and Will Rogers. His lines were always crisp and relevant, smack on the news, and delivered with a good-humored tone and timing that seemed to heat without burning. Early in the campaign season, Leno predicted that the election would depend on the swing voters, and thus "Clinton's got it sewed up." A student of social behavior pointed out that in Europe, extra marital affairs such as Clinton's were an accepted way of life. "Anyhow, we're voting for President, not for Pope."

Bob Orben, the dean of White House humor, who for years had added humor to the speeches of President Gerald Ford (see chapters on Campaign 1976), originated a newsletter encrusted with political humor. When Orben moved to other pastures, the newsletter, called *Current Comedy*, continued to dispense witty comments on the alleged womanizing of Mr. Clinton. Said *Current Comedy*: "When Bill Clinton heard this was 'The Year of the Woman,' he ordered two." The newsletter added, "Women are standing behind Bill Clinton. That's the safest place to be." And acknowledging that Clinton's supporters claimed he didn't have a dishonest bone in his body, it remarked: "It isn't his bones we're worried about, it's his glands." Clinton also took his knocks for Gennifer Flowers on the bumper sticker front. One sticker proclaimed, "Democrats in '92—Too Much Sex, Too Much Gore."

The basis for a splendid TV movie could be found in the love affair between Mary Matalin, political director for George Bush, and James Carville, Clinton's chief strategist. When Matalin issued a vitriolic fax to the media citing Clinton's fear of further "bimbo eruptions," Carville resonded: "If Mary gets fired, she'll have a good career writing fiction."

"Saturday Night Live," that home of slash-and-burn comedy, found gold in the sexual comportment, real and fancied, of the Democratic candidate. Even after Election Day, the writers at SNL continued to flog the infidelity joke. When news photographers lured Chelsea Clinton's cat Socks out of the Governor's Mansion in Little Rock for a photo opportunity, President-elect Clinton, in a rare display of bile, warned them not to do it again. Said the host of "Saturday Night's" Weekend Update segment: "Meanwhile, Socks, who had nothing else to do, decided to kill some time fooling around with Gennifer Flowers's cat Blondie."

David Letterman was busy with his own campaign in 1992, which would result in his signing a lucrative contract to move his show to CBS. Amidst his negotiations, he found time for a few wry comments on the Clinton-Flowers affair. When Clinton's election victory was behind him, the President-elect's two most pressing decisions, according to Letterman, were: "First, what can he do with the economy, and second, who the hell is he going to take to the Inaugural Ball?"

Premiere satirist Mark Russell took the historical view. Womanizing, he said was slow in unfolding as an issue in presidential campaigns. For a long time, the press was just unaware of it. Said Russell: "It took forty years to learn that Roosevelt fooled around a bit. It took five years to learn the same thing about Kennedy. And with Gary Hart, we found out about it before the martinis reached room temperature."

A backup Clinton scandal which was a target for corrosive wit was his draft-dodging: the fact that Clinton had used all his cunning and contacts to stay out of the Vietnam War. The cover of *National Review* pictured Bill Clinton in an easy chair with daughter Chelsea in his lap. Clinton was asking: "What will *you* do in the next war, Chelsea?" With an eye toward Dan Quayle's similar evasions, one wag said: "Clinton admits he avoided the draft. . . . That makes him perfect vice-presidential material." Said one dubious Democrat: "Even though Clinton maneuvered himself out of going to Vietnam, he now says he's in favor of the draft. So am I—let's draft Cuomo." Comedy writer Doug Gamble quipped: "I'd like to know how someone who forgot he received a draft notice can convince us he'll remember his election promises." And Jay Leno cracked, "Bush said that Bill Clinton has not told the full truth, the whole truth, and nothing but the truth about the draft. The trouble is, Clinton thinks those are three different things." And Art Buchwald reported a question from a reader of his widely syndicated column: "Do you think that if Bill Clinton is elected, he will reinstate the draft?" Buchwald's answer: "Bill has always supported the draft and told his friends that one of his biggest regrets is that his number was not called during the Vietnam War. If elected, he may ask for a new number so that he can have one more crack at serving in the armed forces." With a nice economy of wit, Mark Russell summed up the martial picture: "Bush went into the military; Clinton didn't. Gore went; Quayle didn't. It's a perfect example of our system of checks and balances."

Clinton's next Scandal-of-the-Month involved his smoking marijuana at Oxford. With an excess of candor, and oblivious to the statement's ludicrous flavor, Clinton said that though he had smoked marijuana in college, he hadn't inhaled. This led to a number of gibes along similar lines of incredulity. Mocked Dennis Miller: "Clinton said he sipped a glass of elderberry wine but he didn't swallow." Jay Leno added: "A doctor's group has said that drinking milk can be bad for your heart. When Bill Clinton heard about this, he claimed that when he was a child he drank milk but he never swallowed." Wrote one satirist of Tipper Gore's attack on X-rated language in rock music: "Tipper was in a rock band in high school. . . . She said that she moved her lips but never actually sang." Recalling the confirmation hearings of Clarence Thomas in which the judge recalled having smoked grass without pleasure, Miller said: "There are forty million Americans who smoke marijuana and the only two people who didn't like it were Bill Clinton and Clarence Thomas." George Bush marvelled at some of the things Clinton was saying as he travelled about the country. "Maybe he's inhaled too many bus fumes," said Bush. One of the bumper stickers added ridicule along the highway: I SMOKED POT WITH BILL CLINTON AND WE DIDN'T INHALE . . . MUCH.

Indeed, the sheer number of the scandals that beset Bill Clinton in the early days of his candidacy produced an outpouring of humor and scorn. When the shoe of Amelia Earhart, America's most famous female aviator, was found on a South Pacific island as evidence of her crash in 1937, one comic said: "Bill Clinton has taken a lot of hits in this campaign, but his implication in the Amelia Earhart thing hasn't been proven." In *Who's In Charge Here?*, I showed a Clinton aide exulting: "Good news! Bill hasn't had a scandal all week." Dennis Miller recalled that Nixon was the first candidate to campaign in all fifty states, and observed that Clinton "was the first candidate to cover all the ten commandments." And P. J. O'Roarke said the candidate was America's newest superhero: "Scandalman."

George Bush accused his opponent of "waffling" on numerous issues, from the Gulf War to a middle-class tax cut. The President had an arsenal of gaggery on the subject. Said Bush, "There's a reason for having three presidential debates: The first one so Governor Clinton can state his views, and the other two so he can change his mind." On another occasion he said, "One of my grandkids asked me when he could start staying up until eleven o'clock, and I said, 'When Bill Clinton sticks with a position on an issue.'" And on another occasion Bush said, "The Governor is on all sides of every issue. He's been spotted in more places than Elvis Presley. . . . I figured out why Clinton compares himself to Elvis. The minute he has to take a stand on something, he starts wiggling." These lines were provided by Bush's invaluable contributing wit, Doug Gamble. Gamble offered a few other lines on Clinton's waffling that Bush chose not to use: "If they ever put this guy on Mount Rushmore, they'll need two faces for him." And "The way Clinton takes both sides of an issue, he rushes back and forth from one side to the other so fast, he may be the only person in America who could teeter-totter with himself."

Bush made political hay when he made a breakfast stop at a waffle house in South Carolina. He told his audience that Clinton would "turn the White House into a waffle house." This foray into gustatory metaphors backfired. Clinton's strategic staff was quick to react. They handed out bright yellow laminated menus that showed Bush as the proprietor of his own waffle house where they served Iraq of Lamb and Deep Voodoo Pie. The menu declared: "George Bush's White House features Read My Lips Service, Jobs on the Short Side, and a Pay Raise Souffle." The diner who ordered sunnyside up, learned that Bush said, "The American people think we're in a recession and we're not." The Headline on the menu: "Yesterday's Special—Chicken George" and "Tomorrow's Special—Lame Duck." The menu's back page showed a "Going Out of Business" sign across George Bush's Waffle House, and noted that it was established January 20, 1989 but would be closing November 3, 1992. And there was a wry footnote: "Tax not included. Never, ever, ever, ever, ever."

Compared with John F. Kennedy, the president he revered, Bill Clinton seldom employed wit or humor during the campaign. His humor, Doug Gamble observed, ran along lines of "Take my balanced approach between new programs and long-term deficit reduction—please!" Perhaps this was because, for a young man challenging an older one, humor might have seemed like cockiness, disrespect, or trivializing important issues. On rare occasions, Clinton's sense of humor surfaced warily, as when he cited "Clinton's Third Law of Politics—Whenever possible, be introduced by someone who you've appointed to high office." His humor was not at Bush's expense, but more often self-deprecatory, as when he said, "When I was a small boy, I used to stand in front of a mirror and preach, and my mother said: 'You know, you could be a preacher—if you were a better boy.' And so I went into politics." One rare Clinton anecdote recalled those of Lyndon Johnson, another Southern candidate who enjoyed regaling audiences with tales about preachers. Clinton told of a preacher who made the usual invocation, "All those who want to go to the Kingdom of Heaven stand up." The entire congregation stands except for one little old lady in the first row, and the preacher says, "Sarah, don't you want to go to the Kingdom of Heaven?" and she says, 'Oh yeah, I thought you were trying to get up a load to go right now.'" In his speech accepting the nomination at the GOP convention in 1988, George Bush used humor effectively (see chapter on Campaign 1988), but the president seemed more unwilling to use the one-liners that were provided him in 1992. "This time around," complained Doug Gamble, the chief humor-meister of the Reagan-Bush years, "they found little use for wit." For example, Clinton's economic plan seemed a prime target for the deflating effects of humor. Clinton always seemed to have fifty policy options to put a glaze over the eyes. Yet Bush chose not to employ such zingers as these to rebut a wonkish Clinton and his recitation of economic options:

"Governor Clinton's economic plan looks to me like 'Broccoli Economics.' He makes it sound good, but I find it hard to swallow."

"Bill Clinton has more programs than there are problems."

"The economy is like Bill Clinton in jogging shorts. It's in better shape than it looks."

"The president is the Commander in Chief, not Calculator in Chief."

"Governor, I think you're still cramming for that final exam you never took at Oxford."

"This is the pursuit of the presidency, not Trivial Pursuit."

Since Clinton was trying to sound like a new kind of un-liberal Democrat, Bush was urged to say: "We've just seen your impersonation of a Moderate, but you should stick to impersonating Elvis." Or "You look at the taxpayers' wallets like another cheeseburger to be gobbled down."

Of course, Bush did try to tar Clinton with the brush that had served so well on Dukakis and Mondale: that despite his protestations to the contrary, Clinton was a typical "tax and spend" Democrat. There was one Doug Gamble line that Bush was wise enough to incorporate into his standard campaign speech and deliver regularly. "Bill Clinton keeps talking about change. But if his economic policies go into effect, change is all you'll have left in your pockets."

Another sample of the Gamble wit that George Bush did employ was: "If Clinton is elected, lyric sheets will be passed out at the White House Christmas party so staffers can sing such seasonal songs as 'I'm Dreaming of a White Paper' and 'Oh Little Town of Little Rock.'" And "The Clinton Administration will distribute mistletoe to every American home so we can hang it above our wallet and kiss more of our paycheck good-bye." And after the first televised debate, Bush announced, "I enjoyed debating with Ross Perot and Bill Clinton. One of them made three billion dollars and the other made three billion promises."

Bush was not alone in needling the Clinton economic plan. Opined Mark Russell, "Bill Clinton said that his economic plan is endorsed by six hundred economists. The only time six hundred economists ever agreed on anything, it was two plus two equals four—under certain circumstances."

Even Dan Quayle put an oar in, trying to tie Bill Clinton to his party predecessors' tendency to tax and spend. Said the vice president: "I know why Bill Clinton likes football. When he hears the quarterback say 'Hike!' he thinks of taxes."

There was a medley of other issues on which Clinton endured the derision of comics, skeptics, and politicos. Accusing Clinton of acting like Thomas Jefferson, former President Ronald Reagan said. "Let me tell you something. I knew Thomas Jefferson. Thomas Jefferson was a friend of mine. And Governor, you're no Thomas Jefferson."

As Governor of Arkansas, Bill Clinton had little in the way of foreign policy experience, which was George Bush's strong suit. Said bully boy Pat Buchanan: "Bill Clinton's foreign policy experience is composed of having had breakfast once at the International House of Pancakes." Kidding Clinton's hair style, as many had derided Jack Kennedy's in his day, David Letterman jeered: "Political experts believe that if Bill Clinton spends as much time on the country's problems as he does on fixing his hair . . ." Bill Buckley's *National Review*, which had little trouble controlling its enthusiasm for George Bush, had a few darts for Bill Clinton: "Little did Oxford suspect it was harboring our future Commander-in-Chief." But, the magazine conceded, "At least there's no silly footage of

Bill Clinton driving a tank." Some found a resemblance not to the hapless Dukakis, but to an earlier Democrat named Carter. In an editorial cartoon in the *Miami Herald*, Morin showed a voter holding a sign reading "CLINTON FOR PRES. '92" and bearing Clinton's image. Suddenly the face changes and we see Jimmy Carter's teeth in a broad smile. The voter looks startled and screams.

Clinton's sometime feud with Governor Mario Cuomo of New York fed the humorists for awhile. In a phone conversation that had been taped by Gennifer Flowers, Clinton had said that Cuomo acted like a member of the Mafia. Clinton promptly apologized to Cuomo and, said one wag, "When Clinton was in New York, he kissed his hand."

One could perhaps assemble a lively little compendium of sanguinary wit aimed at our First Ladies. Certainly Nancy Reagan had her share of detractors, as did Rosalyn Carter when she attended cabinet meetings. And those with long memories can recall the mockery directed at the compassionate instincts of Eleanor Roosevelt. But it is hard to recall a prospective First Lady (or a sitting one) who came in for the bilious humor that Hillary Rodham Clinton suffered at the hands of America's wits and politicians. Pat Buchanan launched the anti-Hillary movement with a particularly graceless assault at the GOP convention. Some wept crocodile tears for Hillary as they mocked the wandering eye of her husband. Said a scribe in *Current Comedy*: "A reporter asked Hillary Clinton how she'd like being the First Lady. Mrs. Clinton said she'd be happy just to be the only lady." When Hillary responded, in defense of her successful law career: "What do you expect me to do? Stay home and bake cookies?," satirist Mark Russell said, "I thought the issue wasn't her cookies, it was her husband's tarts." And when one of the questions President-elect Bill Clinton was asked was when he thought we'd see the first woman in the White House, Jay Leno cracked, "Well, gee, probably on Hillary's first trip out of town."

The *National Review* printed a poem by their staff poet, William Henry Von Dreel, describing a certain acrimony between Hillary and Tipper Gore, wife of the vice presidential nominee. It described a rancor that never developed. Versified Von Dreel:

Hillary doesn't like Tipper,
Tipper bakes cookies for Al,
Tipper's been censoring lyrics
Boring as "Frivolous Sal."
Bill is aware of the friction,
Hillary couldn't care less.
Al will be getting an earful
Which will be hell to finesse.

When George Bush picked up the strident anti-Hillary theme propounded by Pat Buchanan at the convention, Bill Clinton was ready with a crusher: "You'd think he was running for First Lady instead of for President," said Clinton.

There were many who admired Mrs. Clinton and perceived that the customary relationship of President to First Lady was in transition. Said one Beltway wag, "I'd like to see Clinton elected but it's her husband who's running."

After the "cookie" flap. Hillary Clinton kept a low profile during the rest of the campaign, but once her husband had assumed the presidency the need for such prudence was past. President Clinton positioned his wife in an office in the White House West Wing (first ladies customarily remain in the East Wing, poring over dinner menus), and placed her in charge of fashioning his health-care plan. During the campaign there was little suspicion that she would wield such power. When someone asked Mark Rusell what role he thought Hillary would play in the new administration, he responded that she would be both active and passive. "I see her wearing a frilly white apron while picking the cabinet." Russell recalled that they dubbed Rosalyn Carter "the Steel Magnolia." "An apt title for Hillary would be 'Chief-of-Spouse,'" said Russell.

Once the Clintons, male and female, assumed the mantle of power, a joke began to enjoy wide circulation which recounted how Bill and Hillary were driving through her home state and stopped for gas. When Hillary was warmly greeted by the station attendant, the President asks "Who's that?" Hillary explains that he was a fellow she used to date. Clinton smiles and says, "Just think, if you had married him, today you'd be the wife of a gas station attendant." "No," says Hillary, "if I had married him, today *he'd* be the President of the United States."

The advisors who urged Bill Clinton to select Al Gore as his running mate deserved Clinton's undying gratitude. It was a brilliant stroke of political judgment. The two men, both in their mid-forties, both moderate Democrats from Southern states, possessed a generational power that was as symbolic as it was real. "YOUNG GUNS" headlined *Newsweek* beside images of the two candidates. But humorists must find something to hold the franchise, and in the case of Al Gore, it was his tendency toward a certain stiffness.

Gore himself deprecated his lack of spontaneity. "How do you tell Al Gore in a roomful of FBI agents?" he would ask. "He's the one who looks stiff."

Fred Barnes of *The New Republic* referred to Gore as "that cardboard cutout Clinton brings to press conferences." Jay Leno told of Al Gore and his wife Tipper getting lost after going for a walk in the woods near their home. Suddenly they are confronted by a huge bear. "Thinking quickly," said Leno, "Gore broke into a speech and the bear immediately fell asleep." And Mark Russell, alluding to Gore's colorless, stalwart good looks, remarked: "I always thought, if ever I met Al Gore, the first thing I'd ask him was how Lois Lane was." Then Russell would break into one of his satiric songs that make him the political legatee of Larry Hart. To the tune of "If I Only Had a Brain" from *The Wizard of Oz*, he sang:

My arms are not akimbo,
Don't ask me to do to the limbo,
Not a pretty sight to watch.
People see me and they're swearing
That a body cast I'm wearing
From my head down to my crotch.

In addition to being a vice-presidential candidate, Al Gore was the author of a national bestseller on the environment that, along with Ross Perot's book and Madonna's volume on erotic sex, eclipsed all other books during the election campaign. Said one wag, "It took ten years for Al Gore's book to get on the shelf. Tipper kept burning the thing." The book was used as one more excuse to rap Quayle. Wrote the scribes of *Current Comedy*: "Even Dan Quayle was seen shopping for

Al Gore's book. He said he plans to read it as soon as it comes out on audiotape.''

Gore's preoccupation with the environment and what some said were his excessive plans to protect it, were the subject of humor. Said Doug Gamble, ''With Gore as vice president, the biggest change would be in the Christmas season. You can bet that Gore will want to get to the bottom of why Rudolph the Red-nosed Reindeer has a nose that glows.'' The cover of *National Review* featured a photo of Gore that alluded to his fear of global warming. Gore is shown singing ''I don't want to set the world on fire.'' And referring to Gore's concern about the state of the planet, the magazine headlined Gore's ''Globaloney.'' (It was clear that Bill Buckley's nose had not yet started to glow.) George Bush was provided with a funny line on the subject: ''I understand Al Gore tried to phone his chief environmental advisor, but he couldn't get through. The spotted owl had an unlisted tree.'' In derisive tones, Bush referred to Gore as ''Ozone Man.''

Gore's devotion to the environment would sometimes undermine Clinton's appeal to important constituencies such as the auto workers, and this could prove an embarrassment. This problem was highlighted in an editorial cartoon by Stantis in the *Grand Rapids Press*. Gore and Clinton are shown aboard their tour bus. Gore wears a T-shirt that reads ''SAVE THE OZONE—NUKE A CHRYSLER.'' Says Clinton: ''Al, could you lose the shirt until we get through Michigan?''

Some Bush advisers tried to mock Gore's intellectual gifts but that was a dog that wouldn't hunt. His scholarship was too amply set out in his bestseller. Said John Sears, a GOP advisor, ''Mr. Quayle's only problem was he couldn't spell 'potato,' and Mr. Gore noticing this, went and looked it up.''

Art Buchwald, in a column answering mock letters from his readers, told of a letter he had received asking, ''Should I know who Al Gore is?'' Answered the straight-faced columnist: ''Not necessarily, I'm the only one who knows Al Gore. Al Gore is a friend of mine. And I want to tell you this right now. Al Gore is no Al Gore.''

Gore was not always the target of campaign humor. On occasion he was its originator, as when he said, ''If they made a movie of President Bush's Administration, it would be called

Honey, I Shrunk the Economy. Or considering what he's done to jobs in America, we could call it *The Terminator.*" Then he added: "What we don't need is *Terminator 2.*" When Al Gore appeared on "The Larry King Show," the hospitable program that had launched Ross Perot's candidacy, Gore received an anonymous phone call from a woman who said provocatively, "I know I shouldn't say this, Senator, but I think you're a very handsome man. Are you available for a date on Friday night?" If Larry King's antenna scented scandal, he was disappointed when the caller identified herself. It was Tipper Gore.

Campaign humor aimed at Bill Clinton did not begin when he won the Democratic nomination. It had an earlier season. As is the Democrats' usual custom, there were several candidates feverishly vying for the privilege of representing the party. Because George Bush's approval ratings were so formidable after his triumphant performance during the Gulf War, the Democratic candidates were decidedly second tier. The Cuomos and Bradleys and Nunns had no taste for a lost cause, so the Democratic field was inhabited by people with unfamiliar names, like Kerry and Hawkins and Tsongas—and Clinton.

One name that was somewhat more familiar and that attracted its share of humor, was Jerry Brown, former Governor of California, mystic, hippy, apostle of Mother Theresa, and recent fundraiser for the Democratic Party in California. If America's humorists looked on Campaign '92 as the gift that kept on giving, for decades they had looked on Jerry Brown as the public figure who did the same. He was wonderful for political wags. "I was President of Comedians for Jerry Brown," said Mark Russell. "Governor Brown is America's ultimate teenager," said Dennis Miller. The public perception of Jerry Brown—which was impossible to shed—was of a spaced-out candidate. "Jerry Brown's campaign for the Democratic candidacy looks promising," joked Jay Leno. "The media is paying attention, the unions are supporting him, and Mars is in the seventh house." One comedian quoted Jerry Brown as saying, "I want to make the Earth the cleanest of the planets I've lived on." Said another: "Jerry Brown is concerned about the environment. Funny, he's spent so little time on earth." And during the primary season, which was not especially kind to his candidacy, one comic ruminated: "Clinton vs. Brown, it's a choice between the guy who promises you the moon, and the guy who lives there." In *Who's In Charge Here?* (1992), I showed a photo from a *Star Trek* film, with the crew of the Starship Enterprise sitting for a group portrait. Captain Kirk is saying: "Yes, we sighted Jerry Brown near Pluto."

Back in 1980, when Jimmy Carter was fighting to maintain the Democratic nomination against the onslaughts of Teddy Kennedy, Jerry Brown was much in the news. His romance with singer Linda Ronstadt had set tongues clacking, but the inveterate bachelor had avoided a permanent commitment. Thus, in 1992, political humorist Harry Shearer could say: "Jerry Brown doesn't even have a wife to cheat on."

Feeling that the political system of campaign contributions to presidential candidates was corrupt and corrupting, Jerry Brown set up an "800" number through which supporters could contribute modest sums to his campaign. After Paul Tsongas dropped out, one wit said that if you called Jerry Brown's "800" number, Paul Tsongas answered the phone. Another said that if you called billionaire Ross Perot's "800" number, he gave *you* a hundred dollars. Whenever Brown was on camera, as he often found himself, given the massive coverage produced by the proliferation of cable channels, he would override the protests of moderators by loudly announcing his "800" number. In *Who's in Charge Here?* I show Brown making a direct appeal for funds: "Remember, dial 1-800-MOON-BEAM." Lacking the more substantial contributions of major interest groups, Jerry Brown's campaign was perennially short of funds. Said Johnny Carson: "Jerry Brown's campaign got a fresh infusion of funds this week when his flight was overbooked." Brown was the consummate populist, down to the ubiquitous turtleneck sweater (someone said he'd be sworn-in in one) and the cotton jacket. Said Jay Leno, "Jerry Brown went into the hospital this week to have a UAW windbreaker surgically removed."

As Jerry Brown deplored the fetid system that supported the campaigns of presidents and congressmen at the expense of their independence, he also deplored the deceptions of campaign advertising. In *Who's in Charge* an irate Governor Brown is showing an open newspaper to his staff. He is saying: "This is negative advertising. Vile, insulting, destructive. Keep it up." And I am embarrassed to admit I took some cheap shots at Brown's hippy image. In one photo, he is forcing his way through a crowd and saying, "Come on, who took my beads?"

Jerry Brown's most visible program to repair the ailing economy was a flat tax. Mused Dennis Miller, "Dolly Parton thinks it's a great idea." But most of the public were not entranced by the seeming inequity of placing the same tax on rich and poor. "Jerry Brown's Achilles Heel was his flat tax proposal," said Miller. "Bill Clinton has an Achilles Penis." (Brown insisted that Clinton had an electability problem. One satirist observed that if Brown could get more votes than Clinton in just one state he might prove it.)

Jerry Brown was the one Democratic candidate who stayed with his candidacy right until the Democratic national convention in July. By then the others had dropped out, facing the inevitability of Bill Clinton's candidacy. Jerry Brown was discouraged neither by his lack of funds nor his poor showing in the primaries. Said Harry Shearer: "He did badly in New York because he's not known there, and he did badly in California because he *is* known there."

Perhaps the most incisive derision of Jerry Brown came from political humorist Mort Sahl, who has been offering satiric comment on the political scene since the fifties. Recalling earlier years when Brown was the governor of Sahl's native California, the humorist said: "I used to kid about Jerry Brown studying to be a priest. And he joins an order where he took the vow of silence on the major issues."

With election day, the torch had been passed. As Clinton said with soaring rhetoric, "With high hopes and brave hearts, in massive numbers, the American people have voted to make a new beginning." He might have added that, "With high hopes and brave hearts, in massive numbers, American humorists had decided to make a new beginning." Gone would be the gibes at George Bush, a president who seemed insensitive to bread-and-butter concerns. Gone would be the GOP White House that had fed them material for twelve long

31

years, from Nancy's astrologer to Reagan's catnaps. And, of course, humorists wouldn't have Dan Quayle to kick around anymore.

At the top of the humorists' new agenda were Bill and Hillary Clinton. In a widely seen campaign ad, a beaming teenage Clinton was seen shaking the hand of his idol, John F. Kennedy. And with his victory over George Bush and Ross Perot, the footage reminded some wits that Bill and Hillary had now become, as were Jack and Jackie, the First Family for America's political satirical community—and that, with luck, they might be as fresh and fruitful a source of humor as were the Kennedys.

Some might deplore the fact that Bill Clinton had enjoyed no honeymoon, no respite from attacks by the press and ridicule by the wits. Three days after Election Day, humorist Dave Barry spoke to the National Press Club and said somberly: "I think the big issue facing the nation now is, 'How did the Clinton Presidency fail?'" The press roared; they recognized that even before taking office, Clinton had become a dartboard for the punditocracy and the satirists. Said Barry: "I think the press gave Clinton the benefit of the doubt for the first fifteen, maybe even twenty minutes. But now I think the feeling is that he's not handling the job . . . he has not improved the economy. How long has the guy been in there, right?"

The day before Clinton delivered his surprisingly succinct inaugural address, there appeared on the op-ed page of the good gray *New York Times* some sample inaugural addresses written for the *Times* by some of America's top jesters. One of these was premiere comedy writer Larry Gelbart. In his mock inaugural, Gelbart suggested that the new president declare in part:

> I am opposed to the notion that a woman's place is in the kitchen cabinet. [I have] planned a summit of women who have been harassed by Senator Packwood, providing we can find a hall big enough. . . . I have planned to convene an ex-presidents' retreat, which former Presidents Nixon, Ford, Carter, Reagan, and Bush have agreed to attend and give us all the benefit of whatever is left of their wisdom. . . . [I wish to

extend] special thanks to President Nixon who would participate in a second event—a conference of distinguished Americans who have had the honor of receiving presidential pardons.

On March 18, 1993, President Bill Clinton had been in
office for about two months. While the elderly, the baby
boomers, the doctors, the Wall Streeters, and the National
Rifle Association all looked at him with alarm or satisfaction,
others watched for signs of humor.

Once a man settles into the White House, he experi-
ences a sense of freedom and possibility that encourages an
expansive display of his personality. That includes a greater
display of his sense of humor, which it is often prudent to stifle
during the campaign. Jack Kennedy was at first wary of displaying his audacious sense of humor, remembering how Adlai Stevenson had been criticized for his own. So too, Clinton
had seemed wary of employing humor during his election
campaign.

Thus, once Clinton moved into the Oval Office, observers watched with interest as he addresssed the twelve hundred
journalists of The Radio and Television Correspondents Association that March evening. The affair ran from 8:45 to 11:00
p.m. Fifteen of those minutes belonged to the president. They
served as a useful audition for the more important exposure of
his wit at the prestigious Gridiron Club the following week.
According to one journalist who covered Clinton's first foray
into the hazardous waters of stand-up comedy, "he did not
forfeit his amateur status." Clinton's communications director, George Stephanopoulos, told pool reporters covering the
affair that the president had "winged" half of his remarks,
building them out of his own experience and his own reactions. The other half, said Stephanopoulos, was prepared for
him by in-house wits.

Clinton used the humor in his standup routine in the
time-honored way: to laugh away the criticism that had been
leveled at him by press and public:

Responding to the media outcry that Clinton did not
hold enough formal press conferences but went over the
heads of the White House reporters: "You've been at me to
hold a *formal* press conference. So tonight," he said, fingering
the lapels of his tuxedo, "here it is."

Responding to the rejection of his first two female nominees for attorney general and the acceptance of his third: "I told White House counsel Bernard Nussbaum, who offered me attorney general candidates Zoe Baird and Kimba Wood—when he brought Janet Reno into the Oval Office for an interview: 'This is it Nussbaum. If she doesn't work, you're going to have a sex-change operation."

Responding to Ross Perot's criticism of Mack McLarty, Clinton's old friend who had become his White House chief of staff: "Mr. Perot just resents it because Mack's a short guy with real power."

Responding to the renovations that the Clinton people were bringing to the White House: "Our jogging track is coming along nicely. We expect our own McDonald's to be completed by fall."

Recalling the campaign flap over the search by George Bush's State Department through Clinton's passport files: "British Prime Minister John Major told me during a recent visit: 'You know, you don't look a thing like your passport photos.'"

Responding to GOP opposition to the Motor Votor bill, which would enable citizens to vote when they register their cars: "The Republicans were for it when they thought it was BMWs and Mercedes. But they took the 'Welfare Cadillacs' out of it yesterday."

Responding to fears expressed by some members of the media that he was too young and inexperienced to conduct foreign policy, Clinton said, "You were right."

Responding to a sketch roasting him, he snuck onstage and played his saxophone, then added: "There's nothing like a little sax to get you out of trouble."

And responding to criticism that Hillary Rodham Clinton was exercising inordinate power for a First Lady, he said: "The opinions I will express tonight are those of my wife."

President Clinton's humor, like that of America's leading political satirists, from Leno to Russell to Buchwald, seemed to demonstrate the truth of the axiom that he who laughs, lasts.

After twelve years and three election campaigns devoted to mocking Reagan, Bush, and Quayle, America's humorists felt that they had been denied their birthright when Bill Clinton was elected president.

As Bill and Hillary moved into the big white house on Pennsylvania Avenue, comedians whose job it is to wring humor from the flaws of D. C. notables were left to ponder what they had to handle. Bill Clinton was given to speaking in coherent sentences and, unlike George Bush, was not given to the spastic gestures of Jerry Lewis in *The Bellboy*. And Hillary was unlikely to add an 'e' when spelling potato or to attack some fictional TV character. So there was disquietude in the Beltway.

By the end of the Bush-Reagan years political humor had grown scarce. America's gagmasters and cartoonists were facing an uncertian future. But hope sprang eternal in comedic hearts. Richard Belzer, whose mordant wit had enlivened many campaigns, was already finding humor in the First Lady's clout: "Remember how we used to worry that if something happened to George Bush, Dan Quayle would become president? Now we have to worry that if something happens to Hillary, Bill Clinton will become president."

Comedian Judy Tenuta, like many female comics, struck it rich in the perception of Hillary's prominence: "It's nice that Bill's let Hillary be president. He smiles and she's cracking the whip. She's the dominatrix."

Other comedians were reaping laughs by pointing out the disparity between some of Clinton's campaign promises and his presidential performance. Said political satirist Will Durst, "Clinton promised he'd hit the ground running. We just didn't know it would be away from his campaign promises."

Clinton's brother Roger lent reassurance to many political wits. Said stand-up comedian Mike MacDonald, "I saw Clinton's brother on David Letterman. The jokes wrote themselves. . . . Gore wasn't coming through for us. We needed a new Quayle. Call Roger."

The dean of stand-up comedians, Jay Leno, felt he had found a gold mine in Roger Clinton. "We've hit the mother lode," he said. Leno provides the most widely heard and widely quoted political humor in the country. His lines are invariably crisp and topical, which is somewhat astonishing when one considers that their genesis is this morning's paper.

Leno suffered no shortage of material under the Reagan-Bush-Quayle reign, and with Clinton in power he suffered from no shortage of new targets. "I think it's important to stay on the attack no matter who the president is," he told the *L. A. Times.* "Some of the audience might be confused at first because they think they know my politics. But I'm a comedian rather than a political comedian. It's important to be funny first."

Most of the nation's humorists were as neutral as a mirror. They turned from GOP to Democratic targets in the blink of an eye. George Carlin, the venerable anti-establishment wit, reflected that his subject was not topical events but long-range trends. Carlin is not preoccupied with "the revolving cast of characters in Washington. . . . they're just rearranging the deck chairs on the Titanic."

But most of the best comedians and humorists, from Jay Leno to Mark Russell, tend to deal with topical humor. Like fine food, they consume it while it's fresh. With Clinton's victory, some political satirists had to reinvent themselves or perish. Impressionist Jim Morris was frighteningly adept at duplicating the voice and persona of Ronald Reagan and George Bush. But, remembering how Vaughan Meader had vanished with the passing of JFK, he resolved to replicate the mannerisms of President Bill Clinton. Said Morris: "It's scary starting with a new character. But presidents get funnier with time," he added hopefully.

With the passing of Bush and Quayle, comics worked and prayed for humor with the Clintons. Said Alan Havey, host of Comedy Central's "Night After Night," humorists would have to work harder with the familiar targets of the eighties behind them. "It was easy to make fun of Bush and Quayle, but Clinton's an interesting guy. The humor's out there." The wish may be the father to the thought and the comic optimism may be self-fulfilling.

Comic performance artist John Fleck says: "I'll miss Barbara Bush. I do like the idea of a strong professional woman like Hillary Clinton being in there. . . . I don't really want to make too much fun of her." But chivalry in political humor is not only dead; it is decomposing. Most comedians, humorists, and cartoonists are eager to sink their fangs into America's new president and his First Lady. Said Will Durst: "I still feel that anybody who can be elected president shouldn't be. I spent twelve years taking on the Republicans, but I'm an equal-opportunity satirist."

Most other humorists are too, and Bill and Hillary Clinton are on their scopes.

Chapter 2

Campaign 1992
It's the Economy, Stupid

> The President went over and signed the historic
> trade agreement under which the Japanese govern-
> ment agreed to buy a Chevrolet Caprice.
> —DAVE BARRY

For the past quarter of a century, with the exception
of an aberration brought on by Watergate, Democratic presidential nominees have been taking their lumps on election
day. Hubert Humphrey, George McGovern, Walter Mondale,
and Michael Dukakis all came up losers, as Richard Nixon,
Ronald Reagan and George Bush triumphed at the polls. So
acclimated to defeat had Democrats become, that when Bill
Clinton took the lead in the spring primaries, one jokester
said: "Clinton's so sure of getting the Democratic nomination
that he's already rehearsing his concession speech."

But 1992 was a year when the Democrat didn't need a
concession speech after all. This was due in large part to the
sorry state of the U.S. economy. Clinton's victory was primarily the result of the fact that Americans, desperate for leadership and unshakeably gloomy about their jobs, voted for
change. But, the famous sign in Clinton's campaign headquarters notwithstanding, it wasn't only "the economy, stupid"
that undid George Bush. It was in part that he ran the sort of
hapless campaign that Americans had come to expect of Dem-

ocrats. It was a campaign in which the candidate had the State Department riffle the passport files of his opponent's mother. It was a campaign in which there was a growing whiff of culpability in the candidate's connection with the arms-for-hostage deal. It was a campaign in which the candidate was saddled with a vice president who slandered a fictitious TV character. It was a campaign in which the patrician incumbent felt his best hope lay in identifying with a onetime haberdasher named Harry Truman. It was a campaign in which the candidate was savaged by a member of his own party. And it was a campaign, in short, in which America's humorists—if not its voters—had much for which to thank their President.

Fundamentally, of course, it *was* the economy. Bush's advisers had urged him to develop a more aggressive economic package, but the President was slow to accept their advice. His response was very like his message to the voters: "Trust me—I know what I'm doing." So Bush was the architect of his own demise, and the economy remained stagnant through the election year.

Not so stagnant was the wit with which Bush was attacked by America's humorists. With the departure of Johnny Carson, Jay Leno donned the satirical mantle and his performance throughout the campaign year was always brisk and cogent. When late in the year NBC decided to stay with Leno in the teeth of David Letterman's campaign to replace him, viewers, advertisers and affiliates alike applauded the decision. Whereas Letterman confined his humor to brief remarks, Leno nightly addressed the state of the economy—and other elements of the campaign—with humor and pungency. Here are some of his zingers on the subject:

> The economy is so bad, Hannibal Lector was holding a sign: "I will work for *you*."

> George Bush is worried because unemployed people have a lot of time to get out and vote.

> Ann Landers printed a letter from President Bush. This is amazing to me. The president doesn't have time to write an economic plan. How does he have time to write Ann Landers?

Arsenio Hall, another late-night host (on whose program Bill Clinton would score points with the younger set by donning dark glasses and tooting his saxophone), also showed his feelings about the state of the economy. When there was a proposal that Bush's 1949 apartment in Compton, California, be declared a memorial, Hall said: "These days that actual apartment is filled with people who are very poor, unemployed, and hopeless. Sounds to me like it's *already* a memorial to Mr. Bush."

A west coast comedy writer who had served other Democrats in less auspicious campaigns, provided Clinton with sardonic lines to use on Bush regarding the dormant economy:

Mr. Bush insists we're not in a recession. Mr. Bush is like the fellow who looks at a camel and says there's no such animal. Well, this one has two lumps.

Bush says bad times are just a perception—that a lot of people are working. It reminds me of the guy who says, "I hear a lot about homeless people. But I go to a lot of parties and I don't see any."

America's editorial cartoonists had a field day with the economic stagnancy and Bush's state of denial. Wasserman in the *Boston Globe* showed Bush with an upbeat posture and this telegraphic speech: "Sure, dollar is weak . . . personal income down . . . growth sluggish . . . sales flat . . . but, hey, let's accentuate the positive—food stamps are strong!" Bush's reluctance to give explicit form to his economic plans triggered other gibes. Wasserman showed a woman challenging Bush: "You said you'd cut spending and cap some benefits, but you won't say specifically what will be cut or capped. How can we know your real plans?" Replies Bush: "Read my mind." And when Bush asserted that Governor Clinton had raised taxes 128 times in Arkansas, Pat Oliphant in the *Washington Post* showed a taxpayer in the murderous maw of a huge leopard that is labeled "POVERTY." Only the poor fellow's head protrudes from the beast's jaws as he says to the President: "Hey George, tell me again how many times Clinton has raised taxes." Another witty member of the cartoon fraternity is Jeff MacNelly, whose work appears in the *Chicago Tribune* and elsewhere. MacNelly showed three terrified men in a sinking rowboat, from which Bush is contentedly fishing. The anchor (marked "THE ECONOMY") is stuck in the sand, as an aide says to the chief: "Yessir, it's quite a big one." Perhaps the most caustic of the editorial cartoonists down through the decades has been Herbert Block of the *Washington Post*, known as Herblock. Political junkies with long memories recall his caricatures of a grinning Ike, an unshaven Nixon, a slimy Joe McCarthy. Still at the old stand, Herblock portrayed Bush as a used car salesman, cheerfully hauling a voter out of a demolished car called "BUSH-QUAYLE '88," and pointing him toward a shiny new model that is held together by spit and rubber bands. The sign on the second car reads "THE BRAND NEW USED BUSH-QUAYLE."

Bush suffered from the perception that he was less interested in the stalled economy than he was in matters of foreign policy. Said one satirist: "Mr. Bush should be aware that the average American is as desperate about keeping *his* job as Mr. Bush is about keeping *his*."

Bush's seeming indifference to his domestic duties occupied me in the 1992 edition of *Who's In Charge Here?*, my little election year farrago. In a photo of the Oval Office, I produced some offstage conversation. Says a voice: "This Administration has nothing to be ashamed of." And another answers: "Then what are we doing under the sofa?" Elsewhere in the book, I alluded to Bush's preference for foreign summits over domestic dilemmas. The photo showed a beaming George Bush shaking the hands of a group of followers, and Bush is saying: "So this is America." And in another shot, an ardent follower extends a palm to Bush, saying: "I'd like to shake your hand while you're still president." My favorite is a shot of Bush aloft in Air Force One, declaring: "So that's my strategy. I don't come down till after the recession."

During the House banking scandal, when so many congressmen were shown to have written numerous bouncing checks, one anonymous beltway wag said: "George Bush says the GOP has had no bad checks. Just the trillion dollar debt." And *Current Comedy*, the newsletter of humor for professional speakers, noted with some skepticism Bush's assurance that the economy was improving—but Americans just haven't gotten the word. "I guess the word is traveling by mail," it said. And as the presidential debates approached, *Newsweek* offered a humorous sound bite for candidate Clinton's use should Bush raise the question of his behavior during the draft: "Just say, 'I may not have served in the armed forces during Vietnam, but George Bush has been AWOL from the problems of this country for the last four years.'" Clinton chose not to follow their advice. But when Bush adopted Dan Quayle's crusade for family values and said he preferred a family like the Waltons to a family like the Simpsons, Bart Simpson showed no such discretion. He piped, "We're just like the Waltons. Both families spend a lot of time praying for the end of the Depression."

As the campaign continued and Bush showed no signs of advancing an aggressive plan to restore the economy, the invincible Jay Leno reported that he had just received a chain letter. "It says put $500 in an envelope and send it to the name on the top of the list. And then I realized this wasn't a chain letter. This is President Bush's new economic plan."

Those with long memories recalled the whistle stop railroad tour that had carried Harry Truman to an upset victory over Governor Tom Dewey in 1948. And so it may have seemed strategically shrewd for President Bush to assume the posture of that feisty onetime leader who had pulled off a startling upset. Said Leno: "President Bush spent the weekend on a Harry Truman type whistle stop tour aboard an Amtrak train. . . . Just a year ago who would have thought the Amtrak train would be on track and Bush's campaign would be derailed?" Said a Hollywood scribe: "Mr. Bush compared himself to Harry Truman. When Clark Clifford heard that, he said, 'I knew Harry Truman. Harry Truman was a friend of mine. And Mr. Bush, you're no Harry Truman.' (One Washington oldtimer was reminded of that long-ago campaign. On Election Day, Governor Tom Dewey was so confident of victory that he told his wife, "My dear, tonight you'll be sleeping with the President of the United States." When Truman scored his upset, Mrs. Dewey said, "Let me get this straight Tom. Do I go to Washington or is Mr. Truman coming here?")

But there was to be no upset victory for George Bush. From its highwater mark when he was the hero of the Gulf War, Bush's approval rating had dropped like a Mafia mobster in the East River. One comic said that Bush had complained to General Norman Schwartzkopf: "Next time we start the war closer to the election." And said *Current Comedy*: "This has not been a wildly successful term for George Bush. . . . The country is down to, oh, twenty or thirty points of light." Even by the dubious measurement of bumper stickers, one could perceive a certain lack of enthusiasm for the President. One GOP sticker read: "GEORGE BUSH—I SUPPOSE." Another asked: "ARE WE KINDER AND GENTLER YET?" And a third was more provocative still: "SADDAM HUSSEIN STILL HAS A JOB. DO YOU?"

David Letterman devoted his Top Ten List one evening to signs that, adrift in the lower latitudes of public approval, Bush was panicking. His writers had produced these clues:

7. Has been urging Barbara to show a little more leg.
6. Has been throwing rocks at Bill Clinton's bus.
5. Started hoarding peanuts from Air Force One.
4. Recently shot Barbara in the foot thinking she was a prowler.
3. White House vending machine now stocks Halcyon.
2. Calls Jim Baker "Mommy."
1. Nude press conferences.

Nothing showed Bush's slip in popular approval like the reaction of other Republican candidates at the congressional and gubernatorial level. Mark Russell observed that Republican candidates were suddenly finding themselves on the Bush slate and not delighted at the propinquity. "There is an old political proverb," said Russell. "'When the emperor is naked, he who rides his coattails must bring his own coat.'" Bush's growing desperation—and a desire to be seen sharing the pain of more humble Americans—could be seen in his request that Congress cut his pay by ten percent. Said an unmoved Jay Leno, "I guess this is his final markdown before the big November clearance sale."

The taint of the Iran-contra scandal clung to George Bush throughout the campaign year. He had protested repeatedly that he was "out of the loop" when the decision was made to ransom American hostages by shipping arms to Ayatollah Khomeini, but with the publication of George Schultz's memoirs, the testimony of "Cap" Weinberger, and the stormy protestations of Special Prosecutor Walsh, there seemed room for doubt. The question just would not go away. Cartoonist Mike Luckovich in the *Atlanta Constitution* showed Bush lying supine, a dog labeled "IRAN-CONTRA SCANDAL" standing on his chest and licking his face. Says a beleaguered Bush: "I've never seen this dog before in my life!" C. P. Houston in the *Houston Chronicle* pictured Bush with a hangman's noose labeled "THE IRAN/CONTRA THING" descending around his neck. Bush is terrified. The cartoon's inevitable caption: IN THE LOOP." Said one Beltway wag: "We had trickle down economics. But with Iraqgate and Iran-contra we have trickle down truth."

Newsweek, on its impish Periscope page, offered a sound bite to Ross Perot for his use in the television debates. "When Bush knocks you for jumping in and out of the race," suggested the editors, "you say 'I'm still trying to find out if *you* were in or out of the loop on Iran-Contra. As for Saddam, you weren't in the loop, you were in his pocket.'"

Newsweek's allusion to Saddam Hussein was the other side of Bush's Middle Eastern quandry. The President's prewar dealings with Iraq had become a major campaign issue. So when Bush vehemently denied having built up Iraq's economy before the war, Jay Leno deadpanned: "I don't believe it. We finally find an economy he's improved and now he won't even take credit for it."

Bush may not have shot his wife in the foot as David Letterman mordantly suggested, but he did shoot himself in the foot by permitting the U.S. State Department to go riffling through the passport files of Bill Clinton and his mother. Republican strategists—if that is the word—were seeking evidence that Clinton had sought to relinquish his U.S. citizenship. Comedians had a field day with this wretched excess of zeal. When this story hit the papers, along with a report that Bush had convened a meeting in the Oval Office at which he was urged to imply that Clinton may have met with KGB agents on a student trip to Moscow, you would have thought

45

that Dan Quayle had spelled "potato" with a "q." One Friend of Bill was moved to fax the following gibes to the candidate for his use in responding to Bush's plot:

> Bush said he would do anything to win this election. For the first time I believe him.

> Mr. Bush says I may have met with Russian spies in Moscow. I saw a headline recently that said, SPACE ALIENS MEET WITH PRESIDENT BUSH. I didn't give it much thought, but maybe we ought to look into it.

> The KGB may have wanted to meet with me in Moscow, but unfortunately I was out of the loop.

> I've heard that patriotism is the last refuge of scoundrels. Now I see it's also the last resort of politicians.

> I was just a college student spending three days in Moscow. I'm not able to claim, as Mr. Bush does, that he singlehandedly brought down the Soviet Empire.

Mark Russell, whose satirical and musical gifts are often on display on PBS and before delighted audiences across America, expressed disdain for the State Department's search through the files of Mr. Clinton's mother. Addressing Bush's claim of greater experience, Russsell observed drily: "Bush is right. It takes experience to make those tough decisions—managing the economy, dealing with foreign countries, spying on Clinton's mother." Referring to the entire unsavory ploy as "Operation Mom," Russell smiled: "It will be a big Republican victory once the voters find out that the person who gave Saddam Hussein the okay to go ahead and take northern Kuwait was Clinton's mother." Concluded Russell indignantly: "Using the State Department for campaign purposes is illegal! That's why we have an FBI."

A cartoonist in the *Houston Chronicle* pictured an oafish fellow built like an elephant and adorned in stars and stripes, waving a sign that read: "WHAT WAS BILL CLINTON DOING IN MOSCOW 20 YEARS AGO?" A dismayed bystander carries his own sign which reads: "AND WHAT ARE MEATBALLS LIKE

YOU DOING IN AMERICA IN 1992?" Mike Luckovich in the *Atlanta Constitution* mocked Bush's intemperate attack. He showed Bush holding a photo of trick-or-treaters on Halloween night. The one in the middle wears a sheet and carries a saxophone; another resembles Chelsea Clinton. Says Bush: "I have proof! During Clinton's school years he was a member of the Klan!"

Bill Clinton met the charges more in irony than anger, allowing the ludicrous attack to fall of its own weight. Said Clinton: "The State Department was not only riffling through my files, but actually investigated my mother—a well-known subversive. Brezhnev was calling my mother to get tips on the third race at Oaklawn every night. She had a little shrine in the corner of our home to Joe Stalin."

President Bush had welcomed a shirtsleeved Larry King to the White House for a CNN interview during which he suggested Clinton might have had liaisons with KGB agents. This led Herblock to show a member of the GOP campaign staff rushing about, flourishing a piece of paper: "How's this one for the talk show circuit—When Bill Clinton was a kid, he threw his porridge on the floor."

To some older Americans, Bill Clinton's boyish looks didn't look very presidential. (Neither did Jack Kennedy's or Thomas Jefferson's.) But George Bush looked something less than presidential when, on a state visit to Japan in search of auto trade concessions, he was seized by a momentary indisposition and regurgitated in the lap of the Japanese prime minister. Bush joked about the incident in his State of the Union address when he said, "I noticed that Vice President Quayle and Speaker Tom Foley are laughing. After what happened to me in Tokyo, they're just glad they're sitting *behind* me." Bush had gone to Japan in the company of leading auto executives to seek a relaxation in trade restrictions. One comic said that Bush was learning to beg in Japanese. Said Dave Barry: "The President went over and signed the historic trade agreement under which the Japanese government agreed to buy a Chevrolet Caprice . . . which is now back over here with transmission problems." And said one journalist at the National Press Club: "Perhaps Bush could have won reelection if he had brought a food taster along to Tokyo." *Current Comedy* quipped: "The good news is, President Bush's policies are creating lots of jobs. The bad news is, they're in Japan."

When Hurricane Andrew hit south Florida in the midst of the campaign it was the perfect opportunity for President Bush to show his concern for the needy. Unfortunately, in this uncharacteristically misbegotten campaign, Bush didn't respond promptly enough and came off looking callous and out of touch. Ohlmon in the *Oregonia* showed the White House flying through the hurricane, very much out of control, and a voice crying from within the West Wing: "I'd like to declare this a political disaster area." Cartoonist Mike Peters in the *Dayton Daily News* showed George Bush arriving in a helicopter at the scene of the devastation; disaster and debris are everywhere. Bush waves cheerfully and smiles his lopsided grin. Says an onlooker to his wife: "Have you ever seen such a disaster?" and his wife replies, "No, but his wife Barbara is nice."

Bush appeared something less than bold and presidential when the first two debates were cancelled because he couldn't agree to the format proposed by the bipartisan debate committee. Said Jay Leno: "President Bush insists on increasing the number of moderators from one to three. And if he gets his way, these will be the first jobs he's created in four years." And when the candidates' spokesmen finally agreed on matters of format, Mark Russell said: "We almost didn't have any debates. The president was holding out for multiple-choice questions." Bush took his lumps in the debates. He appeared ill at ease in the town hall format of the second one, and was savaged by maverick Ross Perot who, when challenged on his lack of presidential experience, snapped: "Well, I don't have any experience at running up a trillion dollar debt." As Bush temporized about the format of the debate, Democrats suggested that he lacked the necessary grit. Indeed, at one point they hired a man in a giant chicken suit to appear at Bush rallies. Said Leno: "Michael Dukakis said this was the most degrading job he's ever had." When Bush shouted for the man to 'shut up and sit down," Leno expressed puzzlement about the whole campaign. "Last night," he said, "Mr. Bush said that he'd never do anything to damage the integrity of the presidency. Then he gets in a shouting match with a guy in a giant chicken suit."

Even Dan Quayle was moved to say, after the votes were counted, "If Bill Clinton runs the country as well as he ran his campaign, we may be all right." Most observers felt that George Bush had not run a well organized campaign. Said a sardonic Dave Barry: "I can't blame the president for being a little bitter. It had to be hard being rejected after running such a strong campaign, such a shrewdly organized campaign, with his keen tacticians, Wayne and Garth." Barry alluded to several Bush gaffes including "that shrewd idea of calling Clinton and Gore 'bozos.'" He reflected on what may have happened in the Clinton War Room after this epithet was hurled into the campaign, since the Clinton camp was famous for their quick responses. "To see Carville and all those people sitting around and saying, 'What do we come back with?' I say 'geek.' But there was a big contingent for 'dweeb.'"

One of Bush's major assets was his wife Barbara. Dave Barry recalled meeting the First Lady during the New Hampshire primaries and being mesmerized. "I was truly impressed by her eyes," said the humorist. "They're really scary eyes. . . . She can give you looks that give you dime sized spots in your forehead." Bush acknowledged the popularity of his spouse, which far exceeded his own, at the opening of his State of the Union Address at the start of the election year: "I wanted to make sure that this speech would be a big hit, but unfortunately I couldn't get Barbara to deliver it for me."

When *Newsweek* put Pat Buchanan on its cover, it bore the headline "BULLY BOY." For George Bush, Pat Buchanan, former Nixon speech writer, abrasive CNN broadcaster, and primary attacker from the right, was his worst nightmare. The religious right had never fully trusted Bush, as they did Ronald Reagan, who came from their own ranks. Bush's commitment to their causes seemed more expedient than sincere. And when Bush reversed his much-publicized pledge of "no new taxes," the climate was right for the emergence of a Pat Buchanan to challenge Bush for the nomination. (Bush drew humorous flak for failing to keep his vow. One comic said

Bush had learned his lesson and offered a new pledge: "Read my lips—no new promises!") The right wing was up in arms, so Doug Gamble provided Bush with some self-deprecatory humor with which to charm them. Addressing a religious audience at the GOP convention, Bush said: "If I catch fire in my acceptance speech tonight, it might give a whole new meaning to the story of the burning bush." But the religious right could not be charmed into line by a surrogate Ronald Reagan. They relished the real thing—or at least someone like Pat Buchanan.

Buchanan provoked a good deal of derisive laughter among the White House team and the professional comics, but his gifts as a candidate—an application of the vigorous, combative talents he used on CNN's "Crossfire"—made him a formidable challenger. (A sample Buchanan invective: He called Chairman Deng, who Bush had appeased, "an 85-year-old chain-smoking communist dwarf.") So effective was he as a candidate, and so vital to Bush were his conservative followers, that Buchanan was given a prime-time slot for his speech on opening night of the GOP convention. Mark Russell observed that during the primaries, Buchanan "bashed George Bush more than anybody. More than any Democrat. So who is the opening speaker in Houston? Pat Buchanan. Pat Buchanan— who I think delivered the greatest speech that David Duke ever wrote." "I liked the Buchanan speech," said bestselling Texas author Molly Ivins. "It was probably better in the original German."

After a strong beginning, Buchanan's primary campaign had declined. Said Dennis Miller: "He got his butt kicked on Super Tuesday. I hope it doesn't cause brain damage." Added the ascerbic Miller: "Pat Buchanan doesn't want to create a third party. A third Reich maybe." In my quadrennial photo humor book, *Who's In Charge Here?*, I showed a pugnacious head shot of Buchanan orating angrily. "I have been called an anti-Semite, a racist, a sexist, and a fascist. Well, nobody's perfect." One standup comic pointed out Buchanan's loyalty to the GOP: "Buchanan says he will drop out if he is hurting the party. And Hitler said he would drop out if he was hurting Poland."

Buchanan's criticism of Bush was more strident than

Clinton's or even Perot's. Said Buchanan with bitter irony, "I hope to be the main speaker at the 1994 dedication of the George Bush Presidential Library." And: "Left unscripted, Bush comes off as phony as a novice urban cowboy at Gilly's." When Dan Quayle ventured a criticism of Pat the Hun, as some called him, he responded acidly: "I don't want to say anything critical of Dan Quayle. I don't want to be charged with child abuse."

Buchanan's attacks, whoever the target, were uniformly caustic. Said Jud Pearson, after Buchanan attacked Hillary Clinton as a feminist radical, "If George Bush reminds many women of their first husbands, Pat Buchanan reminds women why an increasing number of them are staying single." And screenwriter/author Nora Ephron seemed to have Buchanan in mind when she said, "As far as the men who are running for president are concerned, they aren't even people I would date." (Buchanan was able to laugh at his own offensive demeanor. Asked why so many people seemed to take an instant dislike to him, he said: "It saves time.")

The GOP convention—thanks to the apostles of the far right who molded its platform, and to Pat Buchanan who spoke of a cultural holy war—led many moderate Republicans to deep misgivings. Said Dave Barry, "The perception on the part of the public was that the convention had been dominated a little too much by the religious right, especially as they opened the second night by burning a suspected witch."

The moment the Democratic convention ended, the matter that numerous Republicans began discussing was the dispensability of Vice President Quayle as George Bush's running mate. After all, Clinton held a substantial two-to-one lead over Bush in the polls, and it was clear to anyone but the most politically naive that the easiest way to reduce that extraodrinary lead was to drop Quayle, who had been a subject of levity and scorn for four years and was seen as a drag on the ticket. This view was thought to be held by many GOP moderates, including Jim Baker. (Since Baker would soon be in charge of the campaign, the abandonment of Quayle seemed quite possible.) But Quayle's loyalists demurred. "It's just not going to happen!" said one of the veep's top aides. Conservatives quickly circled the wagons, with Quayle in their center. "The hard reality that the Quayle-haters can't abide," said the editor of the *Washington Times*, "is that Mr. Quayle's position is actually more secure than the president's."

At the sound of these words, a great sigh of relief went up from America's humorists. What would they do without the glorious flaws of the vice president? He had been a reliable source of humor for forty-eight months. Said David Letterman's head writer, "He's like the Halley's Comet of politicians. Something as good as that only comes along every seventy-five years."

This year Dan Quayle was to outdo himself as a provider of levity for America's wits. When Johnny Carson chose to retire in the spring of '92, he wanted to conclude his decades of humor on the "Tonight Show" in a blaze of glory. So, providentially, a week before Johnny left the air, Dan Quayle launched an attack on a fictional character named Murphy Brown. "You didn't let me down," laughed Carson. Johnny's successor, the talented monologist Jay Leno, was also to profit from Quayle's ineptitude in the months ahead. When a baby threw up on Bill Clinton on the campaign trail, Leno said, "Wait'll you see what Murphy Brown's baby does when he meets Dan Quayle."

Quayle turned the national focus from the election campaign and matters economic to "Murphy Brown" when he lambasted the CBS sitcom for its title character's decision to become a single mother. He blasted the character for "mocking the importance of fathers by bearing a child alone and calling it just another lifestyle choice." It reflected, said Quayle, the dearth of family values in America. But when America's comics directed a stream of ridicule at the veep for his assault on a fictitious character, Quayle tried to be a good sport about the derision. He arranged to watch the season premiere of the show in the company of some single mothers and fathers in a minority section of Washington. (Said Mark Russell: "Next week he will watch 'Cheers' with a group of alcoholics.")

The group of single parents laughed heartily at the show's jokes at Quayle's expense; Quayle was less amused. He laughed the least of the group. The special hour-long broadcast of "Murphy Brown" showed Murphy bringing home the baby. The episode mixed fiction with actual tape of Quayle, so the veep became an unwitting and unpaid supporting player on the show. Quayle came in for some verbal broadsides in the script. Murphy (played by Candice Bergen) reacted to Quayle's 'attacks during an editorial part of the fictional news show. "Some might argue," she said, "that attacking my status as a single mother was nothing more than a cynical bit of election year posturing. . . . I prefer to give the vice president the benefit of the doubt. These are difficult times for our country and in searching for the causes of our social ills, we could choose to blame the media [many did], or the Congress [more did], or an Administration that's been in power for twelve years [sixty percent did], or we could blame me."

Midway through the season-opening show, which had been kept carefully under wraps till airtime—Washington secrets should be so leakproof—the frazzled, unwashed new mother hears news footage of Quayle's speech reproaching her. Says Murphy in exasperation: "I'm glamorizing single motherhood?? What planet is he on? Look at me. . . . And what was that crack about just another lifestyle choice? I didn't just wake up one morning and say, 'Oh gee, I can't get in for a facial so I might as well have a baby.'"

Quayle tried to play along with the jollity at his own expense. He sent Murphy's baby a gift—a stuffed toy elephant. He even filmed an announcement for a Los Angeles station promoting their reruns of the show. Said Quayle on the promo: "I'll be sure to be watching my favorite show, 'Murphy Brown.'" Then he added, a la *Wayne's World*, "not!"

By this time in the race, Bush-Quayle's future did not look promising, so the vice president quipped, "Actually, I'm a little envious of Murphy Brown. At least she's guaranteed of coming back this fall." (Candice Bergen might have replied as Babe Ruth did when it was pointed out that he earned more than President Herbert Hoover: "I've had a better year.") The show scored well in the Emmy Awards ceremony. It's producer hurled some barbs at Quayle and noted that if it took two parents to prevent a dysfunctional household, how did they account for the Ronald Reagan family? Quayle sought to take credit for the shower of Emmys. "Now, Murphy Brown, listen closely," he said, 'because I'm only going to say it once—you owe me." Numberless comedy writers, stand-up comedians, editorial cartoonists, and syndicated columnists felt they owed him too. Quayle's quixotic crusade against Murphy Brown played well for humor. Wasserman in the *Boston Globe* showed Quayle carrying Bush's golf bag as he reads the paper. Says the vice president: "Gosh, George, in recent years family income has been coming down and economic growth is way off. . . . Hollywood sure has a lot to answer for."

At the Oscars ceremony that year, Billy Crystal noted that Disney's *Beauty and the Beast* was the first cartoon ever nominated—since Dan Quayle. And a waggish nominee said that Quayle deserved to win the Oscar for Funniest Man in a Serious Role.

Quayle dropped the forced laughter to express right-eous indignation at this derision by Hollywood's "cultural elite" and said he "wears their scorn like a badge of honor." "That makes sense," said Jay Leno."If you don't have any actual war medals, you have to come up with something."

Art Buchwald, the dean of Washington satirists, cited a letter he had received from a reader of his column, that asked: "What will happen to Murphy Brown once the election is over?" Responded Buchwald, "The inside dope is that if there is a Bush-Quayle victory, Murphy will join the U.S. Navy Tail-hook Association in hopes of finding a suitable father for her child."

Just how much America's humorists were indebted to Dan Quayle may be measured in a book called *The Official Lite Unauthorized Biography of J. Danforth Quayle*, which was pub-lished during the campaign. One might well ask: What other figure in American public life could spawn an entire volume of his gaffes and the humorous responses thereto? What other public figure could have referred to the Nazi Holocaust as "an obscene period in our nation's history," and then try to clarify what he meant by adding, "I didn't live in this century"? What other vice president, on a trip to American Samoa, would ad-dress an indigenous audience as follows: "You all look like happy campers to me. Happy campers you are, happy campers you have always been and, as far as I am concerned, happy campers you will always be."

Quayle seems to invite ridicule with his modest intellectual gifts. Said comedy writer Sandy Krinsky: "If Quayle loses, he plans to become a movie critic. He's anxious to review 'Malcolm Ten.'" In *Who's in Charge Here?* I showed a photo of Bush addressing an audience of law-enforcement officers and displaying a tiny three-inch revolver. Bush is saying, "An attempt has been made to blow the vice president's brains out." Elsewhere in the book, Bush holds his head in dismay and groans, "Dan Quayle bought a Toyota!" And when Quayle had a putting green and a swimming pool installed at his official residence, Dennis Miller said, "You'd think the swing set and the sand box would have been enough." In its "Conventional Wisdom" department, *Newsweek* cited the old and the new perceptions of Dan Quayle:

The old CW on Quayle: Rich, draft-dodging airhead.
The new CW on Quayle: Ambitious, calculating airhead.

The references to Quayle's cerebral deficiencies rolled on. *Current Comedy* said: "The good news is Bill Clinton chose a running mate who is his intellectual equal. The bad news is, George Bush did too." As the vice presidential debate approached, *Current Comedy* reflected that debating Dan Quayle was like playing handball against the Venus DeMilo. And when Bush refused to dump Quayle, it remarked, "that shows admirable concern for the environment." Said another wag in chagrin: "George Bush says he's going to change the world. He won't even change his vice president." Because *Current Comedy's* subscribers are primarily professional speakers, whose audiences include corporate, college, and civic groups, this humor at Quayle's expense rippled out into a hundred forums. When Quayle sought to act with dignity and stature, *Current Comedy* commented, "Quayle acting presidential is like a eunuch in a harem. He's there every night, he watches it happen, he sees how it's done—but he just can't do it himself." And in the final put-down of the Quayle acumen, the newsletter deplored the people who were exhorting Bush to drop Quayle. "Isn't it bad enough that the doctor who delivered him did?"

Dan Quayle did not limit his contribution to the laughter of Campaign '92 to raising the Murphy Brown issue. On a visit to a New Jersey classroom, Quayle misspelled "potato" with a final "e," correcting a youngster who had spelled it correctly. Senator Tom Harken suggested that Dan Quayle might sing the old song "Old McDonald Had a Farm" "e-i-e-i-o . . . e." Murphy Brown ended their season premiere with a shot of a thousand pounds of potatoes being unceremoniously dumped at Quayle's doorstep. And in his acceptance speech to the Democratic convention, Bill Clinton enumerated the things that he had that Bush did not: "He doesn't have Al Gore but I do. Just in case you didn't notice, that's 'Gore' with an 'e' at the end." And after Quayle visited still another school, this one in south central Los Angeles, a youngster added insult to injury. Said 14-year-old Vanessa Marinez with chilling condescension, "He seems like an average type of man. He's not, like, smart. I'm not trying to rag him or anything. But he has the same mentality I have—and I'm in the eighth grade." After Quayle made a speech calling the erudite Governor Mario Como "liberalism's sensitive philosopher-king," Cuomo reflected, "I wonder who wrote all those long words for him."

For those who felt that the press, the comics, and the "cultural elite" were targeting the veep unfairly, it must be noted that Quayle often contributed to their perception of him as an intellectual lightweight. Asked whether he would seek the presidency in the next election, which will be in 1996, Quayle said: "Let us see George Bush reelected this November. Then we'll talk about 1994." This was a patent case of life imitating art. Paul Krassner, in his popular satiric lecture before college audiences, got his biggest laugh by saying, "During the Republican convention, Dan Quayle could be seen marching around the arena, chanting, 'Three more years—three more years—.'"

Why did George Bush lose? Well, from the beginning of the election year, he had scorned continual admonitions from his staff to "come out swinging" and "get fired up" if he wanted to win reelection. Bush was in no hurry. Where electoral warfare was concerned, he had never been (in Dan Quayle's words to the citizens of Samoa) a happy camper. His relish for this particular battle was dampened by the blasting he had taken from the press and public for the rude McCarthy overtones of his '88 campaign—the flag, the Pledge of Allegiance, and other irrelevancies. It was not pleasant to so often recall or be reminded of the distasteful way in which he had beat Dukakis. He was not eager to trod the mean streets again. Like many who hold public office, Bush preferred reigning to running. He would not even be rushed into declaring himself a candidate and diving into the whole grubby process.

As the campaign opened, Bush's behavior looked to many (not just David Letterman) like panic. He made surprising changes of policy. His long awaited mission to Japan was suddenly delayed. And all the while, Bush's approval rating was sliding down a slippery slope.

Bush seemed out of touch with the plight of the voter in general and the inner-city in particular. According to Mark Russell, when Bush went to south central L. A. after the riots that followed the Rodney King verdict, "he spotted someone in the audience and said, 'Pardon me, sir, but are you a social worker?' and the guy said 'No, I'm Jack Kemp, your Secretary of Housing and Urban Development.'"

Why did Bush lose? According to James Carville, Clinton's strategy maven, Bush's defeat resulted from his campaign's distraction by a fevered search for a silver bullet in Clinton's draft records. "That was a mistake," said Carville. "By the general election, people had decided the issue was not important enough to make them change their vote. Yet the Bush people stubbornly continued 'beating their heads against a dead horse.'"

Mark Russell found a simpler reason for Bush's loss. Clinton was "from a place called Hope, Arkansas. You can't make that up. So when Clinton would say—I still believe in a place called Hope, that had a better sound to it than if Bush would say—I still believe in a place called . . . Kennebunkport."

Bush may have depended too much on a declaration of his "experience," forgetting what Oscar Wilde had said about experience—it is the name we give to our mistakes.

In addition, Bush's people never were as bold in their programing of the President on the proliferating TV channels as were Clinton's and Perot's handlers. *National Review's* poet in residence Von Dreel laid down a warning that was ignored, suggesting that the President appear on more innovative television media:

> Put him on Oprah,
> Larry King has space.
> Donahue would take him
> As a change of pace.
> Anyway, don't stand there:
> Move the guy around!
> Otherwise you'll find him
> In the Lost and Found.

Once the election was history, humorist Dave Barry turned an eye to the regrets and disappointments of President Bush, who was manifestly suffering from bitterness and depression after his sweeping rejection at the polls. Said Barry at the National Press Club, as all eyes were on the president-elect in Little Rock: "No one has been covering Acting President Bush, who I think may be harboring a little bitterness tinged with exhaustion as a result of the arduous campaign. I base this on the fact that this morning he declared war on Belgium, appointed Gennifer Flowers secretary of state, and pardoned Manuel Noriega."

Chapter 3

Campaign 1992
The Uncandidate

A lot of people supported Perot. The Perot supporters—I love ya—but you are the new moonies.
—MARK RUSSELL

Perot was a self-made myth. He was always that most
popular of American specimens, the self-made man. Said one
wag during the '92 campaign that Perot turned upside-down:
"He's the ultimate self-made man. A tribute to unskilled
labor."

The seed of the Perot myth was planted when he dispatched a band of mercenaries to get a couple of his executives out of an Iranian prison. Carter dawdled while Perot sent
in the cavalry. It was the perfect premise for a TV movie, and
it became one, a docudrama starring Richard Crenna as Perot,
the reckless hero. "What a Japanese suicide pilot he would
have made," said a Perot employee.

Ross Perot, though he bore little resemblance to Gary
Cooper, called to mind the lone hero of *High Noon*, ready to
take on all comers, be they gunmen or bureaucrats, killers or
politicians. This Horatio Alger acted like Clint Eastwood,
tough, determined, intense. Said one former employee: "He's
the only man I know with clenched hair." He was articulate in
a homespun way, and he dominated any conversation in which
he took part, whether in a corporate boardroom or a presi-

dential debate. Said one associate: "He talks by hour glass and listens by stopwatch."

Of couse, he didn't exactly look like Eastwood or Cooper. As Campaign 1992 began, he was 61, a bantamweight whose most singular characteristic (which fed the humorists and cartoonists) was his jug ears. Said Torie Clarke: "I have a hard time relating to somebody whose wingspan is wider than his total height." Other Perot physical traits that generated laughter included a lacerated nose, a fifties haircut, and a thin, reedy, Texas drawl.

Perot is an extraordinary and idiosyncratic man. Said Bill Clinton's press secretary Dee Dee Myers of the Perot phenomenon: "How do you compete with a pet rock?" Perot provoked more humorous japes than anyone since Dan Quayle. Mark Russell called him "the heir apparent to Emmett Kelly and God's gift to comedians everywhere." And that he was. Satirists, op-ed writers, standup comics, and editorial cartoonists everywhere found food for their mimicry in the cocky industrialist. If Helen's was the face that launched a thousand ships, Ross was the persona that launched a thousand jokes, many of the best ones from Jay Leno on "The Tonight Show." Leno said the country would be better off if more politicians were like Perot. "They'd be too short, too rich to bribe, and they'd quit before they did any real damage." Fred Barnes, the house conservative of *The New Republic*, called him "the Freddie Krueger of American politics."

Ross Perot was the most famous American salesman since Willy Loman, but he was far more successful than Arthur Miller's pathetic creation. Perot's wife would never moan: "Attention must be paid." Perot made you pay attention. He had launched a computer-systems enterprise that made him one of the richest men in the land. As Harry Kurnitz said, "In Budapest everybody lies about how much money they've got. And in Dallas everybody lies about how much money they've got. Only in Dallas they are telling the truth." Perot's worth was between two and three billion, and business rivals said he could be a jagged weapon when he tried to land an important contract. (Bush and Clinton would learn the truth of that.) Perot was that Harold Robbins creation, the cutthroat businessman with a heart of gold. His eyes would cloud over when he insisted that he had "married way above him." "I'm beginning to think he's right," said one comic.

With the help of ghostwriter Robert Novak, Lee Iacocca had captured our imaginations. But he had only created the Mustang. Perot created an army of fevered volunteers, a third-party movement that threatened to topple a sitting president. Perot had wonderful speech mannerisms. Some of his signature phrases included "It's that simple" and "Isn't it beautiful" and "I'm willing to get down under the hood." (Kevin Phillips said, "Ross Perot is running as the National Roto-Rooter Man.") These phrases were a gift to political humorists everywhere. Comics did takeoffs on his speech more often than that of George Bush and his telegraphic syntax. Dana Carvey on "Saturday Night Live" had Perot down pat.

Another trademark Perot colloquialism was that the key to reducing the deficit was "to measure twice and cut once." Said Jay Leno: "Too bad his barber didn't follow that advice.

The attitude of the electorate as Campaign '92 began was one to lend comfort to the heart of any outsider with an agenda. Fifty pecent of the voters felt "a pox on both their houses," and had a balanced detestation of both candidates. So, one evening on "Larry King Live," Ross Perot responded to the people who had been urging him for years to run for president. He said that if the public put him on the ballot in every last state, he'd run. Larry King was a wonderful feel-good instrument for Perot's candidacy. Mike Wallace phoned the show and said, "Mr. Perot, what is it you get on the 'Larry King Show' that you don't get on 'Face the Nation' or 'Meet the Press'? Is it the softballs that Larry throws you?" Since Perot was whacking those softballs over the fence, Wallace's question was the most rhetorical of the year. Cartoonist Danziger in the *Christian Science Monitor* had shown Ross Perot seated by a morose Larry King, talking into King's microphone, his arm around the talk show host. Perot was saying: "Welcome to 'Ross Perot Live' with my guest Larry King." Cher phoned in with a breathless endorsement. Jay Leno was surprised: "You'd think by now she'd be fed up with short, amateur politicians."

Perot's timing was fortuitous—his Larry King declaration came on the heels of the New Hampshire primary. Both Clinton and Bush had hobbled out of that contest looking like the walking wounded. America needed some unbloodied candidate to step up to the plate. When Perot gave his "yes" to Larry King, the switchboard lit up with support. "There were three million calls," said Jay Leno. "They weren't all from supporters. Two million were from AT & T asking him to switch back." People were responding to Perot in enormous numbers—sometimes the most unlikely people. In the *Pittsburgh Press*, a rough looking, beer-bellied guy in a recliner is grousing: "I'm sick and tired of politicians who are out of touch with the common man. I'm voting for that Texas billionaire."

One thing was clear: Perot detested the way politics ran. He said he wanted to create a new political system that didn't attract "ego-driven, power-hungry people." Said *Current Comedy*: "That's like Adolf Hitler saying he wants to create a system that doesn't attract blood-thirsty lunatics with mustaches." And as much as Perot hated politicians, he seemed to hate lobbyists more. Art Buchwald kidded Perot's attacks on lobbyists. "The readers [of my column]," said Buchwald, "don't want to find out what is going on for the next four years from those boys in thousand dollar suits with blow dried hair."

Unfortunately, the little man who wanted to bring redemption to America's corrupt political system was biting off somewhat more than he could chew. Perot had set out to remedy what ailed the democratic system using business know-how and plain talk. Editorial cartoonists were skeptical. Pat Oliphant in the *Washington Post*, showed a magesterial Abe Lincoln, seated in his chair in the Lincoln Memorial, looking dubiously at Ross Perot, seated beside him in a baby chair. Perot is saying: "I'll settle for some of the people all of the time."

Paddy Chayevsky described a broadcaster tapping into the anger of the populace in the movie *Network*. They were "mad as hell and not going to take it anymore." Perot and his free-floating movement was exploiting a similar discontent. He felt disdain for George Bush and for a system so out of control that it could generate a trillion dollar debt.

When Perot offered himself to the public on the Larry King Show, with the qualification of being put on fifty ballots, one comic said: "It was like a love affair. Perot was throwing himself away—but he was taking careful aim." Perot got himself that business necessity, an "800" number, and the calls poured in. In one week, a million people phoned. Tens of thousands volunteered to help. Said Jay Leno dryly: "A lot of Ross Perot's volunteers are unhappy. They just figured out they're doing volunteer work for a billionaire." "A lot of these volunteers," recalled Mark Russell, "left Tsongas to go with Jerry Brown and then went with Perot. They should apply for a nice, steady job with TWA."

Perot would have had to be less than human not to enjoy the great gush of affection that flowed from these volunteers, their phone calls and their petitions. If, as Marshall Brickman said, "Kissing is the most fun you can have without laughing," the electorate's love was the most fun you could have without kissing. The TV talk shows glutted Perot with a banquet of attention.

Perot had little taste for politics. What he liked was talk shows. On talk shows, the queries were friendlier than they would be on inquisitions like "Meet the Press." There were no rude reporters demanding precision. Perot was discovering the experience that Eve Harrington described in *All About Eve*: "It's like waves of love wrapping you up. Imagine, to know every night that different hundreds of people love you." Of course, Perot didn't offer his callers explicit answers, just a dinner of sound bites.

But then two real pros joined the Perot crusade: Hamilton Jordan and Ed Rollins. They were to be co-chairmen of Perot's campaign. But Perot was not about to yield power to the pros. He was like the character in the Harry Kurnitz play who says, "Just because I hire you as an art expert doesn't mean I want you shooting off your mouth about art."

Rollins told Perot that the campaign was going to be tough sledding. He knew what Perot's foes would do: "They'll paint you as some kind of nutty, paranoid billionaire. If anything you do makes you into a kook, you lose."

The comics as well as the GOP did just that. Dave Barry described Perot as a perennial eccentric. He said, "My fear of

Ross Perot involves satellites." Barry described how his dogs responded to a "dog satellite"—they suddenly jump to attention for no apparent reason. "They hear the dog satellite. I think there is a similar thing going on with Ross Perot . . . all of a sudden his ears perk up and he says: 'We've gotta get this deficit down. We've gotta get rid of lobbyists in Washington. . . . The Republicans are putting a giant radioactive scorpion in my basement.'"

Said Mark Russell, reflecting on the idiosyncratic look of the Texas billionaire: "All the candidates have military endorsements. Admiral Crowe supports Clinton; General Schwartzkopf is backing Bush. Captain Crunch is for Perot."

Perot had said that if he were elected there would be no homosexuals in the cabinet or the upper echelons of a Perot Administration. And he had told the executives of his company that adulterers were not welcome. "How can I trust you if your wife can't trust you?" he asked reasonably. Which led the waspish *National Review* to say: "Ross Perot won't hire gays and adulterers for his administration. At last—a practical plan to shrink the size of goverment."

But on matters other than adultery and homosexuality, Perot's style was to prevaricate. When Rollins and Jordan sent him a one hundred fifty million dollar budget, he vetoed it. On the back cover of the 1992 edition of *Who's In Charge Here?* I showed Perot saying: "Okay, everybody turn in their Perot buttons. Those things cost money."

Earlier, Perot had said that he intended to spend one hundred million dollars to win the presidency. Cracked Representative Joseph P. Kennedy II, Bobby's son: "My grandfather only spent ten."

The reporters were elbowing Perot for decisions—how, when, and where would he declare himself a candidate? A shower of memos from Rollins and Jordan drifted to the ground, enough to form a small anthology of frustration. If Clinton would later find his own honeymoon brief, Perot's with the media was even briefer. The press was now pushing Perot on his alleged use of private eyes to spy on competitors, politicians, even his own kids. Mark Russell told of seeing a newspaper headline that read: "PEROT BAILOUT BOOSTS UNEMPLOYMENT. FIFTY PRIVATE DETECTIVES LAID OFF."

The myth was starting to unravel; the little billionaire was beginning to look like a little tyrant. Some people were uncomfortable to learn that if you worked for Perot you wore a white shirt, were clean-shaven, and were faithful to your wife, or else, These biases made a lot of people edgy—especially bearded womanizers in striped shirts. (When Perot attacked adultery and divorce, one comedy writer said, "There are eighty thousand divorces in America every year. There must be something good about it.") Under the growing media barrage, Perot's mountainous pride was injured. He felt betrayed. He mistrusted his high-priced campaign managers and so did the "white shirts" who worked for him. When Hamilton Jordan said that he was going out of town and would return to Dallas with a fantastic speech, a Perot aide said: "Who do you have in the suitcase, Ted Sorensen?"

Jordan and Rollins begged the noncandidate to get beyond the truisms and tell the voters where he stood. Despite their advice, Perot stuck with his one-liners. So all the voters saw was Inspector Perot and his battalion of gum shoes.

Perot's numbers started to corrode and his magic to rust. His press coverage was suddenly turning fiercely unfriendly. Every day he was sustaining more beatings for his brutal business practices. Then Perot delivered his maiden speech: it was to the NAACP convention, and it was a world class disaster. It consisted of a group of patriarchal stories of his youth. They had about them the aroma of the plantation, and included repeated references to African-Americans as "you people." He offended a lot of people that night. One of them was Aresenio Hall, who responded to Perot's "you people" remarks by saying: "Personally, Mr. Perot, I wasn't offended, you no-platform-having, inch-high, private eye, 'Dukes of Hazard'-sounding, gay-bashing, flip-flopping, got-a-million-dollars-in-the-bank-and-still-go-to-super cuts-to-show-off-them-big-dumbo-ears-of-corn. I wasn't offended at all."

Finally, Ross Perot made up his mind. He wanted Rollins and his people out. In a twinkling, security guards were everywhere. Offices were locked, computers went blank, phones lost their dial tones. Shouted one Rollins aide: "The train for Buchenwald leaves at five!" Perot was out of the race. He was history.

In his statement quitting the race, Perot explained that "the revitalization of the Democratic Party" assured that three-way split of the votes would surely throw the election into the House of Representatives, and that would certainly disrupt the electoral process. (A few months later Perot would cite other reasons.)

Comedians and journalists mocked Perot's sudden departure from the race. *Newsweek* called him THE QUITTER. Jay Leno remarked: "Ross Perot said the country would be better off if more politicians were like him. I couldn't agree more. I wish they'd all quit." Added Leno: "A recent survey shows that Ross Perot is still the favorite among young single males. Sure, they can't make a commitment either."

In *Who's In Charge Here? 1992* I showed a photo of Perot seated at his desk with the "Spirit of '76" behind him, addressing his followers: "And to the thousands of people who have worked so hard to put my name on the ballot, I offer this bit of advice. Get a life." Elsewhere in the book he says: "And to my wonderful supporters who I love all around the country I say—don't quit your jobs."

Pat Oliphant greeted Perot's departure from the race with intimations of cowardice. In the *Washington Post*, he showed a tiny Ross Perot standing outside the back door of the Alamo amidst a flock of chickens. Bullets fly. Gunsmoke is everywhere. Perot smiles complacently and says: "Any feller Texans in there need a hand from Ole Ross? Jest you give a holler, heah?" (The Oliphant trademark mouse is saying to a friend: "Watch where you step. Lot of chickens around here.") Said *Current Comedy*: "You don't realize how short Ross Perot's candidacy was until you consider that Liz Taylor's latest marriage has lasted longer."

And after Perot pulled out of the race, Mike Luckovich in the *Atlanta Constitution* pictured an agitated pet store owner. A caged parrot (Perot) at the counter is saying: "Bush, Clinton beware! Awwk! I'm your worst nightmare! Awwk! I'll be back! Awwk!" A sign above the cage reads: "PEROTkeet FOR SALE . . . INCESSANT CHATTER GUARANTEED . . . PRICE REDUCED . . . CLOSEOUT . . . PLEASE MAKE OFFER!"

No doubt the real cause of Perot's exit from the race was personal. He had not believed Ed Rollins when he warned him that running for public office would be no piece of cake. So now he was gone. Again AT & T profited: millions of phone calls poured in. This time the callers were enraged. They wanted him back in the race. Said one local leader: "I feel like I've been stood up by a hooker." In Los Angeles a child faxed Perot: "My parents taught me respect for my elders, but in this situation, if I was in a room with you, I'd kick your ass." Fury and bitterness rained down on Perot. Said Mark Shields: "Ross Perot proves that 'last guys don't finish nice.'"

Ohlmon in the *Oregonian* showed Perot saying, "I'll go wherever the people want me to go." And in the next panel we see Perot surrounded by the flames of Hell. In 1992's *Who's in Charge* I show a photo of a resolute Perot speaking to a group of mugs: "Some people are calling me a quitter. Some people are saying I can't take criticism. I want you to kill those people."

"Everyone wondered," pondered Mark Russell,, "How Ross Perot's followers could have allowed themselves to be conned by him. Perhaps it was because Jim and Tammy Bakker are out of business."

But with the passage of a few months, it appeared likely that Perot had not really quit the race—he had just taken a hiatus from his daily indignities—the abuse of the comics, the barbs of Jay Leno, the pressure of the press. With the summer behind him, Perot returned from his holiday from abuse. He was back in the race.

Doug Marlette, the Pulitzer Prize-winning cartoonist in *New York Newsday*, showed Perot behind a desk with a three-tiered desk tray. The baskets read "IN," "OUT," and "IN." Said Jay Leno: "Are you excited about Perot getting back in the race? That has all the excitement of finding out that Ford is going to start making Pintos again."

Perot's first hurrah had ended in embarrassment and ignominy and the appellation "QUITTER," and in disenchantment for the millions who had been his followers. It was like a Frank Capra movie directed by David Lynch. Said Arsenio Hall: "I've never seen a guy so mixed-up about being in a race since Michael Jackson." And David Letterman, in a Top Ten

List, established a category of Pet Peeves which included: "You spend a week painting 'ROSS PEROT FOR PRESIDENT' on your family car and he drops out. You spend a week scraping off 'ROSS PEROT FOR PRESIDENT' and he's back." Said the wits at *Current Comedy*: "Ross Perot's motto is 'A mind is a terrible thing to make up.'"

With his entry into, his departure from, and his return to the presidential race, Perot was a conundrum wrapped in a riddle inside a perplexity. Art Buchwald cited a question from a reader: "Is Ross Perot as big an enigma to you as he is to me?" Buchwald's reply: "Ross is the kind of person in a family who says he is going out to buy a pack of cigarettes and doesn't return for six years. When Ross said that he was pulling out of the race, both the Democratic and Republican camps said, 'Good riddance.' When he said that he was coming back in, they both said 'Good God!'"

But Perot's last hurrah did not resemble his first one. The second time around, there would be no more self-promoting handlers, no more imagists and bean-counting polltakers. Perot's vacation from strife had apparently been a pageant of pretense intended to avoid the pain of the press. But the on-again off-again performance was a treat for humorists. I said in a lecture to a group at MIT: "After Perot got in the race, pulled out, then returned again, people were starting to ask if he was decisive enough to be president. A reporter from *The New York Times* asked Perot if he was decisive. Perot promised to write an answer to that question for publication, but then he decided against it. Then he said he had changed his mind and he would. But then he said he probably wouldn't— unless it rained."

This time around, Perot made all his own decisions, and when Perot's volunteers were permitted to make a decision it was not substantive. Perot announced that his volunteers would be permitted to select a symbol for the campaign. Jay Leno said, "How about the Yugo? The Yugo is small, it's funny looking, and you never know when it's going to quit on you." The situation brought to mind the Charles Addams cartoon which showed an English warlord addressing his serfs: "We will conduct an experiment in democratic government. The people will vote on the selection of the national bird."

Perot's new campaign was called "United We Stand, America," and his proposals became a little more specific. Under a Perot presidency there would be a 50-cent-a-gallon rise in the cost of gasoline, and the budget would be balanced in five years. *Newsweek* promptly provided a sound byte for Clinton's use in the upcoming debates: "When Perot challenges you on the deficit, say 'Maybe your chauffeur can afford a 50-cent-a-gallon gasoline tax. But most working Americans can't.'"

Perot's reentry in the presidential race was monumental news and it triggered humorous attacks and skepticism from editorial cartoonists. Pat Oliphant, in the *Washington Post*, responded to the vacillating candidate by borrowing from the Brothers Grimm. He showed a bosomy woman seated beside a frog in a forest. Says the lady: "Sure—last time I kissed you, you turned into Ross Perot." The frog, who resembles Perot, says: "Yeah, but this time I'm a real prince." And Oliphant's trademark mouse remarks: "Put not your faith in frogs."

By the middle of September, Perot was prepared to reenter the lists. He polled his Volunteers (like the warlord consulting his subjects) as to their wishes. He summoned his state leaders to Dallas and invited Bush and Clinton to send petitioners for his people to consider. Bush and Clinton couldn't ignore the invitation. Perot represented a great many potential votes. Said Mark Russell: "Only days ago, Dan Quayle was calling Perot a 'temperamental tycoon.' That's been changed to 'potential supporter.' Looks like the party of family values has legalized prostitution." Both camps had the approximate chance of a snowball in hell with the Volunteers. Their questions had all the warmth of a security check. Perot's supporters were not about to turn their back on their messiah, so it was time for "Ross Perot—The Sequel." Jay Leno said, "On Monday Ross Perot will announce that he's back in the presidential race on 'Larry King Live.' The new fall season has just started and already they're showing reruns."

Perot was indeed a new TV phenomenon. He promptly bought twenty-four million dollars worth of television time in the first fortnight. Summarized Mark Russell: "Perot was not a candidate. Then he quit. Now he wants to do campaign commercials. If he was just some poor slob without any money, his family would have had him committed long ago." What the American people saw—and watched in huge numbers—was a kind of programming usually associated with the sale of underwater real estate. Perot's ads were *infomercials*. The candidate presented himself as the network star of a miniseries of thirty-minute lectures, complete with colorful pie charts.

Detractors said it was pure show business. Observed the show-biz trade paper *Daily Variety*: "The presidential election is now less than a week away, meaning television will soon be devoid of all those paid political half-hour ads. Thankfully, 'American Gladiators' and 'World Wrestling Federation' will be around to ensure a continued supply of thought-provoking, high-quality programming."

These ubiquitous displays of salesmanship led Art Buchwald to discuss plans to advertise his newspaper column. "OK, as I said on my half-hour show on NBC last night and will say on CBS tonight, ABC tomorrow evening, PBS next week, the BBC on Sunday, and Radio Free Albania on Inauguration Day, the other American columnists . . . never cared about you." And referring to the diversity of places where Ross Perot was showing up on TV, from "Larry King Live" to "The Today Show," and from "Good Morning America" to "60 Minutes," Dennis Miller said: "I even saw him on the Rodney King video."

It was one more demonstration, if one were needed, of television's Gargantuan power to create overnight stars. It had happened with Robin Williams, Alan Alda, and Milton Berle. And now, as sixteen million people watched the intense industrialist, pointer in hand, charts at the ready, it happened with Ross Perot.

Then came Perot the Debater. Said one journalist: "He is not a person. He is an experience." The little Texan walked off with all the reviews. As the late Lee Strasberg might have said, he had the best lines and the best motivation. It certainly wasn't his preparation, which was trivial compared to his rivals. Bush prepared with aides and briefing books galore. At the Bush rehearsal, former White House chief of staff John Sununu played Ross Perot. He brought along a pair of huge ears (Sununu had not been famous for his gentle humor when he ruled the roost at the White House). A former aide gave Bush some one-liners with which to torpedo Perot, such as: "In the Oval Office, Ross, you can't be a quitter." (It is clear that what was called for was the wit of a Jay Leno or a Mark Russell, not the work of these amateur gag-writers.) *Newsweek* had given its own one-liner to George Bush for use on Ross Perot: "When Perot attacks your record, say: 'You still in this thing, Henry? It doesn't take an army of private eyes to figure out who's got the temperament for the Oval Office.'" Perot showed an example of self-deprecating wit during the debates. When someone challenged his plan for raising the tax on gasoline, he said "If there's a fairer way, I'm all ears."

Unlike Bush, Perot's preparation for the first debate was minimal. On the preceding day, he got a haircut. It brought to mind the cartoon by Szep in the *Boston Globe*. It was a virulent caricature of Perot. In it, along with the familiar jug ears, Perot showed the gap of a missing tooth as he smiled the moronic smile of Alfred E. Neumann, *Mad Magazine's* famous mascot. Perot is saying: "What, me President?"

While permitting Perot to participate in the televised debates, both the major candidates tried to ignore the Texan, and that's how many of the editorial cartoonists portrayed the scene. In a cartoon in the *Houston Chronicle*, the setting is a western saloon. Two cowboys, Bush and Clinton, are playing poker. A tiny cowboy enters—Ross Perot. He starts kicking their chairs, but they ignore him. "Uh-huh, you're back to clean up Dodge City," says Bush. "Do you mind keepin' the racket down?"

In addressing the debates, Ohlman in the *Oregonian* showed Perot at the movies, watching a film showing Bush and Clinton debating. Perot is pictured as that inveterate annoyance, someone who talks in movie theatres. He is saying "Blahblahblah," and a man in the row behind him is complaining, "Will you just shut up and watch the end of the movie??"

The spin doctors of the debate had arranged for a group of undecided voters, each with a dial in hand on which to register their reactions to what they were hearing. It was not unlike the setup in "Sunset House," the Hollywood edifice where they regularly test audience response to new TV shows. The needles often shot upward when Perot spoke.

The first debate had a revivifying effect on Perot's public support. Indeed, one network wit said: "Ross Perot has been doing so well since his debate appearance that he's considering dropping out again."

Perot did well in the first debate; most people awarded him the gold. Some said he was driven by a massive ego. Cartoonist Wasserman in the *Boston Globe*, showed Perot at the podium, saying: "Perot speaking. Bush and Clinton have side-stepped the issue. That is the reason I am running. I will focus the nation's attention where it belongs—on me!!"

The vice presidential debate was a horse of a different color. In it, America got a good look at James Bond Stockdale, Perot's running mate. Stockdale was a Congressional Medal of Honor winner, but he seemed out of his depth. Said one beltway wag, "He looked like a canary that had blundered into a badminton game." Stockdale generated polite humor. In picturing the debate, Jeff MacNelly in the *Chicago Tribune* showed Quayle with a leash around his neck like an attack dog, saying "Why can't Bill Clinton tell the truth?" Al Gore was screaming "Why can't y'll shut up!" And Stockdale was crouching behind his podium thinking, "Why can't I find my seat?" Said one comedian, with a nod to Stockdale's heroic past: "Admiral Stockdale is an American hero—he did something important with his life—so of course he looked out of place on the stage with Quayle and Gore."

Mark Russell said that his favorite debate was the one among the vice presidential candidates. "We made a new friend that night, Admiral Stockdale . . . who seemed to be a nice enough fellow. But he left us with the impression that if anything ever happened to President Perot, we would all be in the unusual position of missing Dan Quayle."

The second presidential debate was staged in the informal style of Phil Donahue examining "Congressmen Who Have Slept with Dwarfs." Clinton, accustomed to this kind of casual format, scored well. Bush was seen consulting his watch, and did himself little good when a woman asked how the recession had affected him personally and he said he "didn't get it." By now, Perot was doing well in the numbers, and Clinton's supporters were smarting. The question was: Had the debates renewed Perot sufficiently to make him a competitor for the anti-Bush votes? Jay Leno expressed the view that "there are enough anti-Bush votes to go around."

But if Perot's threat had once been as serious as *Macbeth*, it ended up as *Much Ado About Nothing*. As a larger-than-life candidate, Perot did not merely shoot himself in the foot, he shot himself in the head. Perot had taken over the wheel of his campaign. Now he plowed it into an oil truck. The explosion was devastating. Whatever good those thirty-minute infomercials had done Perot in presenting him as a wonderful father, husband, businessman, patriot ("also contains Lanolin," said one comic), was undone by a single guest spot on CBS's "60 Minutes" a week before the election, which appeared like a sequel to *The Pink Panther* with Peter Sellers tripping over his trenchcoat. Perot stepped once more into a puddle of plotters and saboteurs. Inspector Perot told the "real" story of why he had earlier quit the race. It was not for the reason he had cited —the disruptive effects of a tied election thrown into the House. Perot now said he did it to safeguard his daughter from dirty-trick artists. The evidence was slight, the details sensational. There was a plot afoot, said Perot, to humiliate his daughter by leaking a phony lurid photo to the tabloids before her wedding. Comedians seized on the paranoid nightmare. Wrote Art Buchwald: "I know that many people are wondering why I dropped out of the National Press Club Presidential race. . . . the explanation I gave at the time was that I had not been invited to Ross Perot's daughter's wedding. Well, that was just a smoke screen for the real reason I quit. I pulled out because Robert Novak's people had vowed to disrupt my 11-year-old grandson's birthday party."

"And now we know the real reason Perot bowed out of the race last July," said Mark Russell. "He had learned that Martians were planning to jump out of his daughter's wedding cake. . . . Further dirty tricks included the distribution of a doctored photograph showing the head of Ross Perot attached to the body of a rational person."

Said *Current Comedy*: "Ross Perot may be a little paranoid. They say that when he was coming out of his mother's womb, he kept looking over his shoulder to see if somebody was following him." And Bush humor-meister Doug Gamble quipped: "Perot accused the Republicans of a campaign of dirty tricks against him. I think the dirtiest trick committed against Perot was by the guy who cuts his hair."

The bizarre story buried the balance of the Perot campaign.

But Perot could not be so easily forgotten or relegated to the distant memories of presidential campaign losers—the Mondales and Dukakises and Humphreys of history. When the election was over, one was left with the feeling that the omnipresent Perot of the infomercials was still somewhere in the neighborhood, somewhere in the atmosphere. . . .

The memory of Ross Perot around Republican campfires was not that of a charming eccentric. Said Doug Gamble, after his patron had lost the election, "George and Barbara Bush are still in the White House for one more Christmas. And if Barbara asks the president if he wants fruitcake after the turkey I hope he tells her he'd rather not have dinner with Ross Perot."

But Perot had made a permanent impression on the populace with his homilies, his fevered populism. He reminded people that the country belonged to them, politicians worked for them. Art Buchwald aped the Perot style in a post-election column. "Let me tell you what I'm going to do for you in the next four years [in this column]. OK, first of all I'd like to say that this column belongs to you, and you have to tell me exactly what you want me to write and I'll do it. You're my boss and I'm not going to take any pay."

The *Mesa Arizona Tribune* said of Perot: "He just doesn't want the spotlight shut off during his fifteen minutes of fame, but guess what, Ross? Very, very soon . . . click."

Ah, but one could not be sure. Perot had won nineteen percent of the vote. And with Clinton in the White House, Perot continued to hold rallies around the country. It appeared the spotlight would not click off on Ross Perot just yet.

Said Mark Russell: "Perot is still with us. People say are you going to miss Perot? Perot took a hiatus of about an hour and a half after the election. He's on now. He's probably on tonight."

Chapter 4

Campaign 1988
Read My Lips

George Bush was born on third base and he thought
he hit a triple.
—JIM HIGHTOWER

Many candidates for the U.S. presidency have owed
their defeat to their vulnerability to campaign mockery.
George Bush owed his *victory* to it. Bush seemed so vulnerable
to ridicule that it led to a basic strategic mistake on the part of
Michael Dukakis and his advisers. For it fed a smugness that
was their downfall.

The fundamental error of the Dukakis campaign lay in
their assumption that all that was required to win the election
was to say the name "George Bush." This would trigger hilar-
ity and mocking laughter. The rest would be history.

The Democratic convention in Atlanta seemed to lend
credence to this dubious thesis. All the speakers needed to do
at that memorable conclave was to utter the name "George
Bush" and thousands of delegates would dissolve in laughter.
There were four solid days of such japery, turning the convention into a veritable laugh-in, a nonstop exercise in derision.

There was so much about George Bush that generated
ridicule—his preppy locutions, his awkward gestures, his propensity for gaffes, his whiny voice—that he seemed invented
for a Johnny Carson monolog.

The Democrats' keynote speaker, Ann Richards, unleashed a string of wisecracks at Bush's expense. Texan Richards declared that she was there to show America "what a real Texan sounds like." She mocked Bush's Texas roots, observing that anyone whose address is a Houston hotel room "is a tourist."

Jim Hightower, a Texas official with a taste for the jugular, ridiculed Bush's pedigree with the comment that he "was born on third base and he thought he hit a triple." Hightower questioned Bush's intelligence with the comment that "if ignorance ever goes to forty dollars a barrel, I want drilling rights on George Bush's head."

Ted Kennedy joined the bandwagon with a litany of questions addressing Bush's absence from the Reagan councils when crucial decisions were being made. Sneered Teddy after each example of Bush's lack of footprints, *"Where was George?"* (One conservative reporter cracked: "He was home with his wife. Where were *you?*")

At the annual Gridiron Dinner in Washington, Governor Mario Cuomo of New York had effectively chastened the vice president with humor. Listening to the crackling Cuomo wit, some Democrats reflected that perhaps the wrong ethnic governor was getting the nomination. Said Cuomo:

> All this talk about the Vice President's silver-spoon upbringing just doesn't square with the facts. George Bush was born in a humble home. His mother was poor, his father was poor, his chauffeur was poor, his governess was poor . . .

Cuomo then addressed Bush's immaculate genealogy. Said the governor: "I was told yesterday that the Vice President said he supported Gramm/Rudman/Hollings because it reminded him of the name of one of his roommates at Yale."

Given Bush's preppy image, his awkward speech, his ineffectual mien, his supine vice-presidential posture, it was perhaps understandable that Dukakis' Harvard-yard advisers would assume their candidate could laugh his way to the White House.

Bush's strangled syntax and verbal gaffes earned the most ridicule, as when he said, "For seven and a half years I've worked alongside President Reagan. We've had triumphs. Made some mistakes. We've had some sex . . . uh, setbacks." On another occasion he said: "I stand for anti-bigotry, anti-Semitism and anti-racism." (Cracked Morton Kondracke: "Well, ányone can make a Freudian slip.") When Bush solemnly declared that September 7 was the anniversary of the attack on Pearl Harbor, cartoonist Jeff MacNelly pictured a member of the American Legion holding a sign: REMEMBER PEARL HARBOR, and George Bush saying: "Great gal! Who could ever forget her?" Satirist Mark Russell explained the error for his younger viewers: "It was actually *December* 7th, a tragic day in our history, when Mexicans attacked Pearl Harbor." Even Michael Dukakis broke his self-imposed moratorium on humor to quip: "I didn't realize there were only fifteen more shopping days till Christmas."

Bob Hope, who usually carries water for Republican presidents, had a wisecrack about Bush's mangled prose. Said Hope: "I think we should have a President who is fluent in at least one language." Cartoonist MacNelly addressed the subject of Bush's whiny voice and frenetic speech with a cartoon in which a robotic Bush stands at a debate podium as some uniformed technicians tinker with his interior circuits. Says one of them: "Here's the problem: We had him set on 78."

Bush had been a loyal and therefore invisible vice president, victim of an occupational hazard for veeps since the founding of the republic. Cartoonist Doug Marlette in the *Atlanta Constitution* showed Reagan in a bootblack's chair, with Bush on his knees, tongue extended above the Reagan wing tips. Says the president: "Just a shine, George." Jesse Jackson underlined Bush's subservient role when he acknowledged that the vice president had met with numerous foreign heads of state—"if you count the dead ones."

Mario Cuomo had needled George Bush about his obsequities and his involvement in the Iran-Contra scandal. Cuomo told of a secret meeting at which both George Shultz and Casper Weinberger had opposed the sale of arms to the Ayatollah. Then Reagan had turned to his vice president and said, "George, do you have something to add?" And Bush replied, "Who gets the tuna and who gets the ham and cheese?"

Bush's country club image made him vulnerable to populist attack. Editorial cartoonists often showed him in a tennis outfit or astride a polo pony. Dukakis referred to the election as a battle between Main Street and Easy Street. Cuomo said: "The Vice President is sensitive to the needs of the poor. He has promised a new program to deal with the economic hardships of America's poor. The slogan is 'Just say No to Poverty.'" And Ann Richards killed two birds—Bush's wealth and his malaprops—with one stone when she cracked: "George Bush was born with a silver foot in his mouth."

What stunned and bushwhacked the Democrats was how adroitly this "goofy" product of privilege was able to deflect these charges with a repertoire of self-deprecatory humor that laughed away all the scalding mockery. The segment of Bush's acceptance speech that reversed the ridicule was the inspired self-disparaging lines in which he cheerfully acknowledged all his flaws—like Reagan kidding his age and Kennedy kidding his wealth and religion. All the lampoonery of Atlanta that painted Bush as a laughable figure of fun was forgotten in the wake of Bush's skillful self-reproach. The hapless wimp turned into Gary Cooper as Mr. Deeds, awkward perhaps but genial and likable; not a caricature but a mellow, modest fellow; one liked him not despite his flaws but because of them. If the Democrats chose to attack George Bush's manliness and personality, he would fight back with the Democrats' own weapon —humor.

George Bush focused a major portion of the acceptance speech on his upbringing, his deficiencies, his awkwardness, his lack of eloquence, his mannerisms. Said Bush: "I'll try to be fair to the other side. Tonight I'll try to hold my charisma in check." Referring to Ann Richards's jovial slander, Bush said that his wife had urged him to "relax, sit back, take off your shoes, put up your silver foot." Kidding his awkward manner of speech, he paraphrased Clint Eastwood, saying: "Go ahead, make my 24–hour time period." Bush conceded: "I may not be eloquent, I may even be a little awkward. But I learned early that eloquence won't draw oil from the ground." (Take that, Ann Richards!)

At the Al Smith Dinner during the campaign, Bush again wielded the weapon of self-deprecating humor. This time he mocked his blue-blooded lineage. The air was thick with Dukakis' invocations of his immigrant parents' voyage to Ellis Island. George Herbert Walker Bush of New England declared that his ancestors landed at Ellis Island when the *Mayflower* made a pit stop on its way to Plymouth. "My people," said Bush, "were the ones waving the Bloomingdale's shopping bags." Addressing the banquet guests resplendent in elegant gowns and white ties and tails, Bush cracked, "I haven't seen so many people so well dressed since I went to a come-as-you-are party in Kennebunkport." Bush reached the zenith of self–disparagement when he kidded his attempts at comedy. A few days before, Lloyd Bentsen had driven a stake through Dan Quayle's ego when the plastic young senator had compared himself to John F. Kennedy. Bush put a twist on that dramatic encounter. He related that his wife had listened while he rehearsed his humorous remarks for the dinner. Bush grimaced. "Barbara said to me: 'I know Johnny Carson. Johnny Carson is a friend of mine. And George, *you're no Johnny Carson.*'"

The chief architect of George Bush's self-deprecating humor was a witty young partisan named Doug Gamble, whom Bush inherited from Ronald Reagan along with his campaign advisers. Gamble kept up a steady stream of jokes to the candidate, which Bush at first disdained to use, then wisely decided to exploit. Here is a brief anthology of the Bush/ Gamble oeuvre:

Sometimes I feel like the javelin contender who won the coin toss and elected to receive.

Every day I live with the reality that I'm just a heartbeat away from Sam Donaldson.

I have good reason to be confident. Shirley MacLaine told me that I was Martin Van Buren in another life.

[After calling Ted Koppel "Dan" in an ABC interview] Now I'm going to have to be very careful that I don't start calling Michael Dukakis "Jimmy."

If Doug Gamble helped George Bush turn aside the mockery of others, Peggy Noonan gave his speeches the grace notes of rhetoric. Sometimes, however, the Noonan prose invited ridicule. In his acceptance speech, Bush acknowledged that he lacked eloquence and often spoke awkwardly. However, said Bush, "I hear the quiet people others don't." Remarked satirist Albert Brooks, "I've got a friend in L.A. who hears the quiet people others don't, and he's got to take a lot of medication." Another of the Noonan images that Bush embraced spoke of "a thousand points of light." It probably referred to private charities replacing public beneficence. But Bush's frequent invocation of the phrase invited confusion and whimsy. A cartoonist in the *Boston Globe* ran a Campaign Quiz that asked:

WHAT DOES GEORGE BUSH MEAN BY "1000 POINTS OF LIGHT"?
CHECK THE CORRECT BOX.
☐ A SWARM OF TV CAMERAS
☐ HIS TOP FINANCIAL BACKERS
☐ A BRAND OF PANAMANIAN COCAINE
☐ A SECRET RELIGIOUS RITE
☐ N.R.A. TARGET PRACTICE
☐ TWENTY AMERICAN FLAGS

George Bush would find it easier to turn aside malicious humor than he would to deflect charges that he was poisoning the political process with his harsh and irrelevant attacks on Dukakis that catered to the sound-bite appetite of television. Editorial cartoonist Ohman in the *Oregonian* ridiculed the sound-bite mentality of the Bush campaign. He showed Abe Lincoln at Gettysburg in two modes:

Before sound bites: "Fourscore and seven years ago our forefathers brought forth on this continent a new nation, conceived in liberty and dedicated to the proposition that all men are created equal . . ."

After sound bites: "Read my lips: No slaves."

Another issue on which George Bush appeared vulnerable, at least early in the campaign, was labeled "the sleaze factor." Dozens of officials in the Reagan Administration had left office under an ethical cloud, and America's humorists and public figures sought to extract critical humor from this phenomenon at Bush's expense. Mario Cuomo, in his sardonic turn at the Gridiron Dinner, addressed this issue. Reflecting on the number of Reaganites who had run afoul of the law, Cuomo observed that the Republican party had learned the wrong lesson from Franklin Roosevelt. "The trick is to pack the *court*," said Cuomo, "not the *courthouse*." Continued the governor: "When they said they wanted to bring back the old values, I never dreamed they meant Watergate." The venality of the administration reminded Cuomo of a Tammany Hall functionary named Fishhooks McCarthy. Said Cuomo: "Fishhooks started every day of his political career the same way— in church on his knees, whispering the same prayer: 'Oh Lord, give me health and strength . . . I'll steal the rest.'" Referring to the possibility of a presidential pardon for the Iran-Contra miscreants, Cuomo said: "Pardons are a dangerous way for a President to be loyal to his friends, and I understand that Mr. Reagan, a longime sports fan, is now considering a better idea —swap Poindexter and North for Noriega and a dictator to be named later."

With somewhat less grace, Dukakis laid the venality at Reagan's door by invoking a Greek proverb to the effect that "a fish rots from the head down." This graphic aphorism, comparing a beloved president to a fish head, generated more sympathy for than suspicion of Mr. Reagan, whose approval rating was on the rise as Iran-Contra receded into the mists of public memory.

When the Democrats directed their arsenal of malicious wit at George Bush in Atlanta, it was an expensive tactic. It squandered all the explosive power of their big guns—Ted Kennedy, Ann Richards, Jesse Jackson, Michael Dukakis—on but one target: the high-born eccentricities of George Bush. When the vice president counterattacked with self-deprecating humor, Dukakis' arsenal was empty. And he had handed Bush an excuse for turning mean, with a campaign of recriminations that centered on furloughed convict Willie Horton and the Pledge of Allegiance. Once again, 1988 demonstrated both the plusses and the perils of political humor.

If the Democrats erred in their convention bombardment of Bush as a cartoon character and a national dunce, at least the Democrats were Equal Opportunity wits: blacks and women joined in the fusillade. Not so the Republican convention, which was uniformly white and male. Pete Hamill wrote of his shock at encountering a black man at the GOP affair and how his initial surprise left him when he discovered the man was a musician in the orchestra. Mike Luckovich, the editorial cartoonist for the New Orleans *Times-Picayune*, pictured a group of lily-white GOP delegates, one of whom gestures toward a black man and a woman. He declares indignantly: "To those that say the vast majority of delegates on the floor are white males, here's two that aren't. What's your name?" Says the black: "Ed Bradley." Says the woman: "Diane Sawyer."

The respectable Republicans who descended on New Orleans for their convention generated a good deal of humor among the media. New Orleans, City of Sin, the Big Easy, seemed a curious home to these defenders of family values. Cartoonist Jeff MacNelly pictured three stolid GOP elephants paddling a rowboat through the lush Louisiana bayous. They wear serious suits and carry golf bags. Says one of the Babbitts: "Well, it sure doesn't look like a place where you'd hold a Republican convention." The dripping trees bear signs that read: "Catfish Festival," "Voodoo Museum," "Cajun Mel's Blackened Lunchmeat," "Nekkid Gator Wrestling," "Hurricanes, $2.50."

Until George Bush captured the willing hearts of the delegates with his splendid acceptance, the convention seemed a love feast for Ronald Reagan. And given the difficulty of transferring love via coattails, this seemed a ticklish situation. Jim Morin, the *Miami Herald*'s editorial cartoonist, showed Reagan addressing the convention amidst a forest of adoring signs. They read: "Ronnie," "Four More Years," "We Love Ron!" As Reagan holds up his hands to the cheering throng, a dismayed GOP official is on the phone nearby. He is saying: "The veep spot? I'll ask him, but don't get your hopes up, George . . ." Don Wright, the gifted editorial cartoonist for the *Miami News*, reflected on the coattails of Ronald Reagan and how they might help the man who had served him so solicitously. Wright pictured a First Family conversation in the dark of their bedroom.

SHE. It's sick!

HE. But I agreed to help Bush with his campaign, Nancy.

SHE. What about overkill?

HE. He's just trying to convince people that he's a vital part of my administration.

SHE. Good night, Ron.

HE. Good night, Nancy. Good night, George.

BUSH. Good night, Chief!

Jokes about George Bush and the perception of him by women were a constant thread throughout the campaign. The classic quip has been traced to Art Buchwald: "George Bush reminds every woman of her first husband." Bruce Babbitt used the line and so did columnist Ellen Goodman, which proves Buchwald's own thesis that copyright protection on political humor lasts about twenty-four hours. (Had Joe Biden been plagiarizing wit instead of rhetoric, his future might have been entirely different.) The *New Republic* was so intrigued by the "first husband" quip that it ran a contest inviting its readers to explain it. There were other cheerful slanders about George Bush and women. Someone said Jeane Kirkpatrick would make the perfect running mate for Bush—she'd add a little macho to the ticket. In my quadrennial *Who's In Charge Here?* book, I pictured the throaty Kirkpatrick musing, "I'm often mistaken for a man on the phone. The same thing happens to George Bush." The problem that all these wisecracks reflected was referred to in campaign shorthand as the Gender Gap. All the surveys showed that women didn't trust George Bush and that unless he closed the gap he might lose the election. Buchwald wrote a delicious column in which he addressed this dilemma. He convened an apocryphal meeting of Bush and his advisers in a New Orleans hotel suite. Bush is puzzled. "I can't undersand it," he says. "I've always been wonderful to women. I let them precede me through a revolving door . . ." An aide laments that their surveys show women think of the candidate as someone they can push around. They must remake his image. Asks an adviser: "Do you mind wearing a green beret when you get off the plane?"

Bush's exploitation of Dukakis' veto of a law requiring schoolteachers to lead the recitation of the Pledge of Allegiance in Massachusetts classrooms was ridiculed by some. The cartoonist for the *San Francisco Chronicle* pictured a suburban home at midnight. Within, the husband is saying: "And now, before we go to bed, I'd like to ask you to stand and repeat after me . . . I pledge allegiance . . ." The wife shouts: *"George!!"* Dukakis explained that he had vetoed the bill because the Massachusetts Supreme Court had advised him it was unconstitutional—it impinged on the freedom of teachers and students. The cartoonist for the *Buffalo News* pictured a youngster, hand over heart, reciting: "I pledge allegiance to the flag of the United States of America, and to the republic for which it stands. One nation, under God, indivisible, with liberty—except perhaps with regard to this pledge—and justice for all." George Bush had made a very becoming garment of the American flag, but he was not the first public figure to wrap himself in Old Glory. In *Who's In Charge Here? 1988* I used a photo of Ronald Reagan standing in front of a huge American flag as he orates:

> I have a little advice for the man who succeeds me. Sometimes the days will be dark. Sometimes the people will lose faith in you. When that happens, make a speech in front of this flag.

Like Gerald Ford, George Bush was not a witty man, but like Ford, Bush recognized the value of humor in washing away his "negatives." So, as Ford had turned to Bob Orben to enliven his speeches with humor, Bush turned to Doug Gamble. Michael Dukakis was a serious man. Perhaps he chose not to trivialize his message with humor. Though a group of writers in his Chauncey Street headquarters churned out a ream of witty one-liners for the candidate's use, Dukakis rarely used them. In examining the product of Dukakis' in-house writers and his ad hoc contributors on both coasts, one finds much that compares favorably with that of the hired guns of the Republican camp. By turning his back on this humorous ammunition, Duakis bequeathed a valuable weapon to his opponent. The reader can decide which of the following lines, which were written for the governor but never used, might have lent spice to his dispassionate delivery:

George Bush is very upset about the Massachusetts Furlough Program. Well, he can be sure I'll never furlough anyone from the Reagan Administration.

George visited Boston recently. He was appalled at the garbage, the sewage, the filth. Then he left his policy meeting and visited the harbor.

After every White House scandal there was an investigation trying to link George Bush to the Administration.

George promised to create 30 million jobs in eight years. It's a strange promise coming from a guy who didn't do even one job in eight years.

George Bush wants to be Ronald Reagan, but he's campaigning like Richard Nixon.

It must be an election year. George Bush has discovered child care and Ronald Reagan has discovered George Bush.

George Bush's proposal to cut the capital gains tax demonstrates his compassion for the second homeless—those Americans without vacation homes.

The cut in the capital gains tax is going to put dollars where we need them most—in the hands of Porsche dealers.

The American people no longer believe in the trickle down theory. They've been trickled on long enough.

George Bush hasn't made a lot of decisions in his lifetime, but he's stood next to people who have.

Since he had no special gift for spontaneous wit himself, Michael Dukakis' speeches and remarks were unfailingly humorless. The one time he chose to employ a barbed, funny line, the remark flew onto the wire services and was widely quoted for days after, refracted in the wit of columnists and cartoonists. During the first TV debate, in response to the opening question, Dukakis derided Bush for vowing to reduce the federal debt without cutting military spending or raising taxes. "If he keeps this up," said Dukakis, "he's going to become the Joe Isuzu of American politics." (The candidate was referring to the devious car salesman of a popular TV commercial.) Reagan won debates in 1980 and 1984 with a deft quip, and Walter Mondale floored Gary Hart with one that was based on a TV commercial. But despite this flirtation with political wit, Dukakis remained immersed in his sober pronouncements throughout the campaign. By contrast, he made George Bush appear a combination of Oscar Wilde and Noël Coward.

Not since Richard Nixon reached far down and far right to choose Spiro Agnew as his running mate in 1968 had the wags had such a fertile field for their jibes. The selection of Senator Dan Quayle for the GOP vice presidential slot brought joy to the writers of late-night talk shows and in other locales where gaggery has become an art form.

Johnny Carson, the Will Rogers of our time, has an immutable law in the monologs that open "The Tonight Show": Thou shalt not do more than three jokes on any one subject. Even such promising subjects as Dolly Parton's bosom and Nancy Reagan's astrologer have fallen to this Carsonian canon. But Dan Quayle was such a feast of comic possibilities that Carson tossed the rule out the window. He did eight minutes on the blue-eyed Hoosier.

Another longstanding rule was violated by George Bush in his choice of Quayle: Never expose a controversy to fifteen thousand idle reporters. For that is what Bush did when on the second day of the GOP convention, with an army of reporters in attendance, he anointed the callow Indiana senator. I was in the media area of the *New York Post* when the story broke of Quayle's use of family influence to seek the sanctuary of the National Guard during the Vietnam War. Said one *Post* columnist: "He'll make a great vice president. Except he'll only work two weeks in the summer." I must have heard a hundred jokes on the subject of Dan Quayle in the next twenty-four hours. In addition to the National Guard story, there were his wealth, his youth, his good looks, his college grades, his right-wing views, his weekend with the beautiful lobbyist, his dangerous closeness to the presidency. Truly a wit's banquet.

As the comic lines floated to earth, they formed a small anthology of humor and malice. Said charismatic populist Jim Hightower, "Dan Quayle is so dumb he thinks Cheerios are doughnut seeds." Said Jay Leno, "Say what you will, when Dan Quayle was in the National Guard, not one Viet Cong got past Muncie, Indiana." Said Mark Russell, "The media is backing off Dan Quayle. They're afraid of another backlash. So they're only asking him questions they think he can handle. Like how many teams are in the Big 10?" The *Boston Herald* printed a cartoon in which George Bush is complaining, "I just wish he'd stop referring to me as 'The Liberal.'" Said one beltway wag, "It's amazing how far down Bush had to reach to find a junior partner." Said Wasserman in the *Boston Globe*, "Dan Quayle—more manic than Jack Kemp, more military than Al Haig, more wealthy than Pierre du Pont, and more pretty than George Bush."

And still the flood of Quayle humor continued. Jay Leno observed that Dan Quayle had two advantages over Lloyd Bentsen—"a blow dryer and a pulse." David Letterman, whose writers were contributing humor, largely unused, to the Dukakis camp, offered a list of Quayle's National Guard duties, including "making explosion sounds when platoon trains with dummy grenades." Johnny Carson greeted an unresponsive audience by saying, "This looks like the kind of audience that would buy Dan Quayle a tape of *Good Morning, Vietnam*." Paul Krassner said the Republican ticket was the start of a great baseball team—a Yankee and a Dodger. Orson Bean said that Quayle had starred in a film about Vietnam called *Full Metal Sports Jacket*. Said Richard Willin of the *Detroit News*, "A 200 million dollar trust fund—is that Bush's idea of balancing the ticket?" Said Bob Orben, "Of course he didn't go to Canada. With his academic record, maybe he didn't know where it is."

Those with long memories recalled how elephant jokes and knock-knock jokes leaped into the public consciousness. Just so did the Quayle joke appear full-born:

What do you get when you cross a hawk and a chicken?
A Quayle.

Why did the chicken cross the road?
To join the National Guard.

What is a Quayle?
A bird that ducks.

What's the difference between a hawk and a Quayle?
None.

What's the Quayle Special at Kentucky Fried Chicken this week?
A bucket of right wings.

Quayle was constantly kidded about his succulent name. There was no end of avian puns. The wags went on a Quayle hunt. Pundits asked whether a bird in the hand was worth two in the Bush. Quayle became the main dish on the menu of America's comedy chefs. The Quayle Roast was the Special of the Day, and every day was a good day to roast Quayle.

Then there was the sexual component. After the bawdy scandal of Gary Hart, Donna Rice, and the Good Ship Monkey Business, the Dan Quayle–Paula Parkinson affair seemed small beer. But never underestimate the power of a whiff of sex to ignite America's humorists. Said Jay Leno of Quayle's alledgedly innocent golfing weekend with the vivacious lobbyist, "Nothing happened between Dan Quayle and Paula Parkinson. She just lobbied his brains out." A Dukakis staff writer offered the governor a joke that the candidate chose not to use. "Dan Quayle's parents have gotten him into everything but Paula Parkinson." A member of an L.A. cabaret group, with a nod to the memory of Mae West, addressed Quayle's insistence that he had spent the weekend playing golf. "Paula Parkinson said to Dan Quayle, 'Is that a putter in your hand or are you just glad to see me?'"

The Quayle humor proliferated at a pace to encourage all those who fear that humor is dying in political life. One comedian called Quayle "Bush Light." Some saw the sardonic wit of Bob Dole lurking behind his praise that Quayle was one of the shining new "lights" of the GOP. Jim Hightower was less subtle in inquiring, "How many National Guardsmen were at the Alamo?"

Dan Quayle even had the dubious distinction of triggering the creation of a short-lived newspaper. In the tradition of the *Harvard Lampoon*'s journalistic takeoffs, the *Washington Possible* appeared. Its headline read: QUAYLE BECOMES PRESIDENT. The sub-head: "'Oh-Oh,' Says Worried Nation." The paper resembled the *Washington Post* and was distributed in six major cities. Another headline read: AMERICANS KNEEL IN PRAYER, REFUSE TO RISE. And one story referred to Bush's choice of Quayle as "impeachment insurance."

Women were offended by the Quayle selection because it seemed evident that his good looks were intended to secure votes from impressionable females and close the Gender Gap. Columnist Ellen Goodman wrote:

> The very finest minds of the Republican Party [have] developed a plan that would win over the hearts, minds and votes of American women . . . Ladies and women, the secret weapon of the Republican Party has been unveiled, the one thing designed to make the fair sex swoon in the voting booth: *The Pretty Face!*

Quayle's "pretty face" generated its own flurry of jibes. The Hoosier senator's campaign literature boasted his likeness to Robert Redford. (Redford protested and demanded the reference be expunged.) Others found a resemblance to a lesser celebrity. Said Johnny Carson: "Another scandal is brewing for Dan Quayle. He just admitted that he had plastic surgery to make him look more like Pat Sajak."

To dispel the same silver-spoon image that had dogged George Bush, Quayle managed to be photographed at home taking out the garbage. This only fed the wags, who said "he's getting ready for his duties as vice president." The Quayle wealth produced a skeptical comment from Johnny Carson: "Somebody said he's worth $200 million and they were shocked that a guy with $200 million didn't go to Vietnam. The only guy with that much money who went to Vietnam was Bob Hope."

If the 1988 campaign was traumatic for Dan Quayle, the

trauma reached its high point in the TV debate with his Democratic counterpart, Senator Lloyd Bentsen. Quayle had been so reckless as to invoke a comparison of himself to John F. Kennedy. Bentsen looked at him with more sorrow than anger and said, "I knew Jack Kennedy. Jack Kennedy was a friend of mine. And Senator, you're no Jack Kennedy." To which Mark Russell added, "Hell, he's no *Caroline* Kennedy."

As the campaign came down to the wire, Senator Quayle was kept out of sight, campaigning in obscure southern towns, well out of the public eye. "They're hiding Quayle!" derided the jokesmiths of the Dukakis camp. Said one: "They're hiding him like the Elephant Man, so as not to frighten the children." He's the "phantom candidate," said another. And a media wag marveled: "I've heard of a secret ballot, but a secret campaign?"

When the votes were counted on November 8, the Bush/Quayle ticket had swept into office on the strength of 426 electoral votes. If Quayle acted as a drag on the ticket and cost George Bush one or two points at the polls, the patrician Yankee could well afford them. As for Quayle, he could laugh all the way to the Old Executive Office Building, where he would soon take over the offices vacated by George Bush.

But if Quayle expected victory at the polls to put an end to what the *New Republic* had called "Veepgate," he was to be disappointed. No sooner was he a heartbeat from the presidency than the Washington wags began to spread an insidious rumor. The Secret Service had received new instructions: In the event President Bush was shot, they were instantly to shoot Quayle.

Chapter 5

Campaign 1988
Zorba the Clerk

The Dukakis campaign had a setback this weekend.
Researchers checked out his family tree. It turns out
Dukakis is the Greek word for Mondale.
—JAY LENO

With only ten days remaining in the campaign, with
Michael Dukakis trailing George Bush and threatened by
landslide, the word went out to the speechwriters at the Dukakis-Bentsen headquarters in Boston: The candidate needs
self-deprecating humor!

The targets for this self-deprecating humor were carefully set by the Dukakis high command: Dukakis' lack of passion and Dukakis' lack of humor. America's wits and Dukakis'
opponents knew no such confinement. They had been deprecating Dukakis since August on a wide range of subjects.
Their targets included Dukakis' Massachusetts prison-furlough program ("Clint Eastwood said 'Make my day,' Dukakis
said 'Have a nice weekend'"); his well-concealed liberal incli-
nations ("He's the Stealth Candidate"); the state of the Massachusetts environment ("That answer was as clear as Boston
Harbor"); the ideological differences between Dukakis and his
running mate ("I can't wait for the big debate between Dukakis and Bentsen"); his shortness of stature ("Bush likes to
get up on a soapbox to be heard, Dukakis likes to get up on a

soapbox to be seen"); his plans for the economy ("Dukakis can't get elected unless things get worse, and things can't get worse unless he's elected"); and his agricultural program ("His farm policy is the Belgian endives and his defense policy is the Belgian waffle").

Dukakis' emotionless, technocratic manner had earned him the appellations "Zorba the Clerk" and "The First Dentist." Columnist Mark Shields quipped that Dukakis' idea of a wild time "is an evening spent straightening out his sock drawer." And GOP consultant Todd Domke reflected that "Dukakis is the kind of guy you'd like to have in your foxhole —if you wanted to study soil erosion."

Back in May, George Bush trailed Dukakis by sixteen percentage points. The headlines were dominated by such depressing matters as the venality of Attorney General Ed Meese, the drug-running of Panamanian ruler General Noriega, and the astrology of Nancy Reagan. Bush's senior advisers decided on a plan of action. They would focus on such red-meat topics as furloughed convict Willie Horton, the Pledge of Allegiance, the pollution of Boston Harbor, the ACLU, and the "L" word.

The approach had so little substance that voters grew disengaged. We live in an age that has grown cynical about politics, but this was more barren an approach than voters had seen in a generation. As always, the irrelevance and boredom of the campaign were lightened by the wit of America's editorial cartoonists. After the final debate, Mike Peters of the *Dayton Daily News* showed a husband and wife asleep at their TV set, snoring loudly as the anchorman pontificates: "Who won the debates? That's an easy one, Dan. The American public won the debates." Jim Borgman of the *Cincinnati Enquirer* showed the public disenchantment with the campaign with a sketch of a presidential candidate being pelted by fruit as voters hoisted signs reading: "A Pox on Both Your Houses," "Boo," "Hiss," "Go Home." Says one campaign aide to another: "Remember the good old days when voters were apathetic?" Premier satirist Mark Russell joined the swelling chorus deploring the campaign's waist-high level. "I saw a poll the other day," remarked Russell, "that said if Bush wins, one million people will move to Canada. If Dukakis wins, ten million people will move to Canada. The big loser in this race is Canada." The substanceless, issueless campaign was best illustrated by Jeff MacNelly in the *Chicago Tribune*. He showed Dukakis and Bush floating gently along the racing lanes of the Olympic swimming pool. Says Dukakis somnolently: "Am not, am not, am not." Says Bush: "Are too, are too, are too." The judges sit listlessly marking off the days of the campaign. Says MacNelly: Dead Heat.

In the *Buffalo News*, editorial cartoonist Toles laughed at Bush's cynical campaign and Dukakis' belated awareness that it was drawing blood. A series of panels illustrated a TV debate.

BUSH. My opponent vetoed the Pledge of Allegiance! (Is he unpatriotic?) And he's a "card-carrying" member of the ACLU! (Is he subversive?) And he thinks naval maneuvers are a Jane Fonda exercise! (Is he a Communist sympathizer?)

DUKAKIS. My only response is that the American voters are intelligent enough not to be swayed by cheap demagoguery.

CRY FROM AUDIENCE. No we're not!

DUKAKIS. Plan B! Do we have a Plan B??

Don Wright joined the media's dismay at Bush's low-road campaign. He showed a spaceship reconnoitering the planet Earth. Says one of the aliens to his colleague: "I've done a quick check on these people. They're in the middle of an election. One guy favors saluting the flag, carrying a gun, using the electric chair, and swears like a sissy. He's ahead in the polls. Let's get the hell out of here."

In the *Washington Post*, the incisive Pat Oliphant derided the vacuous issues blathered by both candidates. His headline read: THE GREAT 1988 DEBATE. Between the two candidates sits a bloated brute, "The Budget Deficit." Blithely ignoring their horrific companion, the candidates burble their views:

DUKAKIS. And we're gonna create jobs! Everyone's gonna have a job! And opportunity! We're gonna create opportunity! An opportunity in every pot! Just like my immigrant forebears used to say way back when . . .

BUSH. And the pledge of allegiance! Why, golly, I'll go to Fist City for that one. And the environment! We're gonna have one, and my opponent fights dirty, the way he picks on little Danforth all the time . . .

Bush's insinuations that Dukakis was less than patriotic because he had vetoed the Pledge of Allegiance bill and Dukakis' indignation at the assault produced merriment. Said Mark Russell: "The other day George Bush made a speech at a flag factory. For a fitting, I assume." Johnny Carson gagged at the patriotic applesauce of the Bush attacks. He observed that with each passing day the campaign was getting more vicious. "Bush is trying to paint Dukakis as unpatriotic," said Carson. "Today he accused Dukakis of mooning Mom's Apple Pie."

The Seoul Olympics provided a pictorial setting for the irrepressible Herblock in deploring both campaigns. He showed the two candidates wearing their Olympic medals as voters looked on in dismay. Bush wears an ineffectual grin and stands ankle-deep in mire. Bush's medal reads: LOWEST-LEVEL CAMPAIGN SINCE NIXON. Beside him stands Dukakis, phlegmatic and morose. His medal reads: DOPIEST PRESIDENTIAL CAMPAIGN. Says a voter dryly: "Couple of winners."

Lest Herblock's comparison to the tawdry Nixon campaigns seem like hyperbole, one must recall the rumors that were raised about Dukakis' mental health. In late July, voters heard the rumble of anonymous rumors from the right-wing press that implied there were bouts of mental instability in the Dukakis closet. When the media failed to carry the scurrilous taunts, President Reagan cracked one of his more tasteless jibes to force the rumors into print. He said, referring to Dukakis' fancied psychic problems, "I'm not going to pick on an invalid." Reagan later pleaded, in a sort of quasi-apology, that he had intended his remark as a joke. This moved Pat Oliphant to produce a cartoon showing Reagan and Bush out duck hunting. Reagan, his gun aimed skyward, is saying: "I think I invalided him, George." Bush's face is blackened with backfire. He says: "Good shot, Sir! A bit low, perhaps . . ." Cartoonist Stayskal in the *Tampa Tribune* showed a husband and wife, slumped in their living room chairs, staring at the

TV screen. The commentator is declaiming: "Dukakis denied today that he has any problems with depression." Grumbles the husband: "See . . . that proves he doesn't know what's going on in the world today."

Jackie Mason, the comedian whose career has been having a renaissance after the blow dealt it by Ed Sullivan, found humor in the fact that the governor's wife, Kitty, was Jewish. During the Democratic convention, Mason wandered about the press area that abutted the convention hall. He prophesied that Kitty Dukakis would make a great First Lady. "She'd bring down the cost of everything," said Mason. "She'd never buy anything that wasn't on sale." As reporters scribbled, Mason continued. "Of course, the President could never get to the hotline. She'd be on the phone to Bloomingdale's." Cynics in the press corps observed that Jackie Mason would soon have a book in the stores, and the publicity would be timely. Tom Hayden was also present in Atlanta, with a coterie of Hollywood stars, promoting his own book. Self-conscious about exploiting the convention for his own gain, Hayden cracked: "Well, the political process is debasing anyhow, isn't it?"

Of course, the GOP convention was awash with small-businessmen exploiting the political process for their own profit. The entrepreneurial spirit was on display at a hundred booths that circled the rim of the massive Superdome. At each of these booths, which elbowed one another like frantic advance men, was a product that attacked the funnybone and the pocketbook, with japes aimed at Michael Dukakis. There was an array of T-shirts bearing messages of merriment and libel. (It reminded one of Fran Gottlieb's remark about message-laden garments: "Why should anyone that I wouldn't think of talking to imagine I want to listen to their T-shirt?") A popular message read: BEWARE OF GREEKS BEARING GIFTS, and another: BEWARE OF GREEKS WEARING LIFTS. The souvenir tables also featured buttons attacking Dukakis with levity. The Duke-bashing buttons included pictures of the governor wearing platform shoes, and one bore the inscription: LET'S KICK A LITTLE DUKAKIS. (This latter message reminded one of George Bush's gaffe after his 1984 vice-presidential debate with Geraldine Ferraro when he boasted to a union official, "We kicked a little ass last night." In 1988, Bush would continue to ripple his colloquial muscles in the hope that beery barstanders would nudge one another and growl, "What a man.") Another genre of souvenirs focused on Dukakis' notorious prison-furlough program, which had freed murderer Willie Horton for a fateful weekend. Merchants did a lively business on "Get out of jail free" cards, "compliments of Michael Dukakis," in the tradition of the Monopoly board game. (Art Buchwald suggested that Bush should pay tribute to Willie Horton, the man without whom he would never have been elected.) One T-shirt was dyed a jailhouse gray and read: FURLOUGHED FROM MASS. STATE PRISON BY DUKAKIS. Had Governor Dukakis seen the relish with which delegates snapped up these T-shirts and buttons, he would have taken the charge more seriously and responded with greater haste and heat.

One T-shirt witticism was never officially sanctioned by the Republican National Committee. It reflected a renaissance fully as surprising as the rebirth of Jackie Mason. The shirt read: HE'S TAN, HE'S RESTED, HE'S READY, NIXON IN '88.

Michael Dukakis' detractors said he deserved what he got. Rather than proclaim his liberal impulses and defend the tradition of Roosevelt, Truman, Kennedy, and Johnson, he ducked and weaved (Elizabeth Dole called it "the Bentsen and Hedges ticket") and declared the election was about "competence, not ideology." Given the incompetence of his campaign when compared to the performance of the GOP professionals whom Bush had inherited from the Gipper, Dukakis' mantra of "competence" seemed particularly ill-chosen. In the *Oregonian*, cartoonist Ohman pictured Dukakis' headquarters in chaos. An aide is nailing up a Dukakis poster upside down. Another is manning a tape recorder that has come unspooled. Another is panicking on the phone. The tableau is a portrait of ineptitude.

The Hollywood wags chimed in with some disparaging one-liners. Joan Rivers turned her attention from the sex lives of the stars long enough to observe, "Nobody wants to end up with a President that has two mustaches for eyebrows." Said impressionist Rich Little, "He's too short to be President and he has no shoulders." Said Mort Sahl, "It's hard to believe that *charisma* is a Greek word."

Republicans mocked Dukakis' position on defense, his readiness to eliminate certain elements of the Pentagon's arsenal. Said George Bush: "He's been against every weapons system since the slingshot." Said Dan Quayle, deriding Dukakis for a photo session at a U.S. Army Testing Ground in which he rode an M-1 tank: 'He went from General Confusion to General Patton." In a concluding remark at their first debate, Bush said with a wry smile, "I had hoped this would be a little friendlier evening. I'd wanted to hitchhike a ride in his tank." Cartoonist Mike Luckovich mocked Dukakis' show of military toughness by picturing the candidate, in the tank turret, declaring: "Voters will know I'm oriented towards a strong defense when they see me ridin' around in this jeep . . ." (One of Dukakis' speechwriters suggested a self-deprecating one-liner to the governor: "I guess I look more at home in a Think Tank than an M-1 Tank." The governor was not amused.)

Dukakis' policy differences with his running mate on such matters as gun control and Contra aid made him a target for levity. Arriving at the New Orleans GOP convention, Ronald Reagan said he felt a kinship with Senator Bentsen, because "neither one of us shares the views of their presidential nominee." (Reagan had admitted a similarity between himself and Mr. Dukakis: "Come this January, neither one of us will be holding a federal office.") Mike Peters in the *Dayton Daily News* reflected on the dichotomy in the Dukakis-Bentsen ticket. He showed a pollster questioning a housewife on her preferences. Says the woman: "I'm a Democrat. So I'm voting for Dukakis. My husband is a Republican . . . so he's voting for Dukakis' running mate."

There was ample evidence, if Dukakis cared to examine it, about the power of political humor in the election of 1988. Pat Robertson, Gary Hart, Joe Biden, and Bob Dole had all felt the sting of humor and had been brought down by it.

Theodore Sorensen, who once crafted humor for the speeches of President Kennedy, managed a line that pinked three candidates with a single rapier thrust. Wrote Sorensen of the GOP primary: "The Republican race has really been rough. In Iowa, George Bush got shot down . . . again. Pat Robertson saw combat . . . finally. And Bob Dole, after being criticized for calling Bush a liar and a coward, adopted a new campaign slogan: 'No more Mr. Nice Guy.'"

Gary Hart had been floored by a maelstrom of raunchy gag lines that left his campaign in tatters. Joe Biden's flirtation with plagiarism, which was exposed by the Dukakis camp, had generated its own scalding humor. And Pat Robertson had been undone by a volley of comic buckshot. Said Mario Cuomo: "Pat Robertson calls for a moral reawakening. He sees debauchery, pornography and prostitution. And things are even worse *outside* the evangelical movement." Robertson had claimed the ability to speak "in tongues," and Cuomo observed, "If he became President we would finally have someone who could communicate with William F. Buckley."

Paul Simon, the candidate who favored red bow ties, took his share of humorous abuse. Said one political operator: "Paul Simon teaches us a valuable lesson. No one can dress like George Will and get elected President." Said an eastern Democrat, "Paul Simon, when he was considering entering the race, asked me if I thought the voters would confuse him with the singer of the same name. He should have been so lucky." In my quadrennial *Who's In Charge Here?* I had Paul Simon saying: "The time has come for America to answer the tough questions, such as What is my name?"

Dick Gephardt preached a protectionist message focusing on the favorable tax status of the Hyundai automobile. Said one observer: "Dick Gephardt realized that the people needed a common enemy and a champion to defeat that foe. This is an old political trick. Roosevelt used Hitler, Carter used Khomeini, Reagan used the Russians, and Gephardt picked a Korean car company." When Gephardt darkened his eyebrows to make them more visible on TV, one wag commented: "I don't see anything wrong with Gephardt darkening his eyebrows brown. It's just that the red, white and blue logo on his forehead is going a little too far." Dukakis knocked Gephardt from the race by pointing out how he had waffled on the issues. This led one cartoonist to picture Gephardt complaining: "They're saying I flip-flop on the issues. I think that's slanderous. But maybe not."

Jack Kemp suffered less mockery for his flawed supply-side economic theory than for more cosmetic matters. Said one observer: "Jack Kemp has not done as well as he would have liked, but at least the media have been treating him well. Ted Koppel lets him use all his old hair."

One political columnist took a swipe at all the Democratic candidates, kidding their sheer number. He said: "I suggested to Paul Kirk that the Democrats could win just by lining up shoulder to shoulder and humming 'The Star-Spangled Banner.' Kirk said he thought that with a little coaching, they could probably learn that."

In the closing days of the 1988 campaign, by the time Michael Dukakis ordered his writers to supply him with self-deprecating humor with which to mock his lack of passion, the damage had been done. America's satirists had anticipated him. Mark Russell pointed out the "passion gap" and Dukakis' efforts to display more passion. "That's a little like watching H&R Block do *Fiddler on the Roof*." Dukakis had advertised his lack of passion beyond reversal. In the second debate with George Bush, CNN correspondent Bernard Shaw asked if the governor's abhorrence of capital punishment would be affected if his wife were raped and murdered. At that moment Dukakis gave self-control a bad name. He answered the question coolly and dispassionately, as America winced at his aloofness. Declared Mark Russell: "He should have said, 'I would come out in favor of the death penalty for reporters who ask such a question!'"

Dukakis' lack of passion, combined with his lack of discernable wit, proved a beatable combination. He tried to say passionate things about his feelings; he tried to say harsh things about George Bush; he tried to say witty things about the issues. But it was not in his nature to effect such a campaign transformation. The *New Republic* described the problem well when it said, "Dukakis doesn't so much deliver red meat to his audience as baked scrod."

The 1988 campaign was not decided entirely on the quality of the one-liners, but the ubiquitous zingers did play a part. They lent color to the candidates and the campaign. The humorous sound bites found their way onto the evening news, adding vividness to an attack, inspiring the faithful, and capturing the attention of the voter. In a presidential campaign like this one, so oddly barren of substance, the zingers played a prominent role.

In 1988 we saw the humorous sound bite become the standard language of campaign communication. Mr. Bush, with the help of a talented cadre of comedy writers, used these sound bites relentlessly and effectively. Comic attack lines became an acceptable and appropriate means of talking to the voter. The Bush strategy, like the Reagan strategy before it, blended wonderfully with the sort of entertainment-oriented journalism of the TV medium. And broadcasters were only too ready to air snappy one-liners instead of more cumbersome analysis.

Creators of comedy make strange kingmakers. It may seem that our electoral process has been hopelessly trivialized when we reflect that Michael Dukakis lost the presidency in large part because he failed to keep his wits about him.

Chapter 6
Campaign 1984
Acting His Age

If Reagan goes to sleep for even thirty seconds during the debate he'll be in a lot of trouble.
—ART BUCHWALD

In his march to inevitable triumph, Ronald Reagan
seemed peculiarly immune to the cuts and slashes of America's
humorists. There was something about this good-natured man
that seemed to soften the edge of humorous criticism and
make him impervious to its assaults. It was as though the country had a love affair with this aging American hero, and the
voters' sensibilities had to be respected—even by the men and
women whose preoccupation is cynical attack. Thus, though
Reagan's views were sometimes eccentric, his statements inaccurate, his friends indictable, and his ideology questionable,
the wits were surprisingly gentle. America was a very tough
room, as the comics say.

There was an irony in the Reagan campaign that was
not lost on the skeptics. Here was, as *Newsweek*'s Peter Goldman said, "an aging warrior offering a springtime of hope."
His bellicosity toward the Russians led one wag to observe, "I
always get a little nervous when a man of seventy-three says
he's ready to give his life for his country." When one counted
the millions who were dubious of his political philosophy, one
might have expected Reagan to be the target of humor that

scratched rather than tickled, that scorched rather than warmed. Instead, the doubters who had savaged Nixon, mocked Ford, and ridiculed Carter came down gently on Ronald Reagan, and the voters, in the words of Mark Russell, "swept Reagan back into office on a landslide of disapproval."

Ronald Reagan's immense popularity made his overwhelming victory a foregone conclusion. His mastery of the television medium, his genial charm and sheer likability, dismissed all criticism as somehow unpatriotic. This gave birth to the appellation, "the Teflon Presidency," a felicitous phrase coined by congresswoman Pat Shroeder. Russell illustrated this remarkable insulation with wit and cogency:

> To give you an example of how the Teflon Presidency works, and how hopeless Walter Mondale's situation is, about a month ago in Washington, a group of demonstrators gathered in front of the White House to burn President Reagan in effigy. The effigy kept blowing out the flames.

One manifestation of the Teflon presidency that was especially galling to Reagan's foes was that the numerous unethical acts of Reagan's aides failed to touch their leader. The wags had tormented Lyndon Johnson with the peccadillos of Bobby Baker; they had mocked Jimmy Carter over the bank frauds of Bert Lance; they had needled Harry Truman over the excesses of Harry Vaughan; but the humor generated by in-house flummery left Reagan untouched and unmocked. There was seldom an administration whose prominent figures had so often been trapped with their hands in the cookie jar or disdaining the public welfare. Interior Secretary James Watt had so little regard for the environment that Reagan himself joked about him "strip-mining the Rose Garden." Art Buchwald reflected that it was hard to tell when one saw Attorney General Ed Meese in court whether he was there as a prosecutor or a defendant. When Meese mounted an attack on pornography and issued a report on its dangers, Johnny Carson cracked that "Meese's next duty is to hire construction workers to sandblast the boobs off the Statue of Liberty." The number of Reagan aides who were guilty of ethical misbehavior continued to mount, but the venalities never touched Ronald

Reagan (until he found himself waist deep in the Iranamok quagmire). Walter Mondale squandered the chance to tar Reagan with the improprieties of his aides when he himself appointed the tainted Bert Lance to a lofty position in his campaign. But it is problematic whether the improprieties of Reagan's staff could have been successfully tied to him.

If Reagan had a legitimate Achilles heel, it was his age. Dwight Eisenhower had once declared that "no man over seventy should sit in the Oval Office"; the job was just too demanding. But Reagan had contrived to make his task extremely manageable by working short hours, taking numerous trips to Camp David and lengthy hibernations at his Santa Barbara ranch, and delegating more authority than any president since Warren Harding.

Much of the wit of the Washington press corps focused on Reagan's odd working hours. Said Fred Barnes of the *New Republic*, "If Ronald Reagan ever faces some terrible crisis, he'll really spend some sleepless afternoons." Recalling that Reagan had slept through a Libyan dogfight, a meeting with the Pope, and part of a cabinet meeting, Johnny Carson cracked, "There are only two reasons you wake President Reagan—World War Three and if 'Hellcats of the Navy' is on 'The Late Show.'" Reagan mocked his own light schedule by observing after a hectic week, "I've really been burning the midday oil."

What became known, in euphemistic terms, as "the disengagement problem"—and, with equal charity under the Tower Report, as Reagan's "hands-off managerial style"—was a source of much irreverent wit. Mark Russell gently inquired: "What do you get when you combine James Dean and Ronald Reagan?" and answered "Rebel without a Clue." A bruising joke that was given wide currency in the first Reagan term had the First Family at dinner. The waiter is taking their order, and the First Lady recites her wishes. "I'll have the shrimp cocktail, the trout almandine, the chocolate mousse, and espresso." "What about the vegetable?" asks the waiter. "He'll have the same," says Nancy.

The public generally laughed away the issue of Reagan's dotage. Even Mort Sahl, whose humor more often burned than singed, laughed on the side of the president on the geriatric issue. Said Sahl, "When Reagan goes to a home for the elderly and meets an 80-year-old man, he thinks, 'When I was your age I was working.'" Phyllis Diller made a virtue of Reagan's antiquity. "There is an advantage for a President being over seventy," she said. "At least he doesn't have to listen to his mother."

The runaway qualities of the Reagan campaign were impeded only once, after the first televised debate with Walter Mondale, when the president sounded bumbling and incoherent. Suddenly, the long submerged question of whether Reagan was indeed too old for the presidency reared its head. Said Mark Russell with an eloquent shrug: "He's an actor. He was acting his age." The *New Republic*'s TRB said, "We should treat the President like a college student and give him a pop quiz." Some typical questions would be: "Who is the President of Honduras?" and "Name your grandchildren." As Reagan prepared for his second TV debate, Art Buchwald said, "If he goes to sleep even for thirty seconds during the debate, he's in trouble." Said Sahl: "Truman proved anyone can be President, Eisenhower proved you don't need a President, Johnson wounded the Presidency, Nixon killed it. Carter buried it. And Ronald Reagan is trying to prove there is life after death." Said Loren Kerry-Walker: "Mr. Reagan said he would take a senility test if he was reelected. But what if he forgot?" When *The National Lampoon* raised the geriatric issue, it pointed out that Mr. Chernenko, the Soviet leader, was about the same age as Mr. Reagan. "Between the two of them," said the *Lampoon*, "they've seen Halley's Comet six times." But those who feared that Reagan had faltered fatally in his first debate by his show of debility and age did not take into account either his popularity or his resilient wit. In the final debate, he disposed of the troublesome issue with a caustic joke. He said, "I will not make age an issue in this campaign. I am not going to exploit . . . my opponent's youth and inexperience." Reagan's immense popularity did the rest. The public wanted to believe that Ronald Reagan was in tip-top shape. As Mark Russell observed:

The consensus after the first debate was that even though the President appeared to be hesitant, nervous, confused and incoherent, as long as he kept remembering to put on his pants, he would be re-elected.

Religion invaded presidential politics in the 1984 campaign. President Reagan associated himself intimately with the Reverend Jerry Falwell, the electronic preacher with special insights into American morality. Reagan announced at a prayer breakfast in Dallas, home of the GOP convention, his belief that religion and politics were intertwined. Geraldine Ferraro, stung by insinuations that she was not a very good Catholic given her dichotomous stand on abortion, questioned how good a Christian the president really was, given his indifference to the pains of poverty and his irregular attendance at church. Addressing Reagan's embrace of the evangelical right, Bob Hope remarked, "On the dashboard of his limousine, Ronald Reagan is reported to have the real Jerry Falwell sitting there." Mort Sahl grew dismayed over the infusion of religion into the secular electoral process. He said:

Mondale says he's a preacher's kid. Ferraro says she's a Catholic. Bush says we're in Nicaragua because they won't accept God. Reagan is close to the Falwell people. Here are four people who could give God a bad name.

When Ronald Reagan declared that in appointing Supreme Court justices he would apply a litmus test of their favorable view about bringing prayer to the classroom, satirist Fran Lebowitz sniped, "My main objection to Ronald Reagan is the religious issue. He's going to want the new Supreme Court Justices to take religious tests. I'd recommend intelligence tests instead."

Though Reagan had done little to enact the programs favored by his far-right religious constituency—school prayer, antiabortion, and so forth—he sought to bond them closely with campaign rhetoric. Columnists and satirists heaped sardonic scorn on Reagan's advocacy of school prayer and its injury to the traditional separation of church and state. Noting the hypocrisy of a man who advocates the nourishment of the soul but is indifferent to the nourishment of the body, one Washington scribe cracked, "Mr. Reagan has been urging prayer in the schools. And if he's successful, the first thing the kids will pray for is hot lunches."

Said Fran Lebowitz: "I've no objection to prayer in the schools if they'll put algebra in the churches." Even Robin Williams, the antic improvisational actor, had an opinion on the overheated subject. "If they vote in school prayer," said Williams, "will it be mandatory to include show tunes?"

To some, Reagan's piety comported poorly with both his irregular church attendance and his indifference to the welfare of blacks. Reagan opposed renewal of the Voting Rights Act and affirmative action programs and favored the distribution of public funds to segregated colleges. Much of Reagan's appeal—and it was handsomely embodied in his TV campaign commercials—was a nostalgic reflection of America's glowing yesterdays. It was an era of kindness and gentility, like a page out of Blanche DuBois's memory book. Some doubted whether this exercise in reminiscence did not resurrect an age only visible through the myopia of sentimental hindsight. One of these doubters was Jules Feiffer, who pictured Reagan reminiscing about the color-blind days of yore. Said Feiffer's Reagan:

> We had a black on my high school football team . . . He was a competitor. He played the game. We became friends . . . I even took him home for dinner . . . My black friend didn't ask for and he didn't receive any favors . . . The Voting Rights Act is a special favor . . . Now, special favors weaken us . . . Special favors would have divided me from my black friend . . . [cheerleading] GO–GO–GO CONGRESS! STRIKE DOWN THE VOTING RIGHTS ACT! . . . Let's win this one for the bigot.

Even after four years of revolutionary politics, during which Reagan had turned the national agenda on its head, escalated defense spending, slashed taxes, built a huge deficit, and attempted to dismantle the federal bureaucracy, there was still some residual doubt about the man's early career as an actor—whether such a background could prepare him for a position of national leadership. "This is a man," said Gore Vidal, "who used to wait for hours on a Hollywood sound stage for some director to say, 'Don't forget to hit your mark, Ronnie.'" America's humorists found it hard to shrug off the idea of a former movie actor leading the free world in its battle with "the evil empire." They were bemused by the frequency with which Reagan would appropriate scenes from movies ("State of the Union" and "Mr. Smith Goes to Washington" are two such examples) and present them as fact.

Often the jokes about Reagan's former career were benign and whimsical, as when Bob Hope said, "Ronald Reagan is not your ordinary kind of politician. He doesn't know how to lie or cheat or steal. He's always had an agent for that." Or when Johnny Carson said, "A lot of people say Mr. Reagan was in Hollywood too long. When he signed the tax bill he signed it, 'Warmest Regards, Ronald Reagan.'" Sometimes the jokes took a gentle swipe at the generally low quality of Reagan's film output, as when Phyllis Diller said, "There are a lot of Democrats who say they are voting for Reagan because they're afraid if he loses he might make another movie." Alluding to his frequent confrontations with a balky Democrat-controlled Capitol Hill, Joan Rivers said, "Reagan is getting less votes in Congress than he did when they voted for the Oscars."

Some of the anti-actor wit was a bit closer to the bone, as when political activist and TV star Ed Asner observed that Reagan was impatient with people who did not agree with his worldview. Said the star of "Lou Grant," "When I made a speech attacking his policy in Latin America, Mr. Reagan said, 'What does an actor know about foreign policy?'" But more often it was innocuous and inoffensive, as when Phyllis Diller said, "Reagan doesn't consider this a second term. To him it's a double feature." Or when Bob Hope said, with the gentleness of a leaf falling, "Ronald Reagan has discovered that the Presidency isn't as easy as he thought. In fact he's going to demand stunt pay." If presidential humor is meant to illuminate and draw blood, Reagan's chums in the entertainment world were attacking with all the ferocity of enraged gerbils. The media were no more belligerent. Looking back to Reagan's pre–movie career in radio, conservative camp follower George Will added his affectionate one-liner: "Ronald Reagan has held the two most demeaning jobs in America—President of the U.S. and radio announcer for the Chicago Cubs.''

In the early days of Reagan's first term, his wife had appeared to be an autocratic woman with a taste for designer gowns and well-set tables. The day after she acquired a new set of china for the East Room, the administration published some depressing figures on poverty in America. But by the time the 1984 campaign had arrived, the magic of public relations and Mrs. Reagan's devotion to the cause of drug abuse had sweetened her image and softened the humor at her expense. By 1984 her autocracy had become a joke that she was ready to accept and even share. White House speech writer Landon Parvin, who had written jokes to enliven Reagan's first-term speeches and provide him with a reputation for wit and warmth, wrote a parody of Fanny Brice's ''Second-hand Rose'' called ''Second-hand Clothes,'' which the First Lady sang at the annual dinner of the Gridiron Club. In the song, Mrs. Reagan kidded her taste for fancy raiments, and her costume was a motley mess of clothes that looked like it had been appropriated from Goodwill Industries. The laughter of the press laid the issue of Mrs. Reagan's aristocratic tastes to rest as firmly as had her husband's joke about his age landed the age issue in the dustbin of history. The theory was that if Nancy Reagan was able to laugh at the issue of designer clothes and pricey china, she could not possibly be as pretentious as her critics claimed. Others joined in the good-natured laughter. Said Phyllis Diller:

> This has been a very stylish administration. For the first time in history we have a designer deficit. Mrs. Reagan bought her fall wardrobe and we had to cancel aid to Bolivia. The Republicans say they're not waging a war in El Salvador. They're catering it.

The jokes about Nancy Reagan were so inoffensive that even Henny Youngman, that antediluvian master of mother-in-law humor, joined the panel of raillery. Said Youngman: ''Nancy was in bed with Ronald Reagan. She said: 'My God, your feet are cold.' He said: 'When you're in bed you can call me Ron.''' (Like many political jokes, this one was an adaptation of an anecdote from another era and another field. The celebrated participants of the original were David O. Selznick and his wife Irene, to whom the messianic producer had said, "In bed you can call me David.") Not everyone was so forbearing of Mrs. Reagan's devotion to the good life. Her indulgences drew a sharp elbow from one Hollywood wag who said, "Mr. Reagan says his heroes are FDR and JFK, but I suspect his *real* hero is Calvin Coolidge. And Mrs. Reagan's is Calvin Klein."

Occasionally, the gibes at Nancy's expense drew blood. The well-publicized schism between the Reagans and their children was the subject of amusement and disapproval. There was a whiff of hypocrisy about a couple that was so full of conjugal warmth and filial devotion and yet had little time for their children. Reagan clearly disapproved of his son Ron writing for *Playboy* magazine or dancing in his undershorts on "Saturday Night Live." (Recalling Jimmy Carter's brother Billy and his taste for beer, Mark Russell cracked on the oddities of presidential relatives: "At least Billy kept his pants on.") It was said that Nancy Reagan, guardian of the gates of her husband's privacy, kept the children at a polite distance. Son Michael had protested that it had been eons since dad had seen his own grandchildren. George Carlin said, "I understand that Mrs. Reagan makes her grandchildren wear name tags." Others needled the First Lady for her devotion to her coiffeur, which seemed greater than her devotion to her own progeny. Said *Punch* magazine: "The Soviet decision to boycott the Los Angeles Olympics . . . was a source of great disappointment to Mrs. Reagan. She's been in training for the four hundred meter hairspray." Added Johnny Carson: "I hear Nancy Reagan fell down and broke her hair."

House Speaker Thomas P. "Tip" O'Neill, who had scant affection for Ronald Reagan (he greeted Reagan after the latter's inaugural with the condescending question, "Well, how does it feel to be in the big time?"), had an equally wounding reference for Reagan's wife. O'Neill speculated that, when Nancy left the White House, she could always become the "Queen of Beverly Hills." Johnny Carson one-upped the Speaker. Referring to the size of his own recent divorce settlement, Carson shook his head, "No, Nancy would *not* be the Queen of Beverly Hills. And I have the royal tab to prove it."

During the 1984 campaign most Americans felt sanguine about the state of the U.S. economy; Reagan had revised the tax laws in a way that benefited the affluent and which his own budget chief dismissed as trickle-down theory —help the rich and the poor will thrive on the crumbs from their table. Not everyone agreed. Conservatives applauded the new tax code. As George Bernard Shaw said, "A government that robs Peter to pay Paul can always depend on the support of Paul." Latino comedian Paul Rodriguez also had his doubts about the Reagan economic plan. Said Rodriguez: "As far as the trickle down theory, we're still waiting for the trickle." (Rodriguez expressed a polite dubiety about Walter Mondale's economic plans as well when he said, "Does this mean we won't have to sell oranges on the freeway?")

Even with as popular a candidate as Ronald Reagan, during Campaign 1984, the Republicans were at pains to shake the public perception of the GOP as the country club party. When asked the difference between Democrats and Republicans, Ann Meara replied, "100,000 dollars." Though Mort Sahl displayed an equal skepticism for liberal Democrats and affluent Republicans, he remarked with a mixture of political acumen and pop psychology, "Liberals don't believe they deserve anything they have. Conservatives believe they deserve everything they've stolen."

David Frost, cocreater of the hallmark show of television satire, "That Was the Week That Was," tried to explain the difference between the two parties by drawing analogies to the British political system. "We have a Labor Party which you in your country would call the Socialist Party, and then we have a Conservative Party, which you in your country would call the Socialist Party." Gore Vidal observed that there is really only one political party in America—the Property party. And Jason Epstein, erudite editor of Random House, pointed out that all issues really boil down to two protagonists —people and property. Columnist Russell Baker came down on the side of the angels when he praised the neutron bomb as the perfect Republican weapon in that it "killed people while leaving the mortgages intact."

The bloated federal deficit and the gargantuan budget were issues that left the electorate unmoved, despite the attention they received from the nation's wits. Said Mark Russell: "Think of a $1.5 trillion budget. If you stood on top of the payment book, you'd experience weightlessness." Bob Hope said of the mammoth deficit, "The President is a showman. He has props for his next economic speech. A hat and a rabbit."

Many voters were uneasy with Reagan's pugnacious attitude toward the Soviets and the fact that in four years in the White House he had never met with any Russian official with a higher position than ambassador. His open-mike gaffe about falling bombs troubled the faithful, and Reagan's staff knew that in the course of the 1984 campaign there would be, well, *something*. They were uneasy about the president. He was prone to mishap when the script had not been carefully rehearsed. As Jeff Davis said, "Reagan is the Fred Astaire of foot-and-mouth disease." Reagan's aides knew that some sort of gaffe was inevitable. And indeed it was.

The president was sitting before an open mike at his Santa Barbara ranch, doing a voice test for his weekly radio address to the nation, when a carefree attitude overtook him. "My fellow Americans," he purred, "I am pleased to tell you today that I have signed legislation that will outlaw Russia forever. We begin bombing in five minutes." Later, Mort Sahl said, "I heard one delegate at the GOP convention say, 'I hope this isn't just another empty campaign promise.'" Said Argus Hamilton: "I covered the Republican convention when the President made his joke about bombing Russia in five minutes. The New York delegates thought he'd flipped his lid. The California delegates thought he ought to, like, apologize and deal with it. The Texas delegates couldn't believe he'd give them five minutes."

Lyndon Johnson had painted Barry Goldwater as indifferent to the needy. Walter Mondale had a more difficult time painting Ronald Reagan with the same brush. Though Reagan's policies were as indifferent to the poor as Goldwater's, Reagan seemed like too decent a man to embody such callous views. Scathing gibes about his myopic attitude to the poor never really stuck. Yet they appeared. Said an editor for *Mother Jones* magazine, "I don't think Mr. Reagan has the proper attitude toward the unemployed. He just thinks they have the wrong agent." And one political wag said, "Mr. Reagan said yesterday that this nation can no longer ignore the suffering of the needy. People started cheering in Watts, but then they discovered he meant Nicaragua."

Reagan campaigned on the formidable achievements of bringing down inflation and interest rates, and, since those twin towers had torpedoed Jimmy Carter four years before, it was no mean achievement. But critics claimed that Reagan had broken inflation on the backs of the poor, producing a recession that had brought pain to the elderly and the working class. Jules Feiffer mocked the Reagan process of gain through selective pain in a cartoon strip in which Reagan is explaining his economic philosophy to a doubting voter. "Recession has its good points," says the president cheerfully. "Recession brings down Inflation. Recession lowers interest rates. Recession will make life more bearable for the middle class." The voter is unmoved. She responds, "But what do we do about the old, the poor, and the unemployed?" Reagan shrugs: "The old die. The poor starve. The unemployed go into the military . . . Not perfect maybe, but it's a beginning."

Reagan's triumph was personal and profound. It seemed to reflect the truth of Edward Bennett Williams's observation about the secret of presidential campaigning and the basic rule for getting reelected. "Politics," said Williams, "is the gentle art of getting votes from the poor and campaign contributions from the rich by promising to protect each from the other."

Chapter 7
Campaign 1984
Walter over the Bridge

Mr. Mondale has said that God doesn't belong in pol-
itics, and apparently God feels the same way about
Mr. Mondale.
—MARK RUSSELL

The motto of the Washington press corps is "If you
don't have anything nice to say—let's hear it," which may account for the fact that a decent, intelligent, stalwart man like
Walter Mondale became an object of raillery and humor in his
campaign for the U.S. presidency. It was not the press alone
that found him a figure of fun. The comedians, cartoonists,
and voters also shared in the bruising merriment. With Ronald Reagan, the wags made sport of his ideological excesses.
But in Mondale's case, the target was most often his ineffectu-
ality. The most amusing thing about Mondale's candidacy was
the curious fact that no one seemed to want him to be president. He was not a victim of the anger he provoked but rather
of the apathy.

Many of the people who laughed most loudly at the anti-
Mondale humor would have liked to see a liberal Democrat in
the White House rather than an aging Republican. They un-
doubtedly liked Mondale's dignity and determination, his
stamina and sobriety. They respected his campaign, which was
encrusted with concrete issues, and were equally dubious of

Reagan's carnival of opiates and free-floating Americanism. But the fact was that, rather than stimulate enthusiasm, Mondale generated ennui and was vulnerable to ridicule for his gray eminence. Fritz Mondale drove Gary Hart from the race with the commercial gag line, "Where's the beef?" but he himself was nullified by the unspoken question, "Where's the spice?"

Mondale did not enjoy the humor he ignited; candidates seldom do. But those who seek the presidency are supposed to be thick-skinned. The gibes and slanders of the professional wits are supposed to roll off their backs. "If you can't stand the heat, get out of the kitchen," admonished Harry Truman. And yet, presidential candidates are all too human, and mockery and scorn are painful. "Thank God I don't read the newspapers," snapped Bobby Kennedy, as he scaled a copy of the *New York Post* across his Hotel Carlyle livingroom. But he *did* read the papers and fumed. "How can they do this to me!" barked John F. Kennedy, as he flung a copy of *Time* magazine across the Oval Office, and Hugh Sidey looked on in discomfort. "I bit the stem off many a pipe," recalled Gerald Ford, thinking of the calumnies of "Saturday Night Live" that ridiculed his clumsiness. "And my own children thought it was funny!"

And so Walter Mondale, that fine and decent man—son of a minister, married to the daughter of a minister—fumed and fretted at the campaign humor that was leveled at him from virtually all quarters—even from his own supporters and from sympathetic journalists. And despite his suffering, the rain of humor continued. Epithets might have been easier to bear than the drumbeat of caustic wit.

One of the basic themes of these attacks was Mondale's purported dullness. On his monthly PBS farrago, Mark Russell said, "Walter Mondale's charisma falls somewhere between a Presbyterian minister and a tree." Mocking Mondale's humorlessness, columnist Marc Shields cracked about the candidate's Scandinavian ancestry: "The three thinnest books in the world are the books on humble politicians, modest anchormen, and Norwegians with a sense of humor."

Mondale's dullness did not escape the attention of Pat Paulsen, the saturnine wit who ran a mock presidential campaign of his own on "The Smothers Brothers Comedy Hour" and resurrected it in 1988. Said Paulsen at the Gerald Ford Symposium on Humor & the Presidency: "Whenever I saw Walter Mondale on television, I thought I had lost the color."

The Mondale grayness was dutifully reported to those members of the British public who developed a taste for following American presidential contests. The Washington correspondent for the London *Times* said, "Walter Mondale is stirring up apathy all over this country."

Early in Mondale's campaign for the presidency, he had communicated with a Hollywood comedy writer to ask if the scribe could provide him with humorous material with which to bloody Ronald Reagan. The writer obliged but discovered to his dismay that Mondale used little of the material that was supplied him. When it was revealed that a Reagan mole had filched President Carter's briefing book to help Reagan prepare for his TV debate with Jimmy Carter, the Hollywood wit sent an assortment of gibes to Mondale, only to have the candidate solemnly respond: "I don't feel that thievery is a proper subject for humor." (Mondale's opponent, on the other hand, felt that nuclear war and farmers' bankruptcies were suitable subjects for humor, and the public seemed to agree with him.)

When Fritz Mondale chose a woman to run for the vice presidency for the first time in American history, even this act of audacity was used as a stick with which to beat the Minnesotan. Said Mort Sahl: "So Geraldine Ferraro will run with Walter Mondale. Women keep getting the crummy jobs." The audience howled, and Sahl went on to reflect on the fate of the distaff entry into presidential politics. "As for women," said Sahl, "running with Walter Mondale is a way to keep them *out* of government."

The perception was always that Walter Mondale was a passive cipher and that Mrs. Ferraro was a ball of fire. One Washington newsman remarked, "Mrs. Ferraro is the perfect running mate for Walter Mondale. She will add a little macho to the ticket." And Robert Klein made a similar point when he cracked, "I'm a little dubious about Walter Mondale. Even if he's elected, I'm not sure Mrs. Ferraro will find enough for him to do." Bob Hope reflected fancifully that Mondale had hired James Cagney as his new campaign manager and that Cagney had advised the candidate to get tough. "Cagney told him the way to look tough was to slap some women around," said Hope. "Mondale tried that and Geraldine Ferraro decked him." Hope dismissed the Ferraro nomination as a trifling threat to the Ronald Reagan steamroller and tossed it aside with a quip. "Mrs. Ferraro's nomination really affected Reagan's strategy," said Hope. "He's fitting George Bush for a dress."

The disorganization of Mondale's campaign was another object of humorous attack. Reagan's campaign seemed serene and effortless, while Mondale's stumbled along in fits and starts. Mondale had been savaged by Gary Hart as the candidates fought through the endless primary process.

Political humorists zeroed in on the logistics and strategies of the Mondale campaign. Reviewing the opening days of the campaign, Mark Russell observed, "Mondale started slowly . . . then he tapered off." Mondale seemed to lack the savvy of Reagan's strategists; he never quite got his operation on track. Eyes twinkling, Russell observed that Mondale's staff handled the candidate somewhat badly. Labor Day is the kickoff date for presidential election campaigns in America. Employing the hyperbole that is the stock in trade of the satirist, Russell said:

The Labor Day Parade in New York begins at noon. So at 8:00 A.M. they had Mondale riding down Fifth Avenue on a garbage truck. Waving at the winos.

The Mondale campaign, with all its glitches and foulups, triggered the wit of professional gagsters who are accustomed to a better sense of organization when you take a show on the road. Said Phyllis Diller: "I admire the Democrats. Here it is a week into the campaign and they're off and stumbling."

Premier attorney Edward Bennett Williams was more sympathetic to the snafus of the Mondale organization. He reminded the candidate that, try as he might to avoid the workings of Murphy's Law, it would inevitably prevail. "Remember," admonished Williams, "in 1895 there were only two automobiles in the entire state of Ohio, and they collided." Williams added another example of the inescapability of Murphy's Law to the hapless campaigner. He reminded Mondale that "the chance of the peanut butter and jelly sandwich landing with the jelly side down is in direct correlation to the value of the carpet."

Fritz Mondale found himself increasingly irritated by hecklers. Of course, hecklers are a traditional part of presidential campaigning, and some candidates learn to deal with them deftly. Anti-heckler tactics call for a strong stomach and a quick wit, which may account for John Kennedy's adroitness with ruffians in the crowd. But Walter Mondale lacked the spontaneity needed to answer them with humor and the staff to arm him with canned responses. Hence, he was rattled by the hecklers who dogged his trail. Art Buchwald noted this painful phenomenon that plagued Mondale and chose to see the curse as a blessing. Said Buchwald:

Heckling has played an important role in the Mondale campaign. If you get heckled, you get covered by the press. With heckling you get on the evening news. The staffs know this. The more hecklers the better it is. Reagan's people are going to bring out their own hecklers to have Reagan heckled. Then Reagan will have some of these great rejoinders to the hecklers which will give him standing ovations. Right now the Republicans are hiring hecklers to heckle Reagan to make him look good. They're holding auditions right now.

Mondale's liberalism was also good for a laugh. His compassion for the poor made for some good punch lines, however decent its inspiration. One might say, with Shakespeare, that "he jests at scars who never felt a wound," but Mondale's compassion made him a tempting target to observers less touched by those in the shadows of life. Said Ronald Reagan, "I just received a Valentine Card from Walter Mondale. I know it was from him because the heart was bleeding."

Mondale's social conscience became a bull's-eye for lampooning. Orson Bean remarked, "At his best, John F. Kennedy made us feel we had class. At his best, Ronald Reagan makes us feel everything's all right. At his best, Walter Mondale makes us feel guilty."

Others mocked Mondale's devotion to heartwrenching causes, as though Roosevelt, Kennedy, and Johnson's similar devotion to the needy was merely quixotic. Said Phyllis Diller:

> The Democrats have a lock on social issues. They're pushing welfare for unemployed whales who suffer the effects of pollution while participating in anti-nuclear demonstrations.

Some lashed back at Reagan's apparent callousness, mocking his selective concern for the "truly needy." Reagan's heart seldom seemed to bleed for the unemployed. His humorous repertoire was full of anecdotes about welfare queens who used food stamps to buy a fifth of vodka at Safeway. On balance, Walter Mondale suffered more for his compassion than Reagan did for his self-absorbtion.

Some compared Mondale scathingly to another bombastic liberal Democrat who was no longer around to resent the comparison. "Mondale is the reincarnation of Hubert Humphrey," said Mort Sahl. Then, after a moment's reflection, Sahl added, "Maybe you have to be reincarnated to displace Ronald Reagan."

Religion became a measurable element of the Mondale-Reagan campaign. It was the first time religion had been a major ingredient in a presidential election since the scurrilous underground attacks on Jack Kennedy's Catholicism. The dais of the Republican convention in 1984 became a resounding pulpit for Jerry Falwell and other television divinities, preaching in support of compulsory morality for the sinners of the electorate. Walter Mondale, in his innocence, did not feel that religion and politics were linked. Here, too, Mondale invited raillery and was whipped by the nation's wits. Mark Russell said, "Mr. Mondale has said that God doesn't belong in politics. And apparently God feels the same way about Mr. Mondale."

When the Democratic candidate took the courageous step of promising to raise taxes as a way to lower the crushing deficit—a step that Reagan mocked but came to embrace after the 1987 stock market crash—he made himself a magnet for jocosity. One White House wag, reflecting on Mondale's opposition to a linkage of church and state and his proposal for increased taxes to retire the deficit, exclaimed: "Mondale has done pretty well so far. He's come out for taxes and against God."

Mondale suffered both ways for his groundbreaking choice to have a female running mate. There were scathing comments that contrasted his passivity with her feistiness. And Mrs. Ferraro was far from immune to humorous attack based on her gender. It was not always tasteful or kind, but perhaps, as Malcolm Muggeridge affirmed, satiric humor must be harsh to penetrate the cynicism of the voter. If so, the antifeminist humor leveled at Geraldine Ferraro satisfied the requirements of political satire.

At first Gerry Ferraro's sex insulated her to insult, serious or comic. Her selection had jarred the political traditions. The GOP was disoriented by a female adversary, and some Republicans reacted with tasteless overkill. Ed Rollins, Reagan's savvy campaign manager, who should have known better, prophesied, "Mrs. Ferraro will end up being the biggest bust in politics." Even the genial Ronald Reagan was unsettled by the blue note of this comment, and when reporters at his next press conference queried him on it—this was back in the days when Reagan used to hold press conferences on occasion —he shrugged his eyebrows and put himself a country mile from the sexist remark.

Barbara Bush, wife of the vice presidential candidate, showed something less than the generosity of spirit we tend to expect from our First and Second Ladies, when the subject of Mrs. Ferraro arose. Asked her assessment of George's opponent in the Veep sweepstakes, Mrs. Bush declined to characterize the lady, except to say that the relevant adjective "rhymes with witch." One did not need the help of the Stephen Sondheim rhyming dictionary to divine the adjective Mrs. Bush had in mind.

When Mrs. Ferraro's personal problems—or, more accurately, her husband's personal problems—burst upon the public press, a good deal of the luster was rubbed off the attractive candidate. Reagan's aides knew all the juiciest tidbits of her financial torment almost as soon as she did and were joyous at the details. No longer would Mrs. Ferraro be in on a pass. Now she was vulnerable to the most scathing attack, and

America's comics found the facts of Ferraro's case equally nourishing. "Geraldine Ferraro has been named woman of the Year," said one wag. "By H. & R. Block."

Gender alone made Geraldine Ferraro a subject of lampoonery for Bob Hope, which must have set Gloria Steinem to grinding her teeth. Said Hope:

> Geraldine Ferraro is having her problems. She is married and has some children. That is undoubtedly why she agreed to run for Vice President. Right now she can only handle a part time job.

Then, employing a familiar slogan for a woman's hair coloring, Hope added: "I've always known that blondes have more fun. Mondale wants to find out if they can get more votes."

Phyllis Diller put a knife in about the candidate's rapid rise from obscurity, ostensibly on the strength of her gender, and by implication her lack of qualifications, for the office she sought. "Until last Tuesday," laughed Diller, "I thought Ferraro was a car."

There was no question that Geraldine Ferraro was chosen as Mondale's running mate because of her sex rather than because of her political experience. Henry Morgan observed that it might be more responsible to have only one criterion in selecting the vice presidential candidate. "It should be the person who would make the best President. . . . Some day we may even choose our *Presidents* that way," smiled Morgan.

Ms. Ferraro was fond of referring to the humble roots of her immigrant parents, and the satirists targeted this for critical attention. At the Democratic convention, Gerry Ferraro was not the only one to boast of her progenitors. Mario Cuomo praised his Italian-born parents, and Jesse Jackson lauded his African heritage. Mort Sahl took a swipe at the pretensions of the New York governor, the minister, and the vice presidential nominee when he said:

> The Democrats had a convention of immigrants. Governor Cuomo said, "My parents came from Sardinia." Jesse Jackson said, "My parents came from Nigeria." Mrs. Ferraro said, "My parents came from Naples." We've been here two hundred years. You would think it's time to unpack.

When Geraldine Ferraro debated George Bush on television in Philadelphia, her Ivy League opponent managed to suppress any humor at her expense. (The next day he was not so successful. A ubiquitous microphone picked up his comment to a labor leader: "I really kicked a little ass last night!") But if George Bush was not sarcastic on camera, he was patronizing, which may in fact have been worse. When the discussion turned to the problems of the Middle East, Gerry Ferraro criticized administration policy. Bush turned an admonitory glance on her—the sort one reserves for backward children and drunken workmen. "Let me help you, Mrs. Ferraro," said Bush with a patient sigh. "Let me help you with the difference between Iran and Lebanon." Mark Russell caught the aroma of condescension in the vice president's tone and cracked:

> You know what he was really saying. You know what the translation was. "Don't you worry your pretty little head about such things. And I believe I'll have some more of those nifty brownies."

At about the time that George Bush was patronizing Ms. Ferraro, Joan Rivers had abandoned her role as stand-in for "Tonight Show" host Johnny Carson to sign a lucrative contract with Fox Broadcasting to host a competing talk show. Carson joked about the new "Talk Show War" and observed that Ronald Reagan was out of the country and Vice President Bush was in charge. Said Carson: "Bush said this would be his last week as guest president, he was starring in his own presidency soon."

Geraldine Ferraro suffered a good deal of sexist slights, comic or sarcastic. If Mondale won, she would be one heartbeat away from the presidency, and Robin Williams speculated on the dubious virtues of a woman president. "We'd never go to war," he said, "and every twenty-eight days we'd have severe negotiations."

Of course, the irony of Bush's insults to Mrs. Ferraro were not lost on the Washington press corps. One White House correspondent observed, "The ultimate slur against a woman vice president is that she would be hysterical, illogical, and highly emotional. Which to my mind rules out George Bush."

There were some limits, of course. No one referred to a romance between Mrs. Ferraro and Mr. Mondale. The days of Gary Hart's reckless liaisons with a Miami model were still a few years away. In the waning days of the campaign, however, as the polls showed calamity ahead, David Steinberg remarked:

> Walter Mondale is getting increasingly desperate. He knows he's in trouble. He just announced that if elected he will marry Geraldine Ferraro. Or, if the people of San Francisco prefer, Gary Hart.

Mondale joined Barry Goldwater, Alf Landon, and George McGovern as victims of the greatest electoral landslides of the century. America's love affair with the genial Californian flattened Mondale and his special interest politics. It was a spectacular victory for Mr. Reagan and his feel-good magic.

But much of the blame must rest with Mondale's dullness and his prosaic style, which were the topics of most of the humor of the 1984 campaign. Mondale would have done better had he employed more humor in his campaign of the sort he displayed the day after it ended. On that solemn postelection morning, Mondale said, "All my life I've wanted to run for the Presidency in the worst way. And that's what I did."

Chapter 8
Campaign 1980
The Easy Target

Sometimes when I look at my children I say to my-self, "Lillian, you should have stayed a virgin."
—LILLIAN CARTER

When the campaign of 1980 began, the presidential incumbent, James Earl Carter, was painfully vulnerable to humorous attack, despite his rectitudinous posture, or perhaps because of it. Inflation raged at 20 percent, the prime rate approached the record set in the Great Crash of 1929, the stock market limped along, the bond market was anemic, the housing business was in shambles, the auto industry was asthmatic, and the trade deficit was at an all-time high. Voters recalled the long lines at gasoline pumps and raged at American impotence in the face of Iranian hostage-takers, and when Ronald Reagan asked, "Are you better off today than you were four years ago?" he provoked a resounding chorus of No's. And Jimmy Carter was history.

Inflation, recession, hostages, unemployment—they combined in a truly beatable combination. It seemed to the electorate that Jimmy Carter was a lackluster president who was over his head in the responsibilities of the Oval Office.

By the time the 1980 campaign began, inflation was so high and Jimmy Carter's standing so low that one member of the Washington press corps joked, "Carter is the first president with poll ratings lower than the prime interest rate."

Carter responded with a bitter humor of his own. Everywhere he went, Carter encountered cool to hostile audiences. His performance had generated scant approval; there was an obvious estrangement between Carter and the public he served, and this manifested itself in crowds that were not shy in showing their disapproval. Carter responded with a sardonic humor that bordered on sarcasm and often stepped across the line of taste. On one rare occasion when Carter was greeted by an exuberant, cheering crowd—"He must have given the city a grant the week before," said an aide—he appeared stunned by the sounds of unaccustomed affection. Carter said to the throng: "It's a pleasure to see people waving at me with all five fingers."

The general perception of Carter's as a failed presidency unleashed a flow of wounding wit from all points of the media spectrum—comedians, satirists, reporters, cartoonists, and even his own aides, who resented his arrogance and sardonic humor at their expense. An editorial cartoonist in the Los Angeles *Herald-Examiner* pictured California governor Jerry Brown speaking to President Carter. "No one thinks more highly of you than I do, sir," Brown is saying, "and I think you're a disaster."

In *Who's In Charge Here?* I made use of a photo of Carter speaking to ABC broadcaster Frank Reynolds. I had them discussing Carter's television advertising campaign:

CARTER. All my TV commercials will present me as an intelligent, efficient person.

REYNOLDS. You going to use a double?

By the time the 1980 election campaign began, the public seemed to have lost confidence in Carter and was willing to embrace almost any alternative. Edward Bennett Williams was clearly referring to Jimmy Carter, the loner from Plains, Georgia, when he observed:

Satchel Paige warned never to look over your shoulder because they might be gaining on you. As President, you've got to look over your shoulder every once in a while, to make sure someone is following you.

Appraisals of Jimmy Carter were so depreciative early in the 1980 campaign that one Washington wag was reminded of Clarence Darrow's acerbic comment—"When I was a boy I was told that anybody could become President. I'm beginning to believe it." Another Potomac wit said that Jimmy Carter's performance brought to mind Mark Twain's line, "Suppose you were an idiot and suppose you were the President of the United States. But I repeat myself."

Carter had made a speech in which he blamed public indignation on a "general malaise." It was not a well-conceived rationale. Ronald Reagan would use that phrase as a stick with which to whack his opponent all through the fall. Comedienne Lily Tomlin referred to public disaffection for Carter when she said, "Ninety-eight percent of the adults in this country are decent, hardworking, honest Americans. It's the other lousy two percent that get all the publicity. But then—*we elected them.*"

Editorial cartoonist Mike Gorrell zeroed in on the Carter record with an illustration in the *Charlotte News* of the White House Situation Room. A map of the world is labeled: CRISIS ZONES—DOTS INDICATE PROBLEM AREAS. The map is pocked with a plague of black dots. Next to the map is a portrait of President Carter—with a black dot on his nose.

The *National Review*, William F. Buckley's irreverent political weekly, was often abrasively witty in its campaign attacks on Carter. When former president Gerald Ford announced he was no longer contesting for the Republican nomination, leaving the path to the presidency open for Ronald Reagan, the *National Review* tucked its tongue firmly in cheek and said, "Jerry Ford's withdrawal from the presidential race severely diminishes the likelihood of a pardon for Jimmy Carter."

As the polls turned against President Carter and the hostages remained unreleased, Carter's frustrations increased. Some thought his attacks on Ronald Reagan grew intemperate and excessive. Carter portrayed his genial opponent as a mad bomber who would surely propel us into nuclear war. This strategy closely resembled that of Lyndon Johnson in his attacks on Barry Goldwater—except in its success. Carter's rhetorical excesses generated what the media came to call The Meanness Issue. Thus, the understated, gentle Georgian suddenly seemed to show a vicious side. A man who heretofore had an image of decency, honesty, and sincerity was exposing a quality of petulance and malice that was not at all flattering. Said one White House press aide who pleaded anonymity: "Some say Jimmy Carter is mean and vindictive. But I work for him and I know he's just the opposite. Vindictive and mean."

Jeff MacNelly, the Pulitzer Prize-winning editorial cartoonist whose work appears in the *Chicago Tribune* and hundreds of other newspapers, focused on Carter's surprising "mean side," as shown by his intemperate attacks on Ronald Reagan. In the midst of the campaign, with Reagan showing strength and Carter desperation, MacNelly pictured Carter in a series of cartoon panels. Carter is saying:

PANEL 1. (calmly) I am disappointed in my opponent . . .

PANEL 2. (calmly) I had hoped that by now we would be engaged in a useful discussion of the issues. But instead, Governor Reagan . . .

PANEL 3. (shouting) WHO HATES POOR FOLKS, AND WANTS TO . . .

PANEL 4. (screaming) ENSLAVE BLACKS AND HISPANICS AND BLOW UP THE WORLD . . .

PANEL 5. (calmly) has resorted to a campaign of slurs and innuendos which insults the intelligence of all Americans.

Carter was stung by the mockery of his vindictiveness. Perhaps he could be forgiven for his growing sense of frustration; he was learning what Walter Mondale would discover four years later—that intemperate attacks on the agreeable Reagan had the habit of rolling off his back in what congresswoman Pat Schroeder called a Teflon effect. Carter saw that he had gone too far with his rage. Here was no Barry Goldwater, to be immobilized by charges of saber rattling and social blindness. Carter was quick to apologize and promised to moderate his comments. The *National Review* responded with its customary wit:

Mr. Carter promises to be very, very good and says he'll try "to be sure that we do not have a lowering of the tone of the campaign." Whether it's possible for him to lower the campaign at this point is far from clear.

Some thought there was method in Carter's meanness—that he was trying to draw attention away from the faltering economy with his vitriolic attacks on Reagan. One of these observers was cartoonist Jeff MacNelly. He pictured Carter as an engineer in the cab of a locomotive that has crashed. The train is a shambles and is labeled THE ECONOMY. Carter is saying: "Uh, not to change the subject or anything, but did you know Reagan is a HATE-MONGERING RACIST?"

As the campaign unfolded, many Democrats viewed Jimmy Carter as unelectable, and they turned their attention to Senator Edward "Ted" Kennedy, the attractive young senator from Massachusetts, whose name evoked the evergreen memory of his martyred brothers. But when Teddy entered the race, encouraged by early polls that showed him devastating Carter, he found himself hounded by the accident at Chappaquiddick, in which a girl had died and Kennedy's behavior seemed less than heroic. The tragic events at Chappaquiddick had triggered a repertoire of wounding jokes that were disinterred when Teddy announced his candidacy on Labor Day of 1979. Said the *National Lampoon:* "Teddy says he regrets the accident but that's all water over the dam." In *Who's In Charge Here? 1980,* I made use of a campaign photo of Teddy pointing down the street and had him saying, "You go down two blocks and drive off the dock." Teddy's hunger for the White House proved abortive, so in another photo I had him remarking to a group of children: "Sometimes I wonder what my brothers would have done." A youngster replies: "They would have won." Said one Washington wag: "Teddy has his eye on the presidential seat, but Mr. Carter has something better on it." In his short-lived, ill-fated campaign to wrest the Democratic nomination from Jimmy Carter, Teddy damaged his chances with a disastrous interview with Roger Mudd in which Kennedy faltered and rambled incoherently on such topics as why he wanted to be president and what had happened at Chappaquiddick, two questions for which one would have thought he could have formulated reasonable answers. As Kennedy fumbled Mudd's questions on CBS, the ABC network was running the Steven Spielberg thriller, *Jaws*. Said Senator Bob Dole, the Kansas senator whose virulent wit had tarnished the campaign of running mate Gerald Ford in 1976 and helped put Jimmy Carter in the White House: "Seventy-five percent of the country watched *Jaws*, twenty-five percent watched Teddy, and half couldn't tell the difference." The famous slogan of *Jaws II* was "Just when you thought it was safe to go back in the water. . . ." After watching Kennedy's embarrassingly inept performance, a Carter aide cracked, "Just when Teddy thought it was safe to go back into politics. . . ."

Teddy's fumbles on CBS recalled the Zeke Bonura Theory of Government, as wittily enunciated by Edward Bennett Williams. Bonura was the clumsy first baseman for the Washington Senators, who each year contrived to end the season with the best fielding average in the majors. He did so by recognizing the baseball rule that you cannot be charged with an error *unless you touch the ball*. Hence, Bonura avoided touching anything that looked the least bit difficult. This, said Williams, was a rule that had been respected by most politicians of our century. Teddy fumbled the two sharp grounders from Roger Mudd that he might have been better off not touching at all.

Kennedy's critics also found him too liberal by half. These preoccupations, they nagged, had become tiresome and predictable. His speeches focused on the sick, the black, the old, and the poor. One reporter, returning from a trip to Capitol Hill to interview the Massachusetts senator, joked about the futility of the assignment. "It was useless," he said. "Whatever I asked him, he answered the same way. If I had asked him about the weather, he would have said, 'When I think about the weather, I think first about the sick, the black, the old, and the poor.'"

The Kennedy brothers had always been adept at joking about their vaunting ambitions. In politics, said Will Rogers, it is essential to be ambitious but fatal to appear so. Bobby had decried his own ambitions for the presidency when Lyndon Johnson occupied the White House. He said, "I have no de-

signs on the presidency and neither does my wife, Ethel Bird."
And so, when Teddy stood in for President Carter at a labor
rally, he said, "Mr. Carter phoned me early this morning and
asked me to fill in for him. I told him, 'I've been trying to do
that for a year.'"

Teddy's campaign to unseat Jimmy Carter for the 1980
nomination was ultimately fruitless, producing some slighting
humor at the senator's expense. In one Second City sketch, a
morose Teddy is commiserating with his mother about his inability to seize the nomination from Carter.

TEDDY. I lost, Mama.

ROSE. Maybe you're adopted.

In his failed attempt to take the nomination from a sitting president of his own party, Teddy's philandering and his
failed marriage drew some ridicule. His wife Joan had joined
her husband on the campaign trail and had done yeoman service in trying to paper over their split. (The efforts of Lee Hart
to camouflage the ruptures in her marriage to husband Gary
seemed a rerun of the Adventures of Joan and Teddy, and
equally doomed. Said Billy Crystal of Gary Hart's reentry into
the 1988 race: "If he's elected, will Donna Rice be the First
Chick?") As Teddy and Joan sought to put a happy face on
their marital hemorrhage, a reporter bluntly asked Rose Kennedy why Joan lived in Boston and Teddy lived in Virginia.
Rose answered, "Who's Virginia?"

During the week of the Democratic National Convention in New York City, the *National Review* puckishly ran a
photo of Carter and Kennedy embracing, wearing transparent
grins. In the balloon captions, Teddy is saying: "What Carter
is saying is that the country is getting better because it's getting sicker at a slower rate." And Carter is saying, in a replay
of his well-publicized prophecy: "I'll whip his ass!" At the apex
of Kennedy's threat to Carter's nomination, the president had
issued this prediction. When he fulfilled it by savaging Kennedy in the primaries, one Washington columnist cracked: "In
whipping Senator Kennedy's ass, President Carter has finally
managed to keep a campaign promise."

Curiously, much of the humor generated by Ted Kennedy's candidacy had nothing whatever to do with either liberalism or Chappaquiddick but with the senator's weight. Kennedy's decision to seek the nomination was a vacillating one. Capital reporters noted that you could tell whether Teddy was running or not on any given week by whether his weight was going up or down. If it was going down, it meant he was running and wanted to be more telegenic. If he was leaning toward beefiness, it meant he cared little about voter image and was not running for president. The insight was a dead giveaway when Teddy decided to make his assault on the Democratic nomination. Several jokes were given wide currency by the Washington press corps about Teddy's tendency toward flab. A reporter for the *Boston Globe* said, "You know where Teddy stands because there's a dent in the ground." Another reporter said he liked to watch Kennedy go into McDonald's and watch the numbers change. Another asserted that Teddy's campaign motto, in a gloss from Truman's famous line, was: "If you can't take the heat in the kitchen, then eat the cookies in the living room." Another media member referred to Teddy as "the Senator from Pizza Hut." Still another said, "There's no getting around Ted Kennedy—except with a high mileage car." And still another gibed, "Watching Ted Kennedy get out of a leather chair is like watching the Russians get out of Afghanistan." Johnny Carson has often expressed his comedic theory that it is perilous to do more than three jokes on the same subject in his monologue. It will be noted that the Washington press corps displayed no such sense of proportion.

To any student of dissembling in government—such as the duplicities of Vietnam, Watergate, and Iranscam—Jimmy Carter's habit of fudging the facts will not seem particularly reprehensible. Like the vicuna coat that Ike's White House chief of staff, Sherman Adams, accepted from a wealthy industrialist, Carter's delinquencies with the truth seem like small beer when compared with scenes of bugging the Oval Office and diverting funds from ransom to rebels. Yet, at the time, Carter's tendency toward what the press called "misstatements" and "disinformation" (but which those with less discretion call "lying") was worthy of satiric attack.

Mike Peters, the talented young political cartoonist for the *Dayton Daily News,* recalls his attitude toward Carter's campaign fibs. "I didn't want to call him a liar," explained Peters slyly. "And so I drew a cartoon of three presidents. Washington was saying, 'I cannot tell a lie.' Nixon was saying 'I cannot tell the truth.' And Carter was saying 'I cannot tell the difference.'"

President Gerald Ford had once referred to Carter's carelessness with the truth. Speaking at a Gridiron Club banquet at which Carter was also a guest, Ford pointed to the Georgia governor who would oppose him in the 1976 election and said, "Governor Carter is sitting over there. You can always tell where he's sitting. But it's hard to figure out where he stands." Ford was deprecating Carter's habit of changing his views to suit his audience.

Referring to Carter's propensity for obfuscation and selective memory, the *National Review* needled candidate Carter in 1980 with an invented news items. Said the *NR:*

President Carter promised a "complete investigation" when reporters questioned his statement that "I do not have a younger brother." A White House clarification the next day stated that what the President meant to say was that he "had no recollection" of having a younger brother.

Carter's strategic vacillations on substantive matters brought a funny broadside from cartoonist Jeff MacNelly. When Carter and Reagan were scheduled to debate on television, third party candidate, John Anderson, sought to join the debate, but Carter rebelled. Cartoonist MacNelly brought his wit to bear on the situation. He showed the TV debate in progress. There were three participants: Ronald Reagan and *two* Jimmy Carters. In front of one of the Carters were papers marked, CANCEL B-1, NO TAX CUT, DELAY MX, CUT DEFENSE and NO DRAFT REGISTRATION. But in front of the second Jimmy Carter were papers labeled BUILD MX, DRAFT REGISTRATION, NEW BOMBER, and $25 BILLION TAX CUT. In the MacNelly drawing, one of the Carters is saying to third party candidate Anderson: "We've already *got* three candidates."

Carter's vulnerability was increased by his reaction to the Soviet invasion of Afghanistan. He expressed incredulity at the Russians' aggression, which led some to mock his naivete. MacNelly showed Carter as a rube in the big city, holding a deed to the Brooklyn Bridge that is signed by Leonid Brezhnev. The shocked Carter is saying, "You mean he *lied* to me?" To show American anger at the Soviet invasion, Carter cancelled American participation in the upcoming Moscow Olympics, which led some to ridicule the president. His reaction seemed tepid and timid to White House watchers. A cartoon in the *Christian Science Monitor* showed an overweight mother serving dinner to her obese son and admonishing him, "How do you expect to make the Olympic Team and boycott the 1992 Olympics if you don't eat your vegetables?"

When the Iranians seized American hostages, the immediate effect on Carter's candidacy was positive—Americans stand behind their president in moments of international distress. But with the passage of time, they stood even further behind him. As the weeks and months slipped by, and with it the failure of a helicopter rescue mission, the public came to blame and mock Carter for his seeming impotence. The Ayatollah Khomeini became a target for caustic humor across the United States. Ballantine Books published *The Green Book*, a paperback containing the eccentric social and sexual philosophies of the ayatollah. His attitude toward women, for example, would have been laughable were it not so venomously sexist. (Speaking at a symposium on Humor & the Presidency sponsored by former President Ford, Pat Paulsen cracked, "The Gerald Ford Symposium on Humor is like the Ayatollah Khomeini symposium on the Sexual Revolution.") With American hostages imprisoned in Tehran, Khomeini announced by way of extenuation that Iran was in "a state of chaos." One columnist cracked, "The Ayatollah was then brought before a Revolutionary Court where he presided as judge, and sentenced himself to execution."

The utter failure of Carter's helicopter raid to rescue our hostages made Carter a target for mockery. When the president called the Republican convention "a debacle," one conservative wag said, "That's high praise from our Country's *Debacler-in-Chief*. Jimmy Carter says the GOP Convention was a 'debacle.' What did he expect—a helicopter rescue mission?" The *New Republic* pointed to the disarray of the Carter administration on the hostage nightmare, citing two headlines it found on the same day in the *Washington Post*: CARTER VOICES OPTIMISM IN HOSTAGE CRISIS and, elsewhere on the page, CARTER OFFICIAL CAUTIONS AGAINST PREMATURE OPTIMISM ON HOSTAGES.

Most presidents offer up their families as hostages to the wit of their detractors and the country's clowns and, frequently, use their kin as subjects for their own humor. Jack Kennedy joked affectionately about the beauteous Jacqueline, his daughter Caroline, his aggressive brother Bobby, his affluent father, and the sheer numbers and naked ambition of the Kennedys. (He once praised astronaut John Glenn by saying, "You're doing pretty well for someone who isn't in the family.") Lyndon Johnson got about as much comic mileage out of his wife and daughters as the comedians who were paid to do it. But Jimmy Carter's family offered even more food for satire than the Kennedy clan or the assorted Birds of the Johnson White House. Most of the humor was produced by the Washington onlookers and considerably less by the president himself. Art Buchwald, who accomplishes the extraordinary feat of being hilarious and relevant three times a week, observed that the Carter family would make a spectacular TV sitcom. He pictured himself proposing the comedy series to a television producer. "It's about a peanut farmer who's also a nuclear engineer and a naval officer and wants to be President. His mother is a member of the Peace Corps, his kid brother runs a gas station, one of his sisters rides a motorcycle, and the other is a faith healer." Concluded Buchwald, "You know what the producer is going to say, don't you? 'Kill the faith healer and we've got a show!'"

Billy Carter, Jimmy's ebullient younger brother, was the butt of most of the jokes, benign and destructive, that were leveled at the president's family. In a revelation that the press predictably labeled "Billygate," it was learned that brother Billy had received $200,000 from the government of Libya to lobby his big brother on their behalf. Congress convened an investigation, and Jimmy mumbled something about having used Billy as a conduit to free the hostages—which stood somewhere near the zenith of diplomatic folly until Ronald Reagan shipped arms to the Iranians for the same purpose. Comedians found humor in Billy Carter, who on one occasion appeared resplendent in a costume made entirely of beer can openers to help promote a brew opportunistically called Billy Beer. Billy's lobbying efforts on behalf of the Libyan regime provoked Bob Hope to remark, "The difference between Jimmy Carter and his brother is that Billy has a foreign policy." Billy remained an embarrassment to his brother throughout the 1975 campaign. In *Who's In Charge Here?* published in that year, I printed a photo of Billy staring perplexedly out of a hot air balloon. He is plaintively asking, "Can I come down after the election?"

Rosalynn Carter invited mirth of a different stripe. She was an intelligent, assertive woman who was the only First Lady to commonly attend her husband's cabinet meetings. Even Nancy Reagan, whose detractors deplore her influence over government policies and personnel, never appropriated a seat at the cabinet table. Nor did Jacqueline Kennedy so directly involve herself in her husband's plans. Jack Kennedy once quipped, "At least I know that Jackie will never greet me at the end of the day by saying, 'What's new in Vietnam?'" I kidded this shared power in the Carter White House in my *Who's In Charge* volume. Two voices were heard from an upstairs White House window:

VOICE NO. 1. Am I or am I not the leader of the Free World?

VOICE NO. 2. You are, Rosalynn.

Jimmy's mother, Lillian Carter, was a feisty, white-haired woman whom America took to its heart. Her unsentimental candor was immensely appealing. On one occasion, when she was more than usually dismayed by the behavior of her sons, she said, "Sometimes when I look at my children I say to myself, 'Lillian, you should have stayed a virgin.'" If Billy was sometimes an embarrassment to the president, Jimmy's daughter Amy did little to enhance his stature. Certainly, she did not bring her father the outpouring of affection that the three-year-old Caroline brought to the New Frontier. The

UPI and Wide World photo libraries abound with shots of little Amy yawning vigorously as her father orates before a variety of campaign audiences. Once she lent unintended levity on the stump. A wire service reporter asked Amy, "Have you any message for the children of America?" to which Amy promptly responded, "No."

If Jimmy Carter was a target for the malicious humor of others—cartoonists, columnists, comics, and his opponent—he was adept at employing humor as a weapon himself. Ted Sorensen, who wrote both speeches and humor for John F. Kennedy told me, "Carter's sense of humor was very much like that of Kennedy's. It was dry and understated." Unfortunately for Carter, his sense of humor was also rather sarcastic, reflecting his hostility to the Washington establishment, which had failed to accept him, and to the Washington press corps, which found him bucolic and unsophisticated. Carter's propensity for mordant, sardonic humor damaged him—unlike Kennedy's ironies and Reagan's anecdotes, which were upbeat and ingratiating.

This sardonic tone was evident on the eve of Reagan's inauguration, when Carter still sat in the White House, bloodied by electoral defeat. Carter called Reagan to brief him on the state of the hostage negotiations, which were ongoing. Carter was thorough in his report to his successor, and when he hung up the phone, Hamilton Jordan asked, "What did Reagan say, Mr. President?" Without cracking a smile, Carter replied, "Well, I briefed him on what was happening to the hostages. He just listened. Then when I finished he said, 'What hostages?'" This nasty little gibe, which implied Reagan's ignorance of worldly matters, typified Carter's humor. It also suggested that even before Ronald Reagan had spent a day at work in the Oval Office, his predecessor suspected he would exercise power in a decidedly hands-off manner. Carter's preconception may have been confirmed by the Tower Commission, as the Iran-*contra* affair unraveled.

A sarcastic wit is not the ideal tone for a presidential candidate. Though it may serve a cabaret entertainer or a moviemaker who seeks to cut and slash his targets, sarcasm is a chancy weapon for a political incumbent or challenger. Robert Dole learned this to his grief as Gerald Ford's running mate and, in the process, helped hand the presidency to Jimmy Carter. (Interestingly, in the 1988 presidential primaries, Dole, who was easily the wittiest of the Republican hopefuls, was careful to suppress his native humor to keep from promoting the appearance of malice.) But though Carter profited from Dole's vicious humor, he did not seem to profit from Dole's example. If experience is the name we give to our mistakes, Jimmy Carter left the White House with abundant experience on the subject of the nuances of campaign humor. All through his four years in office, White House aides had been waving red flags, if Carter chose to see them. They referred in hushed conversations to the chief's "borderline sarcasm." Carter's chief speech writer, Jim Fallows (now a contributing editor for the *Atlantic Monthly*), complained about the draft of a speech that Carter had sent back to him marked simply "A-minus." Joe Califano, Carter's secretary of health, education and welfare, also felt the flick of Carter's sarcastic wit. When Califano brought a group of charts headlined CARTER WELFARE REFORM into the Oval Office to brief the president, Carter twitted his cabinet officer for his well-known egotism. He said "Joe, when you come in here with cards that say CALIFANO WELFARE REFORM then I'll know we're on the right track."

Carter's aides grew gun-shy of the boss's cracks at their expense. When he completed some gentle wheezes to a press dinner that drew scant response, Carter glanced at his chief speech writer and said, "I told my staff I wanted them to prepare a talk for me to make tonight that was funny, but they didn't get around to it." One chastened member of Carter's staff repaid the president for his slights with the comment: "It used to be said that Jimmy Carter was a generous man who, on the occasion of a friend's birthday, would always send a modest gift. And so in time, Jimmy Carter became known as a man of modest gifts."

Carter's cutting wit was so deeply ingrained in his personality that he did not use it merely to singe the people who worked for him. He often directed it at those who supported him with their money and their celebrity. Warren Beatty had assembled a group of cinematic notables at his Beverly Hills home to raise money for the 1980 Carter campaign. To many southern censors and Bible Belt reformers, Hollywood had always been a Sodom with modern plumbing, a hotbed of sex, drugs, and poor table manners. Carter no doubt was reflecting this cultural suspicion when he said to the assembled stars: "It's a real thrill to meet the famous people here tonight. I hope I don't get to know too much about you."

Every candidate who has ever struggled through the exhausting travail of a presidential election campaign knows that the most efficacious kind of wit for a candidate's use is a self-deprecating humor. The public likes a "good Joe" who can mock his own flaws and frailties. Jimmy Carter's performance in the 1980 campaign, however, was quite another matter. In the course of the reelection campaign, one senior aide said, "Jimmy's idea of self-deprecating humor is to insult his staff." Despite the substantial power of the press during an election campaign, Carter did little to ingratiate himself with the reporters who covered his campaign. It was as though Carter felt his superior morality and intellect were such that he need not stoop to conquer the correspondents who had little respect for his gifts. Hence, the Carter campaign humor was sarcastic in its contacts with the press as well. At one briefing along the campaign trail, the president sighed, "I don't have very much for you today, so you can just put away your crayons."

Carter's hostility toward the reporters who covered his campaign was well known. At a White House dinner late in his presidency, Carter concluded his remarks to the assembled journalists by saying, "I want to thank all of you who make my job so easy and enjoyable." Then he turned to his wife and said, "Thank you, Rosalynn." Carter turned his sardonic wit on *New York Times* correspondent Jim Wooten who had often been critical of Carter's policies. "In the White House environment," said Carter, "it is difficult to separate fact from fiction, which reminds me of my friend Jim Wooten here—the Erica Jong of the *New York Times*." His vitriolic humor reached a new plateau when, near the completion of his abortive 1980 campaign, Carter said to an assemblage of newsmen, "I've had a lot of setbacks and a lot of troubles, as you know, and you reporters have been kind enough to make them clear to the

American people." What Carter and so many of his predecessors in the Oval Office failed to perceive was that this is precisely the function of the Washington press corps—to report the travesties along with the triumphs, not to behave as though criticism was a subtle form of sedition.

Even Carter's running mate, Walter Mondale, was not immune to Carter's glancing wit. In one campaign speech, Carter turned to his vice president, who sat beside him on the dais, and said, "I am very grateful that my associate, Walter Mondale, is here. I've done the best I could to find something for him to do." Not content with that remark—since Veeps are notoriously sensitive about their inactivity and impotence—Carter continued:

> I would like to ask you to keep Walter Mondale from getting lonesome in the White House. . . . If you have any questions about the Concorde, Northern Ireland, abortion, gay rights, downtown parking. . . .

In *Of Thee I Sing*, George S. Kaufman created the prototypical vice president, Alexander Throttlebottom—underworked, ignored, and sent out for sandwiches. At one point, when someone observes that Throttlebottom doesn't look well, he says, "I'm having a breakdown. Underwork." Walter Mondale, Hubert Humphrey, Lyndon Johnson, George Bush—all the good and worthy men who have occupied the vice presidential office—have known the agony of that empty position. But only Jimmy Carter would ridicule the vacuum of the vice presidency to the man who held it.

Carter's critics in the 1980 campaign taxed him as a president who knew the words but not the music—if his pronouncements had the ring of action, too often they failed to produce any meaningful change. Mr. Outsider was now on the inside, but he had failed to augment his cadre of Good Ole Boys with any of the establishment types he loathed. Hence, Carter seldom seemed able to turn good intentions into good works. (Ironically, President Kennedy was often unable to turn his soaring rhetoric into the hard currency of legislation. It took Mr. Insider, Lyndon Johnson, to transmute JFK's sterling rhetoric into law.) Carter's inability to match words with deeds led political cartoonist Jules Feiffer to pillory him with his syndicated strip. Said a ruminative Carter:

> I give a strong talk on the environment. And do nothing about it . . . I deliver an innovative speech on disarmament. And do nothing about it . . . I issue a clarion-call on energy. And do nothing about it . . . I may not be much of a President . . . But I am a hell of a political columnist.

Carter's born-again rectitude brought him close to arrogance. But it also gave him a calm, cool demeanor that the public found particularly welcome, especially after the overheated atmosphere generated by such activists as Kennedy and Johnson and the corruption fostered by Richard Nixon. The soft southern drawl, the sly, understated humor, the gentle smile that bore no relation to the solemn message of his words —all this provided a gentling air that the electorate welcomed —at least until the gas lines stretched to the horizon and America was held hostage by Iranian terrorists. Jules Feiffer gave Carter's coolness one-handed applause in a memorable series of panels during the 1980 campaign. Said a placid Carter:

> I do not panic in crisis . . . I use statements in a crisis . . . I preach normality in a crisis . . . I hide out in Camp David in a crisis . . . I act passive in a crisis . . . And after a while, the crisis goes away . . . Or would you prefer the Bay of Pigs [and] Vietnam? . . .

President Lyndon Johnson's mixture of liberalism and conservatism was vexing to many of his supporters and invited charges of hypocrisy. President Carter produced similar angry humor as he ran for reelection against Ronald Reagan. The former actor was quite clear about his position and his principles, while Carter was ambivalent and calculatedly imprecise. Feiffer pinpointed this tendency in a strip that pictured a man wearing a hood over his face. The cartoonist offered RIDDLE:

> "I am smiling . . ."
> "I am crying . . ."

"I am weak . . ."
"I am strong . . ."
"I am liberal . . ."
"I am conservative . . ."
"I am leaving . . ."
"I was never here . . ."
"Who am I?"

Whereupon the man whips off his hood, revealing himself to be Jimmy Carter. "I am a political cartoonist's nightmare," he concludes.

The 1980 campaign ended with Jimmy Carter rejected by the public he sought to serve. Inflation, recession, hostages, and unemployment had led to popular disenchantment with James Earl Carter. During the frantic week that followed Election Day 1980, the Associated Press reported that Carter was planning to write his memoirs. "Fine," chirped the *National Review*. "We'd rather he write than be President."

Chapter 9
Campaign 1980
The Actor

There was a fire in Ronald Reagan's library and
both books were destroyed.
—PAUL KRASSNER

Running for president, said Garry Wills, is a delicious wound inflicted on willing sufferers. And much of the
pain derives from the insights of humorists. Nineteen-eighty
proved a painful race and a fast track for those who sought the
GOP presidential nomination. There was Howard Baker, the
bantam media star whose easy eloquence had dominated the
Senate Watergate hearings. There was Bob Dole, who had
made an indelible if not altogether positive impression as Jerry
Ford's running mate with his abrasive wit. There was George
Bush, with a resume as long as Chile and memorable indict-
ments ("voodoo economics," for example) that he would later
have to swallow when he joined the ticket of the target of his
contempt. There was John Connolly, the charismatic Texan
who took a bullet from the rifle that killed John F. Kennedy
and who poured a fortune into a campaign that would bring
him a thimbleful of votes. And then there was the husky-
voiced star of three dozen B-pictures on the Warner Brothers
lot and a forgettable Western TV series. The outcome of this
colorfully casted contest is history.

When Ronald Reagan took on incumbent Jimmy Carter, it was natural for America's chorus of wits and clowns to focus on his former career in films. If there is any profession that Americans view with more disdain than politics it is acting. It seems like such a trivial way for grown-ups to spend their time. After all, how could the electorate decide that a former movie actor was a "serious person"? Reagan was not a luminescent star in the tradition of Gregory Peck or James Cagney. As Jack Warner smirked when he first heard that Ronald Reagan was contesting for governor of California, "No no, that's all wrong. It's Jimmy Stewart for Governor and Ronald Reagan for Best Friend."

Reagan had made a career out of being the best friend to his cinematic betters in an array of Hollywood second features. Yet, jokes about his former calling had as little effect on his candidacy as rain on the ocean. Like the Teflon presidency that would later make him immune to the misdeeds of his administration, jokes about his thespian beginnings simply failed to stick. Most such jokes were more friendly than malign. Indeed, comedians and humorists who sought to make light of Reagan's film career found that the candidate had cut them off at the pass. Reagan skillfully co-opted the issue, defusing whatever problems it contained by laughing away his Hollywood years with good-natured aplomb. But on occasion, Reagan's critics were able to invoke his celluloid beginnings by linking them to his approach to affairs of state. Jules Feiffer turned his acid pen to the task in one series of panels in which Reagan is speaking to the public. In Feiffer's strips, Reagan never opened his speeches in the mandatory political idiom, "My fellow Americans. . . ." In the world of Feiffer, Reagan began his orations, "My fellow audience. . . ." After that he becomes a walking trailer for a new superproduction, saying,

We are about to release "MOVIE-AMERICA" . . . As the producer of "MOVIE-AMERICA" let me lay out the story line. Boy meets girl. Girl gets marriage and family . . . Father gets a new job and a tax cut. Mother gets a drop in grocery prices . . . Children pray and go to church socials. Business sky-rockets. Russia can't keep up in the arms race and unconditionally surrenders . . . Black and white, yellow and brown, young and old, mend their differences and go to the prom . . .

142

[An explosion of lights illuminates the White House like a Hollywood premiere.]
Watch for "MOVIE-AMERICA." Coming soon to the White House.

If any of the gibes about Reagan's palmy days before the movie camera should draw blood—which was most unlikely—his loyal advocates on the right were prepared to dismiss the derision as irrelevant, immaterial, and left-wing. W. H. von Dreele, the sardonic poet laureate of the *National Review* wrote:

Now watch the Walter Cronkite types
And every last detractor
Remind the folks that Reagan is
A former movie actor.

Reagan's other target of vulnerability was his ultraconservative message. Like Barry Goldwater in 1964, Reagan ran against the government he sought to lead. He would get the government off the people's backs. He would dismantle the social machinery of the New Deal, the New Frontier, and the Great Society. That message had been an irresistible target for America's humorists when Goldwater articulated it. It had produced a landslide victory for Lyndon Johnson. But Jimmy Carter was not Lyndon Johnson, and Ronald Reagan was not Barry Goldwater.

For one thing, it was Reagan, not America's professional humorists, who was the most visible joke teller, and they were *his* gibes that were engaging the public's funny bone. Oppressive, bloated government became the target for Reagan's humor, and Reagan was much more adroit in attacking the bureaucracy than America's funny men were at attacking Reagan's message. This should not be surprising to political junkies who have long known that, next to the media, the government is the favorite target for angry humor. When Reagan ridiculed the excesses and stupidities of government, he found a most receptive audience. Many laughed so hard that they lost sight of the support and security that these "bloated" government agencies offered them.

Reagan had a huge repertoire of scathing jokes and anecdotes that pictured congressmen and bureaucrats as a pack of mendacious prodigals and government as the original evil empire, an institution berserk in a blizzard of paper. The quality of Reagan's anti-Washington humor, as expressed in the 1980 campaign, had been honed during a thousand roasts, when he acted as spokesman for the General Electric Corporation. There was little subtlety to this government-bashing humor. Some of his one-liners and anecdotes sounded like retreads of ancient wheezes from the *Reader's Digest*. Some of it had the aroma of Hollywood, which was not surprising, since throughout his primary and election campaigns, Reagan was fed a steady stream of jokes by the premier gagsters of Hollywood. But all of it, vintage or fresh, was delivered with the impeccable timing and genuine humility of Reagan the performer. Adlai Stevenson spent an inordinate amount of time *writing* his own speeches. Ronald Reagan was more astute. He spent an inordinate amount of it *rehearsing* his speeches—particularly the jokes that were crafted for his campaign and his ideology. (His opponent, President Carter, made the lethal mistake, according to his top White House aides, of spending virtually no time at all in writing, reading, rehearsing, or embellishing his campaign speeches or in guiding his speech writers.)

In targeting government for his humorous attacks, Reagan was doing much the same thing that his opponent had done four years before in riding a wave of antibureaucratic loathing to power. Carter was as much an outsider in 1976 as Reagan was in 1980, but when they met at the turn of the decade, the former actor was the master of the game. After all, Reagan was still an outsider, while Carter had been on the inside for four years.

The popular contempt for government is regularly fueled by well-publicized scandals. Politicians themselves attack the government that they are meant to serve. Senator Eugene McCarthy, between naps and effete pontificating, said, "The only thing that saves us from the bureaucracy is its inefficiency." The brilliant curmudgeon H. L. Mencken observed, "It is inaccurate to say I hate everything. I am strongly in favor of common decency. This makes me forever ineligible for any public office." Said Edward Langley; "What this country needs is more unemployed politicians." Given the slanderous things that witty men have been saying about it for centuries, government makes an irresistible target for public figures like Ronald Reagan who want to reach the White House.

Reagan's witty antibureaucratic one-liners in 1980 included the following:

> Where else but in Washington would they call the department in charge of everything outdoors the Department of the Interior?

> There are two ways of doing things—the right way and the way they do it in Washington.

> When you mention common sense in Washington, you cause traumatic shock.

> The Washington establishment believes that the only good dollar is one taken from a taxpayer's pocket.

> In Washington the economists have a Phi Beta Kappa key at one end of the watch chain and no watch at the other.

> Washington is the only city where sound travels faster than light.

> Washington didn't have the same problems other cities did. . . .
> They grabbed hold of the fastest growing industry in America.

Much of Ronald Reagan's antigovernment wit pandered to the popular repugnance to the income tax. Running in favor of motherhood is no more secure a position than running against taxes. Reagan's joke book of antitaxation gibes served him well in 1980 and led him to a solemn vow never to raise taxes—a vow that he would reluctantly abandon after the stock market crashed in 1987. To imply that taxes are excessive is as unassailable a position as recommending that a starving man eat more.

Humorous one-liners are the ideal instrument for discrediting taxes—if somewhat more irresponsible than reasoned debate. When laughter is engaged and the emotions are aroused, there is little opportunity to assess the merit of the programs that the taxes fuel. Indeed, there is not a little irony in the fact that Reagan and his tax-blasting repertoire won him major support from the people who benefited most from the programs the taxes financed. Reagan's grab bag of antitax levity included the following:

> To paraphrase Will Rogers, in government they have never met a tax they didn't like.

> There is an old saying: In levying taxes as in shearing sheep, it's best to stop when you get to the skin.

> The big spenders in Washington would have been right at home with Oscar Wilde. He's the one who said that the only way to destroy a temptation is to yield to it.

> Government is like a baby—an alimentary canal with an appetite at one end and no sense of responsibility at the other.

> Balancing the budget is a little like protecting your virtue. You just have to learn to say "no."

> Feeding tax dollars to government is like feeding a stray pup. It just follows you home and sits on your doorstep asking for more.

The enormous outpouring of affection that Ronald Reagan generated among the public outraged his opponents. Barry Goldwater and his antediluvian policies drew a small army of adherents who could be disdainfully dismissed by liberal members of the media and the public. But this fellow Reagan was adored—not because of his views but despite them. Thus, Reagan was a magnet for good-natured insult. But the effect of the humor on Reagan's mounting popularity was practically nil.

The Republican convention met in Detroit in 1980. Reagan had swept to victory over his numerous rivals in the primaries—Dole, Baker, Connolly, and Bush had all tasted his dust. His nomination on the first ballot was as secure as the Oscars for *Gone With the Wind*. The one question mark centered on Reagan's running mate, and the other candidates could foresee his choice's value in Reagan's electability. The spot meant becoming heir to the Oval Office in eight years or, given the vagaries of health and age, in four. For a moment former President Ford seemed "a definite possible," as Sam Goldwyn used to say. It would be a dream ticket, said the cigar-wielding power brokers. "Terrific," said Mort Sahl—"the Gipper and the Tripper." But the romance was a brief one, and after Ford was briefly hustled between the microphones of Walter Cronkite and Barbara Walters, and the clamorous talk of increased responsibility for the former president ("a co-presidency" they called it), Reagan decided that there would be no Ford in his future. Jerry Ford, who never entirely got along with Ronald Reagan, slipped out of the picture, and the cameras focused on George Bush, who quickly laundered his positions to blend with the man at the top of the ticket. Bush's moderate perceptions on economics and abortion underwent a quick convention conversion, and he happily took up the mantle of running mate. Editorial cartoonist Paul Conrad of the *Los Angeles Times* showed a supplicative Bush on his knees, gripping Reagan about the calves with ardor. Bush is saying: "By golly, gee whiz, it's sure good to serve this President!" (Bush never quite shook this image of subservience and genuflection. Eight years later he was still fighting the look of an obedient cheerleader, as he sought to win the presidential nomination in his own right—without the explicit endorsement of the man he had served so long.)

One of Reagan's primary rivals, John Anderson, formed a third party to run against Reagan and Carter in the general election. Anderson was a witty, intelligent man, cruelly hampered by lack of funds, staff, and hope, yet he was not entirely without assets. He stung his opponents with humor, as when he referred to Ronald Reagan, his Hollywood past and conservative views, as "a product of Eighteenth-Century Fox." Anderson derided Reagan's plan to balance the budget while cutting taxes and increasing defense spending. "How do you do that?" asked Anderson rhetorically. "It's very simple. With mirrors." When critics called Anderson a spoiler for running against his fellow Republicans, he smiled, "What's to spoil?

Spoil the chances of two men at least half the country doesn't want?" Anderson's caveats were prescient, as were George Bush's, who called Reagan's monetary program "voodoo economics." The combination of a substantial tax cut and greatly increased Pentagon spending failed to balance the budget; indeed, it created a gargantuan deficit that helped precipitate a market crash. But in the euphoric days of 1980, the plan seemed entirely plausible and Anderson's gibes the querulous carpings of a loser.

When Jimmy Carter learned that the TV debate planned by the League of Women Voters would include John Anderson, he refused to participate, and he was mocked by the press for his decision. They suggested he was afraid to face the articulate Anderson, but the president stuck by his guns. When League president Ruth Himerfeld reported, "There will probably be an empty chair in Mr. Carter's place," Pat Oliphant, editorial cartoonist for the *Washington Star*, drew a telling picture of the debate in progress, with a baby's high chair in place of Carter to illustrate the president's infantile pique. Responding to the possibility of an empty chair, Johnny Carson quipped, "What if the chair wins the debate?" Another wag described President Carter's arrival at the debate: "An empty car will pull up to the station and Carter will get out." Given the hectic atmosphere of the debate and the uncertainties as to who would be debating whom, Ronald Reagan cracked, "A funny thing happened on the way to the studio." Ultimately, Reagan debated Anderson sans an empty chair.

When President Carter finally debated challenger Reagan, he doubtless thought that Reagan's controversial positions opposing programs like Social Security would make him easy pickings. The script didn't quite unfold that way. George Kaufman used to mock the traditional Hollywood story line thusly: "Boy meets girl, girl gets boy in pickle, boy gets pickle in girl." The Reagan-Carter story line was also an unexpected twist on the traditional story. Part of the cause of this unexpected turn of events was not revealed until three years later, when it was learned that just before the debate, a Reagan mole had stolen a copy of Carter's briefing book and passed it on to Ronald Reagan. Thus, the challenger knew every point the president planned to make and could prepare a seemingly spontaneous counterpoint. An editorial cartoon in the *Milwau-kee Journal* showed the two candidates in the TV studio at their respective podiums. Carter is about to speak when Reagan interrupts, "I know exactly what you're going to say."

To those innocents who find this thievery analogous to Nixon's "dirty tricks" and wonder why the public did not reproach Reagan for this deplorable strategy, it should be recalled that Nixon never possessed a fraction of Reagan's immense likability. The pilfered papers were considered a tempest in a teapot. Ron Zeigler called the Watergate break-in "a third rate burglary" without too much success. Reagan's press secretary dismissed the theft of Carter's briefing book as much ado about nothing, and the voting public seemed to concur. Reagan had cooked the books and gotten away with it. He even had columnist George Will coach him for the debate; Will then appeared on TV in a postdebate analysis without disclosing his partisan role and solemnly declared Reagan the winner. But it is doubtful whether the stolen briefing book or the secret Will assist was crucial to Reagan's triumph in the debate. Reagan's polemic victory was the product of his charm and Carter's sanctimony. Whenever Carter glared furiously at Ronald Reagan ("he looked like he was going to slug him," said one observer), Reagan was affable and agreeable. When Carter reached a shrill crescendo of attack on Reagan's past positions, Reagan simply chuckled and said, "There you go again." The audience laughter seemed to wash away Carter's argument and mock his wrath. This lighthearted reaction disarmed the audience, which burst into laughter—as four years later Reagan would disarm Walter Mondale with irrelevant humor on the issue of Reagan's age.

Carter's humor during the debate was mainly unintentional. Late in the confrontation the subject turned to arms control, a field where Carter could properly have felt he held an advantage over the Russophobic Reagan. Carter's aides stared dumbfounded and reporters laughed as President Carter suddenly said, "I was talking to my daughter Amy the other day, to ask her what the most important issue was. She said she thought it was nuclear weapons and the control of nuclear arms." The image of the nine-year-old Amy, stifling a yawn and pontificating on nuclear proliferation, was laughable

—an example of unintended campaign humor that damaged Carter beyond remedy.

Despite Reagan's easy affability with audiences of all kinds—he always seemed to have an anecdote that was felicitous and flattering to the group he was addressing—Reagan tended to commit unfortunate gaffes when answering questions of the press. When the scenario was not carefully scripted, Reagan was likely to produce a howler that sent his aides rushing for their typewriters to produce an explanation. (As the campaign progressed, reporters were kept further and further away from the candidate to prevent these calamitous misstatements. One correspondent, quoting the famous line from the film *Love Story*, said, "Covering Ronald Reagan is never having to say you've seen him.")

Reagan's chief ally in the campaign of 1980 was the TV camera. It was no secret that in the Age of Television, the personality of a presidential candidate had become more important than his positions, a dangerous triumph of matter over mind and image over issues. (In the seventh year of the Reagan era, screenwriter/director James Brooks would display the dangers of cosmetics over facts in his film, *Broadcast News*. But, by the time it appeared, the battle between substance and aesthetics had become a cliche; seven years of Ronald Reagan had schooled even the most primitive voter in the power of personality over program on TV.) Television had given fame to Lucille Ball, Jackie Gleason, and Johnny Carson. It would now give ultimate power to Ronald Reagan. In what other presidential campaign would a Republican aide run up to a campaign manager (in this case Bill Casey) after the candidate had made a substantive policy statement, and exclaim, "My God, Bill—he was wearing a white shirt!"

Image was important to Ronald Reagan, and President Jimmy Carter quite properly felt flummoxed by the ineffable warmth and charm of his opponent. Cartoonist Jeff MacNelly took careful aim at the image issue. He showed Carter looking like Herbert Hoover, wearing a prim Hoover collar and a Hoover/Carter button, and looking at a poster of Ronald Reagan who wears an FDR grin and holds an FDR cigarette holder at a jaunty angle. The poster reads: HAPPY DAYS ARE HERE AGAIN, Roosevelt's old campaign slogan. And the Hooveresque Carter is moaning, "WOULD SOMEBODY PLEASE EXPLAIN WHAT'S GOING ON? . . . ."

Ronald Reagan generated a great many jokes about his intellectual deficiencies. It was said he did not read books and had little taste for the study of history. The books in his library were chosen for their color, said the wags. It was bruited about the beltway that reports on policy matters had to be compressed into one-page memos (a slur that was retailed about President Eisenhower before him). Said satirist Paul Krassner: "There was a fire in Ronald Reagan's library and both books were destroyed." And author/editor Vic Navasky said, "There's a side to Ronald Reagan that people don't know. When he was a young man, Reagan read the complete works of William Shakespeare. Of course, when Reagan was young, Shakespeare hadn't written all that much." Ted Sorensen told a story that also called Reagan's cerebral gifts into question. In it, Reagan asks his barber to place a black dot on his forehead. The barber protests that a dot on one's forehead is a decoration in India, but Reagan is insistent. "I just met the Indian ambassador," says Reagan, "and after our conversation he turned to a friend, tapped his forehead, and said 'Nothing there.'"

Reagan laughed away the question of his meager intellectual qualities. He deflected the matter as deftly as he dealt with matters of age—by acknowledging it. Visiting a grammar school during his campaign, he told a classroom full of children, "I thought you asked me here to a remedial English class because you heard my speeches." Returning to Eureka College where he had earned his sheepskin by way of the pigskin, he kidded his modest academic record by saying, "I only came back to clean out my gym locker. . . . But I am excited to receive this honorary degree. I had always figured the *first* one was honorary."

Ronald Reagan had created a rocky road for Gerald Ford when the latter sought the presidential nomination in 1976. But in 1980 Reagan would not be denied. The former governor's assets were daunting. He had enormous charm, was an able public speaker, and the camera was kind to his face. The Goldwater circle comprised his loyal clique. On occasion a liberal Democrat, outraged by Reagan's artful simplicities, would protest, as did Hubert Humphrey: "Ronald Reagan is George Wallace with eau de cologne." But these quibbles were drowned in a chorus of cheers.

In the election campaign of 1980, political observers were aware of what has since become known as Ronald Reagan's hands-off management style. In the blunt lexicon of the Washington press corps, this was referred to as "Reagan's tough four-hour-days." Newsmen grinned that, if he ever faced a really formidable crisis, "Reagan will have to spend some sleepless afternoons." Or the derisive suggestion, on the occasion of a visit from a chief of state; "Reagan is taking a working nap." By 1987, *Time* magazine was emblazoning its cover with the rude question, WHO'S IN CHARGE? as the stock market collapsed and the Congress rejected Reagan's Supreme Court nominee; a vacuum seemed to cry out for the filling in the West Wing. But in 1980, as Reagan ran for the presidency against a chief executive in whom the public had lost faith, the disengagement issue was not widely observable. Of course, a few perceptive satirists noticed something. Jules Feiffer pointed a finger at Reagan's tendency to delegate too much authority as he cleared brush on the ranch. In one series of pen-and-ink panels, Feiffer showed Reagan speaking to a vast unseen electorate:

> My fellow audience, I'm gonna run a committee-style government . . . With me in the Oval Office supervising lotsa little governments . . . We're gonna have a State Department Government . . . An' a Defense Department Government . . . An' a CIA Government . . . An' a Budget Bureau Government . . . An' they're all gonna run themselves an' leave the President alone . . . Go, Go, GOVERNMENT FELLAS! [Reagan falls back into his chair in an ecstacy of withdrawal] . . . I'm gonna take a nap.

The humorists who had been laughing at Reagan's Hollywood beginnings and Carter's waist-high administration had expected a lame contest, reflecting their doubts about both candidates. But Mae West, that padded temptress of the twenties, had called the turn when she murmured, "If I have to choose between two evils, I pick the one I haven't tried." That advice portended trouble for Carter. The American people picked the man they hadn't tried. Ronald Reagan was swept into office. His plurality was eight million votes, and he garnered 489 electoral votes, while Carter won a scant forty-nine. It was a humbling defeat for a sitting president, the worst since Herbert Hoover bowed to another charismatic charmer fifty years before. It was an arresting change of direction for the U.S. government, since Ronald Reagan articulated the views of the far right, stating quite clearly that he planned to dismantle the welfare state of Roosevelt, Truman, Kennedy, and the rest. He would cut taxes for the rich and be more scrutinous of welfare cheaters; in short, he was adopting the agenda of the conservatives at a time when the nation was moving inexorably rightward. The *National Review* greeted Reagan's election with the joyous impudence that had long characterized its conservative voice in the wilderness and that of its coruscating founder, William F. Buckley. Suppressing a chuckle and a cheer, it wrote:

With the election of Ronald Reagan, The National Review assumes a new importance in American life. We become, as it were, an establishment organ. . . . This is therefore the last issue in which we shall indulge in levity. Connoisseurs of humor will have to get their yuks elsewhere. We have a nation to run.

Chapter 10
Campaign 1976
"No Problem!"

> I feel rather embarrassed about the way I treated
> you on "Saturday Night Live" and I'd like you to
> pardon me . . . Oops!
> —CHEVY CHASE

It was said that Jerry Ford gave America three years
of good government and eight years of comedy material. This
was doubtless the result of Ford's singular vulnerabilities to
humor. In the presidential election of 1976—when Ford first
wrested victory from Ronald Reagan in the primaries and
then lost the general election to a grinning Georgian named
Jimmy Carter—Gerald R. Ford was a perennial target for the
wit of satirists. Ford squirmed under much of the mockery.
Ten years later, when he convened a symposium on Humor &
the Presidency at his presidential museum in Grand Rapids,
the outpouring of affectionate mirth at Ford's deficiencies was
still at torrent strength, though his sensitivity to it seemed to
have lessened.

The chief flaw that America's wits, journalists, and cartoonists found in Ford's persona was clumsiness. Ford's pedes-
trian mind and phlegmatic ways were other targets for raillery. In his incisive book, *A Ford, Not a Lincoln*, Richard Reeves
quotes a *Washington Post* poll that revealed Ford's friends characterized him as "slow, plodding, unimaginative, poorly

staffed, out of touch and inarticulate." Said one comic, after reading the *Post* results: "Ford has his friends and he has his enemies. Some think he's dull, slow, and boring. And those are his friends." The qualities elicited by the *Post* questionnaire made Ford a lightning rod for deprecatory wit. During the 1976 presidential campaign, these uncharitable gibes led Ford, as he told it, to bite the stem off many of his favorite pipes. When Ford prematurely freed the Polish people in a famous gaffe during a TV debate with Jimmy Carter, the mistake became the topic of another outpouring of caustic humor. Ford's full pardon of the sins of Richard Nixon also produced ample humor, somewhat less benign than that produced by Ford's clumsiness or intellectual lethargy.

Ford's perceived clumsiness was a target for humor, both amusing and destructive. Week after week, "Saturday Night Live's" youthful audience—most of whom were of voting age—observed Chevy Chase aping Ford, crashing through doors, falling down stairs, knocking over tables, collapsing on the floor, disappearing from view behind a podium, and promptly reappearing to purr, "No problem, no problem!" Not only did the public find the humor hilarious, but President Ford's own teenage children were vastly amused. In one of the show's most famous sketches, Ford's press secretary (played by Buck Henry) explains to the president (portrayed by Chevy Chase) that they have devised a fresh tactic for fighting the perception of Ford's clumsiness. The strategy is called "Operation Stumblebum," and the plan is brilliant in its simplicity. Each time the president stumbles, all his aides will stumble too. Thus, the president's stumbling will appear to be the sort of thing that could happen to anyone. As the skit unfolded, the presidential aides and Secret Service men are bumbling about the Oval Office like drunks and spastics, crashing into the furniture and one another.

There is some humor that strokes its object—one thinks of the humor directed at Kennedy's clan, Reagan's Hollywood roots, and Johnson's steers. There is other humor that diminishes its target by making him the object of sneers and ridicule. One thinks of Gary Hart's philandering and Joe Biden's plagiarism. The gaggery about Ford's clumsiness was of the latter variety. Ford was powerless to either ignore or to laugh away the clumsiness issue. The unshakable image of oafishness was particularly galling to Ford and his advocates since it was basically "a bum rap." Richard Nixon and Jack Kennedy had ridden the bench at Whittier and Harvard football games, but Jerry Ford had been a legitimate gridiron star. He had led his team to the Rose Bowl with regularity. This suggested an extremely well-coordinated man, not the awkward, bumbling fellow of the comedian's image. But satire is a matter of exaggeration. Humor does not always reflect the truth; sometimes it feeds on it for humorous effect. "You would sacrifice anyone for an epigram," a friend once said to Oscar Wilde. And the humorist *would* sacrifice anyone for a laugh. If truth is the first casualty of war, it is also the first casualty of comedy. Whether Jerry Ford was actually a cluster of aberrant motor reflexes is somewhat irrelevant. The comics and cartoonists had found a "schtick" that could assure laughter, like Nixon's jowls and Jack Benny's pusillanimity. Though Ford did not relish this mockery, he realized that it came with the territory. He also recognized that one cannot protest such indignities without irrigating them.

Editorial cartoonists thrived on the Ford clumsiness. Mike Peters of the *Dayton Daily News* pictured him with a ubiquitous band-aid on his forehead. Pat Oliphant showed him in constant disarray from some recent calamity. The cruel canard all began when Ford fell down the ramp as he and Betty were emerging from an airliner in Munich; then he gilded the lily by butting his head on a helicopter door. Both events occurred before a phalanx of photographers and TV cameramen, who were quick to register the happenings on film and tape for the amusement of posterity.

It was not only the editorial cartoonists who mocked Ford's clumsiness—though Peters, Oliphant, Paul Conrad, and Jeff MacNelly were in the forefront of the attackers. Cartoonist Garry Trudeau relied on the Ford palsy for his laughter. One Trudeau strip pictured Ford at the White House indoor pool. President Kennedy swam daily with his pal, Dave Powers, exchanging bawdy stories as he did laps to ease his aching back. President Johnson swam naked with uptight establishment types to shock their prim sensibilities. President Nixon had the pool covered and turned into a commodious press room, ostensibly for the reporters' convenience, but more likely to keep them a greater distance from the Oval Office. President Ford opened the pool again, and this in turn opened the door to Garry Trudeau:

PRESS SECRETARY. Mr. President, the workmen have finished reconverting the press room back into a pool.

FORD. Oh, good, good! Let's try it out!

PRESS SECRETARY. Ladies and gentlemen, the President of the United States!

[We see a volcanic SPLASH! The final panel shows a group of eager correspondents brandishing microphones.]

REPORTERS. Mr. President! . . . Mr. President! . . . Wow! Didja see that gainer?!

Ford tried to laugh along with the comics who were kidding his disorientation. To the Washington Press Club he said, "I don't agree with those who have called me the Evel Knievel of politics." He even invited Chevy Chase, his chief tormentor, to the annual dinner of the Radio and Television Correspondents Association. Then, when Ford was introduced, he "accidentally" caught the tablecloth in his trousers and tumbled a ton of silverware into Chase's lap. "Oops!" said the president in mock chagrin—"Oh, by golly. . . ." As Ford approached the microphone at the center of the dais, he pretended to trip, and his fifteen-page speech went flying over the audience. Dan Rather, Walter Cronkite, and the rest went rushing to retrieve the speech. Havoc reigned and laughter exploded. When the audience stopped roaring its delight, the president produced the real script from his breast pocket, pinned his celebrated guest with a sharp eye and said: "Good evening. I'm Gerald Ford and you're not!" The inspired sight gag was the product of Don Penny, the former TV actor/director who was brought to the White House to enliven the president's oratory. Penny overcame the opposition of the West Wing traditionalists in promoting this buffoonery and endeared himself to both Ford and the Washington journalists. Of course, the amusing antidote failed to work entirely, and the mockery of Ford's clumsiness, justified or not, acted as a brake on his hopes for election in 1976.

The power of campaign humor is such that Ford and his aides spent a fair amount of time trying to defuse this particular target for ridicule. Ron Nessen, Ford's amiable press secretary and a former TV journalist, developed the idea of appearing on "Saturday Night Live" as a guest host. His aim: to show that the president didn't take their mockery very seriously and neither should the voters. After all, went the rationale, Jack Kennedy had laughed away the ticklish subject of his religion and his father's wealth in winning the 1960 election. Why couldn't Ford laugh away an issue that was far less cosmic than God and money? So Ron Nessen appeared on "Saturday Night" in one of the most memorable episodes of that iconoclastic series. Nessen played along with the stumbling mystique, telling the audience that his work as presidential press secretary had been an invaluable training ground. He had learned, for example, to remove the president's necktie from the helicopter blade, while Mr. Ford was still wearing it. He smiled indulgently as Chevy Chase impersonated Ford by stumbling around the set, talking to a stuffed animal, stapling his ear, and signing his hand instead of the tax bill. Nessen's appearance tended to disprove the maxim, "If you can't beat 'em, join 'em." The president of NBC and numerous columnists all thought Nessen's appearance on the show was ill-advised and insulting to the president. Some senior White House aides went so far as to suggest that Nessen resign.

If Ron Nessen was trying to defuse a destructive issue in the midst of an election campaign, it was counterproductive at best. The *Washington Post* printed a letter to its editor that carried a chilling message. Ford, after all, had granted permission to his press secretary to participate in the unseemly farrago. Wrote an irate *Post* reader: "I don't know how I can vote for a man who could be so dumb."

Another vulnerability that generated campaign humor was Gerald Ford's general lack of charisma and imagination. Ford's own minister had said of the most distinguished member of his congregation: "Gerald Ford is a normal, decent, God-fearing man, but you can say that about a lot of people." This is known as damning with faint praise, or in the case of a minister, praising with faint damns. Lyndon Johnson was less gentle in his attack on Ford's modest cerebral powers. Said Johnson, in a splendid example of the mean spirit and barnyard aroma that characterized the Johnsonian wit: "Jerry Ford couldn't fart and chew gum at the same time." Ford did little to dispel the image of an intellectual lightweight. He even acknowledged it. On one occasion he joked, "If Lincoln were alive today, he'd roll over in his grave." If Jack Kennedy brought poetry to politics with his rhetorical flourishes, Jerry Ford brought a sort of dull blank verse. He displayed his deafness to the glory of words when he named his campaign organization, which would joust with Jimmy Carter. He named his election team "The President Ford Committee"—PFC—one of the lowlier ranks in the U.S. military.

In 1976 members of the Republican electorate had to choose between two men who no one was ready to acknowledge as intellectual Goliaths. Both Gerald Ford and Ronald Reagan, who fought for the GOP nomination, were not renowned for their mastery of history, biography, economics, or the complex issues that informed the final third of the twentieth century. Ford declared that his favorite TV program was a shoot-em-up detective series called "Cannon," and Reagan was a fervent fan of "Mission: Impossible."

Ford's gaffes were dismaying to his staff to a degree that has seldom been approached within the beltway and that would not be seen again until Ronald Reagan moved into the White House. (Reagan's howlers were more blatant and more numerous than Ford's and led his aides to keep him away from any microphone or TV camera unless the script had been well rehearsed and the backdrop carefully selected. But curiously, owing perhaps to Reagan's personal appeal, the blunders that tarred Ford merely rolled off Reagan's well-tailored back.)

Ford had a problem with names—a curious failing in a politician—and this too brought gibes from the gallery. Campaigning for Dr. S. I. Hayakawa, the GOP candidate for the U.S. Senate in California, President Ford referred to him as "Dr. Haya-kama." A Ford aide grimaced at the error but then looked at the matter in a more cheerful light. "It was better than what he called Hayakawa when they met privately. Then he called him 'Hiawatha.'"

Ford's occasional vacuity was pricked by Garry Trudeau in a "Doonesbury" strip that tightened jaws in the West Wing on the eve of the TV debates with Jimmy Carter. Trudeau has the president consulting his chief of staff, Dick Cheney:

FORD. Dick, how do you think I should handle that opening statement tomorrow [in the TV debate]?

CHENEY. Well, sir, I certainly think you want to touch as many bases as possible . . . It's important that you underscore the considerable progress made by the Administration, particularly in restoring trust in government and faith in the economy.

FORD (weighing the advice). Maybe I should give my Acceptance Speech again.

During the late 1970s Johnny Carson turned the force of his wit more and more to politics. It was a lamentable turn of events for Jerry Ford, who more than once felt the sting of a Carson one-liner in "The Tonight Show's" opening monologue. The political zingers were most often the product of the cool, wry wit of Hal Goodwin, Larry Klein, and Ray Siller, Carson's top writers. Through the medium of their comic perceptions and Carson's impeccable delivery, the comedian had become middle America's contemporary Will Rogers. During the Ford-Carter campaign of 1976, Carson regularly riddled the foibles of both candidates. To Carson, President Ford looked like "the guy at Safeway who okays your checks."

There was no question that Gerald Ford was boring, bland, and somewhat limited in his perspicacity. In the words of one political columnist, he was "giving decency a bad name." Ford was not clever like Kennedy or cunning like Johnson. David Steinberg suggested that Ford seemed destined to join Jimmy Carter and Richard Nixon on "a Mount Rushmore of Mediocrity." Thus, in that peculiar autumn of 1976, satirists and cartoonists alike found Ford's passivity fed their funnybones if it did not stimulate their cerebrums. They were amused by the gap between the good guy character and bad guy programs (much as they would react to the same dichotomy in Ronald Reagan). Comics were nourished by his bumbling good nature and his mental lassitude. He was like a soothing Valium after the evil prodigies of Nixon and Johnson.

Jules Feiffer said of Ford: "He fills spaces like a vacuum." For three decades, Feiffer has been exposing us to the political inanities of our times. He always illustrated Ford with a tin can on his head and drew him as Happy Hooligan, the lunkhead hero of the turn-of-the-century comic strip character. "Another creation he closely resembled was the Frankenstein monster," said Feiffer with more mirth than malice. Feiffer had begun his career under the benign aegis of Harvey Kurtzman, the creator of *Mad Magazine*, but he found his true forte in his incisive mockery of America's presidents, from Eisenhower to Reagan. Ford must have often squirmed at the Feiffer panels that flowed from the President's TV debates with Jimmy Carter. The cartoonist once showed Ford behind his lectern, a sign proclaiming: GREAT DEBATE.

QUESTIONER. Mr. President, critics claim you don't care about the poor.

FORD. The who?

QUESTIONER. The victims of rising unemployment.

FORD (alarmed). The unemployed are rising? Call out the guard!

QUESTIONER. Describe your views on civil rights.

FORD (puzzled). Who's Sibyl Rice??

QUESTIONER. Describe your views on civil liberties.

FORD (brightening). On individual liberties? I know that one! Any corporation has the right of free choice to make as much profit as they want as cheaply as they can . . .

MODERATOR. This ends our rehearsal, Mr. President. Two minutes to air time.

FORD (ecstatic). HOORAY! BRING ON JIMMY CARSON.

Bob Orben, the premier comedy writer for Red Skelton and Jack Paar, who President Ford brought to the White House to enliven his often soporific speeches with crisp, relevant one-liners, had equal reason to blanch at Ford's wayward way with words. On the campaign trail in 1976, Orben would often find that his presidential patron had inadvertently substituted the wrong word at a critical point in the punch line. The *New Republic* called the candidate "Jerry the Joke Killer," as the president trashed the humor of a well-turned phrase. Here is an example of Ford at work in dismantling the wit of an anecdote:

> As I was walking through the lobby a friendly lady came up to me, shook my hand and said, "I know you from somewhere, but I can't remember your name." So in a friendly way I tried to help her out. I said, "I'm Jerry Ford." She said "No, but you're closer." [The proper punch line: "No, but you're close."]

Ford again undermined his own humor on the campaign trail when he addressed the National Athletic Association, an organization comprising athletic directors from the most prestigious colleges in America. Said Ford:

> I feel very much at home here today, because the athletic director of any college and the President of the United States have a great deal in common. We both need the talent, we both need the cooperation of others, and we both have a certain lack of performance in our jobs. [Proper punch line: "We both have a certain lack of permanence in our jobs."]

If the voters of America viewed Gerald Ford as less knowledgeable than Kennedy or Johnson or Nixon, and if columnists and cartoonists focused joyous attention on his shortcomings, Ford tried manfully to shrug aside the petty slanders. He appeared at the annual Alfred E. Smith Memorial dinner in New York City. It was a propitious platform. It was at this dinner in 1960 that John F. Kennedy had used his delicious wit to turn a political embarrassment into a popular triumph. Ford tried to replicate the Kennedy trick at this famous Manhattan banquet, when he said:

> Let me say first how busy it is, running the country and the campaign at the same time. We seem to go from one place to another without pausing. Sometimes it gets confusing, but it is always nice to come back here to Philadelphia.

Kennedy's and Roosevelt's intellectual fire exploded in their oratorical skill, but even Ford's staunchest advocates admitted that he was not an exceptional speaker. He would often flub his lines during a critical campaign speech. These misadventures in the text occurred so often that Bob Orben pasted a 3X5 card on the inside cover of the presidential speech binder. It bore a line to be used by Ford on those occasions when he blew a line. It read:

> I told my wife I knew this speech backwards, and that's how I'm delivering it.

In show business, such a line is called "a saver," and no comedian is without one. Ford found that it invariably brought laughter and applause from his audience; it carried a measure of modesty that was most appealing. Ford grew to like the line so much that he would purposely flub his lines in order to use it.

Ford's use of a professional comedy writer within the White House drew its share of ridicule. Though Kennedy and Johnson both pressed their regular speech writers into service as gag writers (Ted Sorensen for JFK, Ben Wattenberg and Liz Carpenter for LBJ), only Ford hired a writer exclusively for these comic creations. This seemed to many like excess in image making. Barry Goldwater had said that extremism in the defense of liberty was no sin. Ford seemed to be saying that extremism in the promotion of humor was no sin either. Not everyone was so forbearing. Garry Trudeau found the hiring of a presidential comedy writer a phenomenon worthy of his attention. In one of Trudeau's strips, President Ford is reading a letter inscribed in the unformed handwriting of a child. It reads:

> Dear Mr. President . . . I read that you pay a man to write your jokes for you. So I made up a joke. Here it is. You say, "I'm a Ford, not a Lincoln, and Ford has a better idea." Please send me $10.00 for this joke. Your friend, Billy R.

Not every public figure need be a Cicero or Demosthenes. Indeed, there are some who say the era of rhetoric is leaving us. If so, Gerald Ford anticipated the change. As even his best friends would attest, Ford was not a terribly moving speaker. An election campaign makes demands on the nominee's stamina and judgment, but it makes its maximum demands on his oratorical skill, and Ford's were modest. Don Penny, who doubled as Ford's speech coach, told of training the president in delivering his acceptance speech to the GOP convention, and Penny's description stands as one of the funniest monologues in the history of presidential life. "I played Bugs Bunny to his Brer Bear," said Penny, who had brought a videotape camera into the Oval Office. Ford improved under Penny's tutelage and his convention address was splendid. But on the campaign trail, with Bob Orben consigned to editing speeches and removed from his job of writing humor, Ford's speeches once again had the ability to empty arenas faster than the Chicago Cubs on a bad day. Ford acknowledged his own rhetoric deficiencies with engaging humor. He told of giving a speech in Omaha during the campaign, after which he was taken to a reception elsewhere in town. Said Ford: "At the reception a sweet little old lady came up to me, put her gloved hand in mine, and said, 'I heard you spoke here tonight.' And I said, 'Oh, it was nothing,' and she said, 'Yes, that's what I heard.' "

As Gerald Ford prepared to debate Jimmy Carter on TV, his oratorical shortcomings came into the gunsights of Garry Trudeau. Like Al Capp and Walt Kelly before him, Trudeau has managed to turn his daily strip into an entertaining battleground for frauds, fools, and ideologues of all colorations. (Most recently he has been featuring an invisible George

Bush). The public figures savaged by the insightful Trudeau seldom appreciate this form of recognition, though they often have the wit to importune him for the original artwork. In spotlighting Ford's rhetorical flaws, Trudeau pictured the president behind his desk in the Oval Office. He buzzes his secretary on the intercom:

FORD. Call Dick Cheney [White House chief of staff] and tell him I want to have my debate briefing at noon . . . And has my speech coach arrived yet?

SPEECH COACH (entering). Hi, Chief! Ready to run through some warm-up drills?

[Ford tells his secretary to forget it.]

SPEECH COACH. After me, Chief! The RAINS . . . in PLAINS . . . fall MAINLY on . . .

FORD (interrupting). Hold on. I gotta loosen my tie . . .

The televised debate with challenger Jimmy Carter was doubtless the turning point of the 1976 campaign and sealed the fate of Jerry Ford. His memorable declaration that Poland was free of Soviet domination was one of the Great Moments in Unintentional Humor and a gaffe from which Ford never recovered. Said Art Buchwald, in reflecting on his profession as a political humorist: "Are American Presidents providing us with enough humor? Well, just when I think they aren't, Richard Nixon says 'I am not a crook.' And Jimmy Carter says, 'I have lusted after women, but God has always forgiven me.' Or Jerry Ford says, 'I have just freed the Polish people retroactively.'"

It was the second Ford-Carter debate, and Ford's misstatement was triggered by a question from Max Frankel of the *New York Times*. Frankel asked the president about Soviet influence in Eastern Europe, and Ford blundered into an answer that would feed a hundred comedy writers from downtown Burbank to Rockefeller Center. Said Ford with the solemnity of a grandfather clock striking the hour fifteen minutes late: "There is no Soviet domination of Eastern Europe, and there never will be under a Ford administration." As aides winced, reporters gasped, and viewers rubbed their eyes, Ford plunged on, like Al Campanis explaining why blacks "lack the necessities." "I don't believe, Mr. Frankel," continued Ford, "that the Poles consider themselves dominated by the Soviet Union." Said one political observer: "If Ford believes the Poles are free, there's a bridge I want to show him in Brooklyn."

If the Ford campaign caught a cold with his Polish gaffe, his pardon of Richard Nixon gave him pneumonia. It haunted him throughout the debates and the entire campaign. In an editorial cartoon in the *Boston Globe*, Paul Szep showed a laughing Jimmy Carter and a grim-faced Jerry Ford before the television cameras. A relaxed Carter is sitting in a rocking chair, while a tense Ford is dressed in convict's stripes that recall Nixon's felonies and his possible fate, had it not been for Ford's pardon. In the cartoon, Carter is saying: "I'LL BE JACK KENNEDY. WHO DO YOU WANT TO BE??"

Paul Conrad, the Pulitzer Prize–winning cartoonist for the *Los Angeles Times*, tweaked the confusion and ambiguity of Ford's political statements. Conrad showed two Jerry Fords standing behind their respective lecterns at the debate. The first Ford is pointing indignantly at the second and shouting: "MY OPPONENT IS DELIBERATELY DISTORTING MY POSITION!"

If Garry Trudeau kidded Ford and his performance at the great debate, he had little taste for the satiric attacks that "Saturday Night Live" mounted on the president. Trudeau characterized the NBC show as "screw you" humor and "slash-and-burn" comedy. To Trudeau, "Saturday Night" reflected "a sort of callousness" and might lead, he said, to a society that is "intolerant of failure and uncompassionate in the face of suffering." Certainly, "Saturday Night" was intolerant of Ford's failure and indifferent to his suffering at their hands. There is some evidence that even Chevy Chase, the chief purveyor of this slash-and-burn humor at Ford's expense, felt twinges of guilt at his mockery of the president. When he met Ford ten years later, Chase said, "Mr. President, I feel rather embarrassed about the way I treated you when you were president, and I'd like you to pardon me . . .Oops!"

Trudeau did not stoop to slash-and-burn tactics after the Ford-Carter debate. He brought to it his gentle ironies, which were more effective for their understatement. In the Trudeau strip, the debate is in progress, and a viewer is watching it on his livingroom TV. The announcer is saying,

Direct from Philadelphia—THE PRESIDENTIAL DEBATE! Tonight's debate is being broadcast live from the Walnut Street Theater, which has been chilled to a previously agreed upon temperature of 68 degrees Fahrenheit! In the interests of fairness, both candidates have been made up and lit exactly the same way. They're also sitting behind matching lecterns, and are wearing identical blue suits . . . Now, then, which of you is Governor Carter?"

In 1976, the hearts of many conservative Republicans were betrothed not to Jerry Ford but to the charismatic governor of California, Ronald Wilson Reagan. The popular former actor was seeking the Republican nomination in 1976, and, despite his incumbency, Ford found Reagan a formidable rival. The usually amiable Ford turned bilious where Reagan was concerned. He said on one occasion, "There is a rumor to the effect that Ronald Reagan dyes his hair. That is ridiculous. He's just prematurely orange."

Ford had his hands full with Reagan in the Republican primaries. Reagan was armed with a covey of conservative gag writers in his old Hollywood home, so it was at this moment in history that Ford summoned Don Penny to his campaign train to feed him strategic anecdotes and one-liners. One of these tried to puncture the cinematic gloss of the California challenger. Said Ford: "Governor Reagan and I *do* have one thing in common. We both played football. I played in Michigan. He played for Warner Brothers."

Reagan's assets were, paradoxically, similar to those of Democrat Jimmy Carter's; he had never served in the nation's capital and so could attack the government and the bureaucracy with vigor, and he had no links, as did Ford, to the scorned Nixon team. As John Dean, the whistleblower of the Watergate scandal, said of Ford: "[He was] the unquestioning soldier and servant of the Nixon White House." Dean was maximizing his exposure by covering the GOP convention for *Rolling Stone.* As the *National Review* observed, mocking the self-promoting former Nixon aide, "John Dean's own story will be told in the forthcoming book, *Profiles in Chutzpah.*" But *NR* was not always supportive of Ford; generally, they came down on the side of the genial former governor of California. Ford had been far too tolerant, they felt, in permitting the growth of government during his watch, and that rankled the opinion makers at the *National Review.* Said the *NR* in their witty "This Week" review of recent events:

> President Ford last week opened a Centennial safe containing among other nostalgic mementoes, a list of all the federal employees in 1876—80,000 of them, presumably ancestors of the 2,800,000-strong swarms of them in 1976, and if that doesn't confirm your worst fears about bureaucratic breeding habits, get out the calculator.

If Carter and Reagan were outsiders, attacking from the woods, Ford was the insider, firing from the dubious safety of the wagon train. Like the middle-aged movie actor who became an overnight political success after two decades on the Hollywood sound stages, Ford's political career took a meteoric leap as well. His surge came in the mid-seventies with Nixon's flummery. From House minority leader, Ford became, in a rapid series of escalations, first an instant vice president, then an instant president, both without the messy requirements of a general election. Ford joked about his hasty ascendency, saying: "The Marine Corps Band is a little confused. They don't know whether to play 'Hail to the Chief' or 'You've Come a Long Way, Baby.'" As Ford sought the presidency in his own right—as had LBJ in 1964, after reaching the Oval Office adventitiously—he looked back on his early indifference to his office. As congressman from Grand Rapids (where rumor had it a sign reads, "Gerald Ford Slipped Here") he had often protested that he had no interest in the presidency. He had a safe seat, a handsome family, a loving wife, and that was enough. When pressed on the subject, Ford would say, "I must admit that late at night, when I'm driving home to Virginia and I pass the White House, I sometimes say to myself, 'If I lived here, I'd be home by now.'" But Ford seemed sincere in the modesty of his ambitions.

It was said by Washington wags that the reason Nixon chose Ford as his vice president was that Nixon couldn't believe the American people would impeach him since it meant handing power to Jerry Ford. Nixon's calculation was faulty, as was his decision not to burn the tapes. But shortly after Ford redecorated the Oval Office, bringing "an end to our long national nightmare," he issued a full, free pardon to his predecessor "for any and all crimes he may have committed in office." Many Americans felt they were not prepared to have their national nightmare ended so abruptly and turned on Ford as though he were the network programmer who had cancelled "Star Trek." Watergate had, indeed, taken on the appeal of a long-running TV series, and its abrupt cancellation by Jerry Ford injured our sense of theater as well as our sense of justice. The public uproar was deafening, and it says something of Ford's political antenna that the firestorm profoundly surprised him. If much of the public screamed in reproach, America's satirists reacted with a mixture of hostility and mirth. In the edition of *Who's In Charge Here?* for 1976, I showed a photo of President Ford at his Oval Office desk reading a letter. It said: "DEAR JERRY, THANKS FOR THE PARDON. BY THE WAY, I HAVE JUST RECEIVED THE ENCLOSED PARKING TICKET. . . ."

Garry Trudeau pictured Ford on the phone:

FORD. Get me Mr. Nixon on the line! . . . Dick? This is the President.

NIXON. Jerry! How thoughtful of you to call. How's everything at the Oval Office?

FORD. Not all that it could be, Dick . . . Quite frankly your pardon has turned out to be quite a headache!

NIXON. Oh, now you mustn't mind what people say! I never did!

FORD. Well, I probably wouldn't, Dick, if you had gone the contrition route. But you didn't—even after massive incriminating evidence!

NIXON. Well, that's the way it has to be . . .

FORD. How so, Dick?

NIXON. Jerry, you've got to try to understand—for me to apologize would simply be inappropriate! It would set a precedent that would *compromise* the office of the former President.

FORD. Huh?

NIXON. You see, it's not *me* I'm thinking of, Jer—it's *future* Presidents!

Jules Feiffer zeroed in on the pardon with telling effect. In the midst of the 1976 campaign, Feiffer pictured a grim, befuddled Ford, head in hands, behind his Oval Office desk, ruminating:

I was right on federal spending . . . I was right on inflation . . . I was far right on busing . . . Where did I go wrong? . . . THE PARDON! . . . [In the next panel, Nixon's bedside phone rings, awakening him. He seizes it, listens, slams down the receiver]

PAT NIXON. Who was that, Dick?

NIXON. An obscene call.

As the 1976 campaign unfolded, the public seemed particularly ambivalent about Jerry Ford. It liked his obvious decency and disliked his policies. It was the good cop–bad cop within the same uniform. Feiffer addressed this dichotomous dilemma by showing Ford staring at his image in a mirror and pausing to reflect.

FORD. Mirror, mirror on the wall, who is the best candidate of them all?

[The reply summed up two years of the Ford presidency with pith and perception.]

MIRROR IMAGE. Well, you couldn't care less about the unemployed but you're candid . . . You bomb Cambodians but you're humane . . . You're for ravaging the environment but you're decent . . . You have an 18th Century view of economics but you're honest . . . You have a liking for dictators but you're good natured . . . You think secrecy in government is nobody's business but you're open about it . . . You think civil rights is wrong but you're a terrific dancer . . . Accordingly *you're* not so hot but I, your image, am the best candidate of them all.

For a candidate who, in the words of his chief confidant and speech writer, Bob Hartmann, "was tone deaf to humor," Jerry Ford tried hard throughout his 1976 campaign to bear the gaggery of others with grace and respond to it with humor. He used the surrogate whimsy that Bob Orben created for him in the time-honored way. Politicians from Cromwell to Churchill have sought public office with self-deprecating wit, sensing that voters like the man who can mock his own flaws. So Ford kidded himself about everything from his paunch to his golf game. About the latter, he said,

Arnold Palmer has asked me not to wear his slacks except under an assumed name . . . They say you can tell a good golfer by the number of people in the gallery. You've heard of Arnie's Army. My group is called Ford's Few . . . My problem is that I have a wild swing. Back home on my home course, they don't yell "Fore," they yell "Ford" . . . The Secret Service Men you see around me today—when I play golf, they qualify for combat pay . . . In Washington I'm known as the President of the United States, and in golf I'm known as the Jinx of the Links.

As Gerald Ford's campaign train wound across the map of America, his humor of self-depreciation reached new heights, or rather, depths. To a convention of skiers, he said, "I can ski for hours on end." To an assembly of recreational sailors, he said, "Is there any correlation between the fact that sailing needs a great deal of wind, and your invitation to me? . . ." At Ohio State, he said, "I met Woody Hayes at the airport. We had our picture taken . . . and the caption read: 'Woody Hayes and Friend.'" Of his awkwardness on the dance floor, he said of the days he was dating Betty: "We had a problem. Betty had studied modern dance and I was a football player . . . She had a theory as to why I played center rather than quarterback. She said it was one of the few positions where you don't have to move your feet." To a Rose Garden gathering, he modestly averred: "I told the Republicans I had a safe seat in Grand Rapids—and look what happened." To another group, he protested, "You don't need to have a pool at the White House to get in deep water." And to a fund-raising dinner, he announced, "I didn't know the honeymoon was over until the [subway] started to build a new station in the Oval Office."

Beyond the lacerating damage done by Ford's pardon of Richard Nixon, his campaign suffered from his controversial secretary of agriculture, Earl Butz. Butz had resigned in embarrassment after telling a particularly repellent joke that was offensive not only to the blacks it ridiculed, but to a great many nonblacks as well. The joke, if it may be so dignified, dealt with the evacuative and sexual pleasures of the black man. The fact that Ford took an inordinate amount of time to ask for Butz's resignation was taken as a sign of his insensitivity. Butz had given the president fair warning that his humor was an accident waiting to happen. On an earlier occasion, Butz's untethered wit brought long faces to the White House staff. Commenting on the Pope's restrictive views on birth control, Butz affected a broad Italian accent and cracked, "You no playa the game, you know maka the rules."

Ford tried to laugh away Butz's corrosive wit during a speech to the Radio and TV Commentators Association, where he shared the dais with Bob Hope. Said Ford: "I have only one thing to say about a program that calls for me to follow Bob Hope—it's ridiculous. Bob Hope has stage presence, comedy timing, and the finest writers in the business. I'm standing here in a rented tuxedo—with three jokes from Earl Butz!"

Washington cartoonist Pat Oliphant found Ford too forgiving in his toleration of Butz's comic offenses and drew a pattern of behavior that went beyond forbearance to callousness. In the first panel, Ford is pinning a FORGIVEN button on Richard Nixon; in the second, on Earl Butz; and, in the third, on himself. Many voters felt that none of the three deserved absolution from the consequences of their mistakes.

Ford was not forgiven for his—the Nixon pardon, the Poland gaffe—and on Election Day 1976, the born-again Georgian they called "Jimmy Who?" took a four year lease on the impressive public housing on Pennsylvania Avenue.

Chapter 11
Campaign 1976
"Jimmy Who?"

That's Governor Carter over there. It's easy to see
where he sits. Now if we could only figure out where
he stands.
　　　　　　　　　—JERRY FORD

Could George S. Kaufman and Moss Hart have cre-
ated a more lovably eccentric clan in *You Can't Take It With You*
than Jimmy Carter's family? Probably not. And it was small
wonder that as Jimmy Carter emerged from the Democratic
pack in the primaries of 1976, America's wits emerged from
their hibernation. They had not really reveled in a First Family since the Kennedy years. Of course, there was some humor
to be found in the Johnson ménage—all those birds, the jokes
about the cattle grazing on the White House lawn, Lyndon
baring his surgical scar to his secretaries, Lyndon roaring
through the Texas hills in his Lincoln Continental. But there
was scant humor in the Nixon household, except for the irony
of daughter Trish marrying one of Nader's Raiders. And
daughter Julie wedding Ike's jug-eared grandson. Or, for
those with a taste for black humor, the stricken president beg-
ging Henry Kissinger to kneel with him in prayer for an unlikely salvation. The Ford family had been a source of occasional merriment. Betty Ford's outspoken advocacy of
premarital sex produced snickers from the Hollywood crowd,

and so did Jerry's battles with the law of gravity. Official White House photographer David Hume Kennerly produced some brazen wit. On the day Saigon fell, Kennerly scurried into the Oval Office to declare, "The good news is the war is over. The bad news is we lost." There was also the canned laughter that Bob Orben brought to Ford's speeches and the indiscreet appearance of press secretary Ron Nessen on "Saturday Night Live." But not since the Kennedy years had a First Family been so ripe for the scalpels of America's wits as when the Carters emerged from the obscurity of Plains, Georgia.

Carter's southern accent spawned its share of humor as he took to the campaign trail. Kennedy's Boston twang and Lyndon Johnson's Texas drawl had both lent themselves to the impressionists, giving Vaughan Meader and Rich Little food for fun. Indeed, so had Nixon's harsh vibrato. But when Kennedy spoke of "Cuber," the electorate at least knew the subject of discussion. The Carter drawl was so thick that two separate books were published in the form of mock dictionaries to help the citizenry know what the gentleman from Georgia was saying.

In *The Jimmy Carter Dictionary*, written by William Maloney and published by Playboy Press, the author presents various familiar words and the meaning that Carter attributed to each of them:

HAR: a growth covering the skull.

STOW: an establishment with goods for sale.

PIN: a writing instrument using ink.

MILE: letters or items sent via the post office.

JEW: the second person pronoun.

TAIL: to relate, narrate, recount.

TOAD: past tense of the verb "to tell."

RETCH: having a great deal of money.

176

Carter joked about his drawl in many of the speeches he delivered throughout the south. In Atlanta, Birmingham, and Biloxi, he smiled, "Isn't it time we had a president without an accent?"

After all, Jimmy Carter was the only man from the Deep South to be nominated for the presidency by one of the two principal parties in the past century. He displayed the modesty of the obscure outsider with a nice mixture of humor and humility. When he received the Democratic nomination, he opened his remarks with a wry line that he had often used in the bruising primary battles. "My name is Jimmy Carter," he said, "and I'm running for president."

Garry Trudeau addressed the Carter drawl with amusement while drawing a bead on Jerry Ford, as both candidates prepared for their first TV debate. In the "Doonesbury" version, an aide is briefing President Ford on the ground rules:

AIDE: Sir, the debate will last 90 minutes. Each of you will first make a statement, and then field questions. You will be permitted to rebut . . . On your opening statement, sir, just try to be yourself and play it as presidential as possible. When Carter's up, be sure to make hard eye contact.

FORD: And in my rebuttals?

AIDE: Take charge. Flaunt your superior command of facts. Use classified information if you have to.

FORD: Can I do that?

AIDE: Uh-huh. And don't be afraid to *make fun of his accent.*

Carter's principles and policies seemed unsettlingly flexible; they changed with his audience. The GOP castigated Carter's chameleon views by asking: "Why not a debate between Carter in New York and Carter in Atlanta?" Once Carter reached the White House, Jules Feiffer showed the new president rationalizing his vacillating views. Said Feiffer's Carter:

Originally I campaigned against a tax cut. But my experts are for it, so I'm for it . . . I campaigned in favor of wage and price guidelines. But my experts oppose it, so I oppose it . . . I campaigned against the B-1 bomber. But my experts want it, so I may want it . . . If these decisions turn out to be wrong don't blame me—I'm the President, not an expert . . . It's not as if I'm qualified.

On the heels of the corruption and cynicism of Watergate, Carter seemed to protest too much about his own probity. "I will never lie to you," he insisted at hundreds of campaign stops throughout the primaries and the campaign. Carter aide Jody Powell saw some of the humor of this insistence when he cracked, "We're going to lose the liar vote!" Carter's mother snapped, "Well, I lie all the time. I have to— to balance the family ticket."

The uncertainty of who and what Jimmy Carter represented was sardonically limned by cartoonist Herblock. He pictured a grinning Carter as the groom in a wedding ceremony. The apprehensive bride, her gown labeled "Democrats 1976," hovers outside the chapel, chattering to her bridesmaids as she eyes the groom waiting at the altar. "But I don't think I *know* him!" she gasps.

Like Reagan in 1980, Carter won his way into America's heart in 1976 by attacking Washington. After the tragedy of Vietnam and the travesty of Watergate, Washington was the ideal joke for a candidate's campaign humor; Carter realized that attacking Washington was the best way to get a job there. In traveling about the country, he perceived the dismay and disgust the voters felt toward the capital, the bureaucracy, the Congress, and the White House. Hence, like George Wallace and Ronald Reagan, Carter developed a repertoire of Washington-bashing jokes. His mocking humor carried the southerner through the primary battles. Carter launched his speeches by proposing to catalog his assets and liabilities. He would smile his toothpaste grin and say, "Well, my assets are all in my campaign literature. So perhaps I'd better start with my liabilities. [The crowd tittered] I'm not from Washington. [Laughter from the crowd] I'm not a member of Congress. [Hoots of derision] I've never been part of the national government. [Laughter turning to applause]." Jody Powell recognized the wisdom of ridiculing the capital. "In most of the primary campaigns," he said, "we benefited from being able to joke about Washington."

Carter's gaffe in *Playboy* magazine generated abundant campaign humor. Since sex and politics are said to be America's two greatest focuses of interest, a story that combined the two—as would Gary Hart's escapades in the 1980s—created a geyser of printer's ink. Though the public likes its leaders to be religious, it does not like them to be *too* religious. And Carter was anxious to persuade the mainstream voter that this born-again Christian was not a sanctimonious fundamentalist. Thus, in his interview with *Playboy's* Robert Scheer, Carter was open-minded to a fault. As the interview concluded and reporter Scheer packed up his tape recorder and headed for the door, the candidate seemed to feel he had not laid to rest the electorate's view of him as a pious, narrow-minded fellow. He stopped Scheer and continued the conversation in an unexpected direction that produced snickers across the country. Said the candidate: "I've looked on a lot of women with lust. I've committed adultery in my heart many times. This is something that God recognizes I will do—and I have done it—and God forgives me for it." Carter was swept along by his ruminations, and Scheer's tape recorder gobbled up the confessional. "That doesn't mean I condemn someone who not only looks on a woman with lust but who leaves his wife and shacks up with somebody out of wedlock." (Carter may have had in mind certain members of his own staff of whose sensual excesses he was said to disapprove.) "Christ says, 'Don't consider yourself better than someone else because one guy screws a whole bunch of women while the other guy is loyal to his wife.'" Carter's views on sex produced laughter and mockery —as did Ford's on the freedom of Poland.

If Carter regretted his *Playboy* remarks, America's comics did not. The bumper sticker manufacturers prospered as well. Recalling the famous Barry Goldwater slogan of a dozen years before, IN YOUR HEART YOU KNOW HE'S RIGHT, luminous stickers started appearing on bumpers that read, IN YOUR HEART HE KNOWS YOUR WIFE. A rhapsodic female supporter at a New Orleans rally waved a placard at the candidate that read: I LUST AFTER JIMMY CARTER FOR PRESIDENT. Ford exploited the episode with understated irony. When Jerry Ford's face appeared on the cover of *Newsweek*, his supporters ran a newspaper ad juxtaposing the *Newsweek* cover with the one of *Playboy* that had hyped the Carter interview. Said the ad's headline: ONE GOOD WAY TO DECIDE THE ELECTION— READ LAST WEEK'S *Newsweek*. READ THIS MONTH'S *Playboy*. SEX, SIN, TEMPTATION—CARTER'S CANDID VIEW headlined the *Chicago Sun-Times*. CARTER ON SIN AND LUST screamed the *Washington Star*. The individual members of the press were more ribald than the city editors who wrote the headlines. Some members of the media covering the Carter campaign sang a parody of "Heart of My Heart" that amused their listeners more than it did the candidate. It went:

Lust in my heart, how I love adultery.
Lust in my heart, it's my theology.
When I was young, at the Plains First Baptist Church,
I would preach and sermonize
But oh how I would fantasize.

Oh, lust in my heart, who cares if it's a sin?
Leching's a noble art.
It's okay if you shack up
'Cause I won't get my back up,
I've got mine
I've got lust in my heart.

The Carter lechery story brought out the best and brightest in editorial cartoonist Paul Conrad. Conrad has the uncanny ability to express outrage and humor with a minimum of symbols and a minimum of text. When *Playboy* hit the stand, spreading the Carter sexual philosophy across America's newsstands, Conrad captured the humor of the situation in a cartoon in which a grinning Jimmy Carter is mentally undressing the Statue of Liberty. In Carter's fantasy, the old girl is bereft of her robes and in voluptuous form. Carter's reference to lusting after other people's wives provided a wag at the *National Review* to remark: "We'd trust Jimmy Carter with our wives any time. What we don't like is the way he eyes our paychecks." Then as public attention passed on to other issues, the *NR* cracked, "Well, maybe he's weathered this one. But wait for the *Hustler* interview." Carter tried to laugh away the *Playboy* storm, with scant success. Introducing Andrew Young, who was actively supporting him in his election campaign and who had also been the subject of a *Playboy* interview, Carter said: "Andy Young has helped me a lot. He made it clear that I was not the only one that gave a *Playboy* interview. And he pointed out to the *Playboy* people that I still was filled with lust, but I didn't discriminate."

On balance, Carter's *Playboy* declaration probably helped him more than it hurt, in allowing the candidate to display a refreshing honesty to Americans who feared his excessive piety. In 1988 the American public would be confronted by minister candidates in both parties—Pat Robertson and Jesse Jackson—and both carried the albatross of religiosity and the confusion of church and state. Carter's born-again Christianity carried this same risk, and his *Playboy* interview, while generating abundant ribald humor, may have relieved the doubts of many.

Carter revealed another insight into his secular tastes when he met Elizabeth Taylor at a dinner party. "I couldn't take my eyes off her," he acknowledged. When she asked the candidate a question, he failed to respond, continuing to stare fixedly at the glamorous star. When she repeated the question, Carter finally replied. "I'm sorry, Miss Taylor," he said. "I'm sure you were talking to me, but I didn't hear a word you said." Neither history nor journalism reveal whether Elizabeth Taylor was undergoing the same fanciful inspection that Paul Conrad showed Carter giving to the Statue of Liberty.

Billy Carter was the target of humorous attention throughout the campaign. He was a corpulent, gimlet-eyed, fun-loving young fellow who ran a gas station in Plains, Georgia, while sharing responsibilities at his older brother's peanut farm and factory. Billy parlayed his fifteen minutes of fame—in the jargon of Andy Warhol—into a product called Billy Beer, and promoted it assiduously. He posed for news photographers in a costume made entirely of the rings from beer cans, cradling a six-pack in his arms. Billy relished the eccentricities that ran rampant in the Carter family. Said Billy to a fascinated pack of reporters as the 1976 campaign began: "I got a mamma who joined the Peace Corps and went to India when she was sixty-eight. I got one sister who's a Holy Roller preacher. I got another sister who wears a helmet and rides a motorcycle. And I got a brother who thinks he's going to be president. So that makes me the only sane person in the family."

If Jimmy Carter sometimes found his kid brother to be something of an embarrassment, he managed to conceal his irritation. And if the elder Carter's jokes at his brother's expense seemed at times to be somewhat close to the bone—questioning Billy's mendacity as well as his intellect—that was Jimmy's cautious form of reprisal. Speaking of plans to reorganize the government, Jimmy said, "I'd like to involve Billy in the government. I've been thinking of reorganizing and putting the CIA and the FBI together. But Billy said he wouldn't head up any agency he couldn't spell."

Some Washington observers dismissed Billy as a bumpkin; others called him "a loose cannon." This latter appraisal was prophetic. When Carter moved into the White House, Billy embarrassed his brother by accepting a $200,000 fee from the Libyan government to lobby his brother on their behalf. When influential Jews objected to Billy's behavior, he declared that "the Jews can kiss my ass." This was nearly as offensive as Jesse Jackson's reference to the "Hymies in Hymietown" (that is, the Jews of New York) that raised a ministorm during the 1984 campaign. But as Carter's popularity declined in the later years of his presidency, he ruefully observed, "A lot of people criticize Billy, but his standing in the public opinion polls is substantially above my own." And, as the election campaign unfolded, Billy Carter was a reliable source of humor for his candidate brother. On one occasion, when Billy's beer interests were reaching a head, the elder Carter observed, "Billy is doing his share for the nation's economy. He's put the beer industry back on its feet." When Billy was invited to Montreal to help publicize a new public swimming pool, the candidate remarked, "My brother has found another way to make a living other than growing peanuts. He can go to Canada and do a belly-buster in the swimming pool and make more money than he made all year on the farm. . . . When I mentioned that to Billy, he said, 'Well, you forget, Jimmy, that I don't know how to swim.'"

Students of sibling rivalry find little odd in Billy Carter's resentment of his older brother's achievements. So Billy's response was unsurprising when a reporter asked him on election eve how he would be changed if his older brother became president. Billy weighed the proposition and said, "If Jimmy becomes President tonight, I'm gonna make everybody call me *Mister* Carter for the first twenty-four hours." When Ford made his concession announcement late on election night, Jimmy Carter approached the podium, eyed his brother and declared, "*Mister* Carter, I want to thank you for waiting up all night to greet me." The day before Jimmy Carter took the inaugural oath the following January, Billy Carter kidded his brother's religious ties, saying, "I hear it's gonna be forty degrees here in Washington tomorrow for the inauguration. Jimmy must've been talkin' to the Lord again."

The Jimmy Carter grin produced a great deal of campaign mirth in 1976. Recalling the toothy grin of a famous First Lady of an earlier era, one irreverent wit cracked that Jimmy Carter looked like "the illegitimate son of Eleanor Roosevelt." Carter himself mocked his expansive smile with its rows and rows of gleaming teeth when he said, "My tax audit is coming out okay. The only thing they questioned so far is a six hundred dollar bill for toothpaste." Paul Conrad took a page out of *Alice in Wonderland* in his editorial cartoon in the *Los Angeles Times*. Twitting Carter's frequent avoidance of the issues, he pictured the huge, toothy, disembodied smile of Jimmy Carter poised overhead in the foliage of a tree, and a perplexed Alice studying it from below. "WELL! I'VE OFTEN SEEN A CAT WITHOUT A GRIN," THOUGHT ALICE. "BUT A GRIN WITHOUT A CAT! IT'S THE MOST CURIOUS THING I EVER SAW!"

Carter's splay-toothed grin became famous during the primary and election campaigns of 1976. Perhaps Teddy Roosevelt's tombstone teeth, as Gore Vidal called them, could approach the Carter smile, but no other presidential candidate of this century could compare. Of course, the hard-driven aides who took Carter's orders and who were often subjected to his icy stares of disapproval could tell that there was a distinction to be drawn "between Jimmy's good smiles and his bad smiles."

When the campaign struggle of 1976 concluded with Jimmy Carter the victor, the White House took on a new look. Carter put the imperial pretensions of Richard Nixon and the country club resonance of the Republican party far behind him, taking care to be photographed carrying his own suit bag and addressing the nation in a cardigan sweater. Mike Peters in the *Dayton Daily News* pictured the government in transition most effectively by showing the famous facade of the White House, and in place of the familiar portico were the huge, gleaming teeth of Jimmy Carter.

Chapter 12
Campaign 1972
So I Made a Mistake

Where does Richard Nixon stand on the great issues
of our time? Aside.
—DAVID FROST

Richard Nixon has always provided an irresistible
target for the malicious humor of American satirists, playwrights, novelists, essayists, and monologists. Other presidents
have inspired the benign laughter of the one-liners of Bob
Hope and Johnny Carson. But only Nixon has become the
nemesis of America's counterculture, providing an opportunity for millions of Nixon-haters to ridicule his remarkable career. Given the controversial aspects of his long political struggle—his "Six Crises" plus one—Nixon has generated a
spectacular outpouring of toxic humor.

If Nixon had the crackling wit of a Jack Kennedy or the
genuine humility of a Ronald Reagan, he could have responded to these libelous attacks by slipping many of their
punches. But he lacked the gift of humor that so many of his
assailants possessed. He was cursed, in the words of Theodore
Sorensen, by "a bitter mind-set" that ill-equipped him to fight
fire with fire or humor with humor. Hence, as the satire of his
detractors reached its zenith in the 1972 campaign, Nixon
could do little more than crouch in the imperial cocoon of the
West Wing, displaying a solemn mien, his shoulders hunched
and his jowls waggling in self-pity.

The siege mentality that developed in the Nixon White House was irrigated to a large extent by the steady stream of mocking humor that issued forth from the media and the entertainment world. Nixon was its perennial target, and if the eye sees itself but by reflection, as Shakespeare tells us, Nixon must have grown bitter at the image his tormentors threw back at him. He was quick to protest that "you can't let your enemies defeat you [with slander and ridicule]." But can any man withstand the steady onslaught of caustic wit?

Richard Nixon's lack of humor made him a perfect butt for the wounding humor of others. His paucity of wit was exemplified by Lou Cannon, venerable White House correspondent for the *Washington Post*. Cannon told a story of a congressman who had been a cohort of Nixon when the latter had been in the House of Representatives. When Nixon reached the White House, a number of legislators wanted to throw a party to laud the former friend who had risen so high. They needed some funny stories to brighten their lauditory speeches. So the congressmen phoned Nixon's private secretary, Rose Mary Woods, telling her, "Rose Mary, we'd like some funny stories about Mr. Nixon." There was a lengthy pause on the line. Finally Rose Mary Woods spoke. "There *are* no funny stories about Mr. Nixon," she said.

The humor of John F. Kennedy was laconic and elegant. The humor of Lyndon B. Johnson was earthy and anecdotal. But the humor of Richard Nixon was largely unintentional. And this obliviousness to humor inspired Nixon's critics to prodigies of ridicule. Comics had a field day with Nixon's desire to act the "good Joe." The most famous such display was when Nixon greeted David Frost, the journalist/satirist who was interviewing him for a series of syndicated interviews in his post–Watergate days. Nixon greeted Frost with a one-of-the-boys question: "Well, David, did you do any fornicating this weekend?" A less familiar display of Nixon's forced humor occurred during the 1972 campaign when a motorcade was carrying Nixon through the streets of Denver. The motorcycle of the lead policeman overturned, breaking the officer's arm and leg. As he lay on the pavement writhing in pain, awaiting the arrival of the ambulance, Nixon leaned over the stricken officer and said: "How do you like your job?"

Nixon's lack of humor invited scathing wit from his political opponents, to which he was unable to respond in kind. Jack Kennedy's alter ego Ted Sorensen, in an address before the National Press Club, fabricated a display of Nixonian wit that, though clearly apocryphal, was accepted as fact by a credulous reporter from *Time* magazine. It was reported in that magazine as evidence that Mr. Nixon "had not lost his sense of humor." Said Sorensen:

> I ran into Richard Nixon last week and he said to me, "I watched the Kennedy Inaugural and I have to admit that there were some words he said that I wish *I* had said." And I said to him, "Well, thank you, sir. I guess you mean the part about 'Ask not what your country can do for you.' And Nixon said, 'No, I mean the part about I do solemnly swear.'"

Just as Barry Goldwater was a target for malicious humor in 1964, Richard Nixon proved an inviting target for caustic wit in 1972. The difference lay in the outcome of the two campaigns. In 1964 the target was swept away in a humbling defeat, but in 1972 the target was swept back into office on a seeming landslide of ridicule. In effect, Nixon laughed all the way to the White House. If their boss was the subject of scathing wit—from Buchwald, Russell, Baker, Oliphant, Feiffer, and the rest—Nixon's aides could not have cared less, as the candidate continued his triumphal march to reelection. With the polls showing Nixon running far ahead of the hapless George McGovern, a Nixon aide laughed, "We're running scared . . . for about an inch." It was doubtless the shortest run of panic in electoral history. Joked Bob Dole, then the chairman of the GOP campaign committee, and already the repository of the most brutal wit in public life: "We aren't saying we'll win all fifty states, but we aren't conceding anything." Even Nixon's buttoned-down, uptight press secretary, former Disneyland guide Ron Ziegler, could laugh at the prospects for a Nixon runaway. Mixing his humor with his antimedia animus, Ziegler reflected on how the Nixon-hating press would handle the McGovern debacle that unmistakably lay ahead. "I can picture the headline in the *Washington Post*," cracked Ziegler. "McGOVERN SWEEPS D.C., with the sub-head NIXON CARRIES NATION."

(Ziegler was the source of unintentional humor a year later when he reviewed the accomplishments of Nixon's presidency in the year 1973 for a White House reporter. It was an impressive list of achievements. Ziegler concluded the list by saying, "So it was a really terrific year except for the downside." "What downside?" asked the reporter. "Watergate," said Ziegler.)

Certainly the 1972 campaign between Richard Nixon and George McGovern was one of the most bizarre contests of the century. Johnson v. Goldwater was incongruous, and Eisenhower v. Stevenson was anomalous, but the contest between Nixon and McGovern exceeded all others in its offering of contrasting candidates. The point was not lost on America's wits. Never had two men more diametrically different sought the White House. Nixon was suspicious and paranoid, McGovern was forthright and accessible. Nixon was hostile to the young, while McGovern rode to prominence on the shoulders of youth. Nixon sought honor in Southeast Asia, while McGovern wanted us out as quickly as possible.

Much of the humor at Nixon's expense flowered from his perceived character. He was a loner, humorless and manipulative. Many remembered with distaste the pink circulars he used to discredit his opponent in his race for the Senate. They recalled the secret slush fund that nearly got him jettisoned from the Eisenhower ticket and the maudlin speech about his wife's cloth coat and his little dog Checkers that retrieved his career. They remembered his tears on that occasion and the vitriolic comment after his loss of the California governorship, "You won't have Nixon to kick around anymore." And so, fifteen years before the so-called character issue decimated the ranks of presidential candidates in 1987—with Biden's plagiarism and Hart's adultery—the character issue plagued Richard Nixon and generated a campaign of particularly nasty humor.

Said one Washington correspondent of Nixon's maudlin sentimentality: "When Nixon read an article on his boyhood years, he cried for two hours. They spelt his name wrong." Reflecting on his sore loser speech after the gubernatorial loss, one reporter cracked, "Nixon sent a very sportsmanlike message to Kennedy conceding the '60 election. He wrote,

'WARMLY CONGRATULATE YOU ON YOUR WELL-EARNED VIC-
TORY AND CHARGE FRAUD IN ILLINOIS, MARYLAND, AND
TEXAS.'" A wire service reporter said he had heard how
Nixon deals with pressure. "He has a little trick when the tension is too great. He closes his eyes and people can't see him."
To protestations that power had mellowed the old campaigner
and there was a "new Nixon," the correspondent for a British
daily remarked, "Is there a new Nixon? Absolutely. The old
Nixon was sly and opportunistic. The new Nixon is just the
opposite. Opportunistic and sly." The view of Nixon as a loner
spawned other jokes. Said one San Francisco monologist: "I
hear a lot of talk that Nixon doesn't have any friends. That's
absurd. He has a lot of friends. In fact, he recently went on a
lengthy tour visiting all his friends. And since the weather was
good, he walked." Mocking the imperial adornments that
Nixon had brought to the White House during his first term,
a correspondent, looking ahead to 1976, said, "One wonders
whether Nixon will make Agnew his successor. Probably not.
White House insiders say that when Nixon leaves office, he's
planning to take the United States with him." David Frost
summed up Nixon's personality problems with the sardonic
observation: "President Kennedy proved that a man could not
be prevented from being President simply because he was a
Catholic. Nixon went him one better. He proved that a man
could not be prevented from becoming president simply because he was Richard Nixon."

Nixon ran for reelection by citing the accomplishments
of his first term, and none had more luster than his opening to
Red China. Inevitably, some American president would have
recognized the reality of China and established relations with
that most populous state, but to his credit, that president was
Richard Nixon. It was a laudable achievement, especially for a
man who had spent a lifetime vilifying the communist Chinese
and slandering the opposition party for "losing China." But
even this extraordinary icebreaking brought laughter in certain circles. Roy Kammerman created a book of captioned
photos that kidded Nixon's China trip unmercifully. Said another humorist: "What is Nixon's position on Red China? He
is opposed to their admission to the Diners Club. And what is
his position on the Great Wall? No handball playing."

Given his lifetime of exertions as a professional Communist-hater, it was hard for the public to accept Nixon's conversion to detente—just as Reagan's infatuation with Mikhail Gorbachev was a crash cut from his "evil empire" orations. The voters of 1972 asked with strained credulity: Does Richard Nixon really want improved relations with the Russians? Sometimes the answer was sardonic. Said a Manhattan nightclub comedian: "I believe Nixon does want better relations with the Russians. I hear he's planning a trip to the Soviet Union to cement relations. The State Department has worked out an extremely fair exchange with the Russians. The Soviets say that if we send Nixon there, they'll send him back."

There was a whiff of arrogance about Richard Nixon that triggered campaign attack. A correspondent wrote to *Ramparts* magazine: "I hear that Mr. Nixon is deeply sympathetic to Israel's national aspirations. I understand he is planning to provide Israel with an important new irrigation project. He'll shortly go to Tel Aviv to smite a rock with a rod."

Another allusion to the Nixon pomposity zeroed in on his work habits. It was said that the presidency had not made him the least bit pretentious. His workday was just what it had always been. "For example," said one White House wag, "this past week he worked at his desk for six days, and on the seventh day he rested."

Others thought Nixon had little to be arrogant about. Said novelist Peter De Vries: "I used to think that Nixon was deep. But now I see that deep down he's shallow." There was a cold quality about Nixon. His apparent remoteness to the needy prompted the witticism: "'What are the things closest to Nixon's heart?' 'His lungs.'" Nixon's political foes assumed that he was indifferent to the plight of the poor, in America and elsewhere around the globe—despite the fact that he had certainly not grown up in affluence. Said TV commentator Lindsay Gardner: "Nixon is deeply concerned about the area of the world where the streets are crowded with teeming masses and where men struggle to escape the bonds of misery and ignorance. San Clemente."

Hubert Humphrey said that a government must be judged by how it treats those in the dawn of life, its children; those in the twilight of life, its elderly; and those in the shadows of life, its poor and disabled. Nixon's fancied callousness, said some, extended to those in the twilight of life. The preoccupation of Kennedy, Johnson, and Humphrey with the aged was well documented. George McGovern had spoken passionately about his plans for the elderly. But Nixon had been mute. One D.C. satirist cracked: "Have you heard about Nixon's amendment to the Medicare Act? If you're over sixty-five and you need an operation but you can't afford it, the doctors retouch your X-rays."

If Richard Nixon was perceived to be indifferent to the plight of the poor, the homeless, and the elderly, his attitude toward the jobless was also in question in the campaign of 1972. Said one Democratic critic: "Oh yes, Nixon cares about the unemployed. He's put hundreds of computers to work to analyze the data and find a solution to the problem of five million unemployed. In a few weeks, these computers can do the work of five million men working for years."

Nixon had taken office in 1969 with a pledge that he had a "secret plan" to end the war in Vietnam, but four years later, as American campuses and cities continued to explode with fury, the war ground on. McGovern called for the instant withdrawal of U.S. forces from Southeast Asia, while Nixon and his secretary of state, Dr. Henry Kissinger, continued to seek an elusive "peace with honor." This situation spawned a black humor among the country's satirists. The following exchange brought gallows laughter at a cabaret in Los Angeles:

"Nixon failed to fulfill his election pledge to stop the war, end the killing, suspend the draft, and bring peace to America. What excuse does he have for this?"
"He didn't say positively."

A west coast improvisational group picked repeatedly at the scab of American dismay at the Vienam War. In one sardonic sketch, two citizens discuss their views:

"Do you think Nixon really wants to get out of Vietnam?"
"Absolutely. He's seen this war first hand. He's been a witness to the dirtiest kind of guerilla warfare imaginable—

sniping, stabbing, and sadistic barbarism. So now he's ready for the 1972 election campaign."

The chief instrument of Nixon's peace-seeking efforts was Henry Kissinger, a man with all the sparkling wit that Nixon and the Haldeman-Ehrlichman team lacked. On one of his trips to Southeast Asia that sought a negotiated peace, Kissinger's security escort picked up rumors of a plot to kidnap the secretary of state and hold him for ransom. Kissinger's favorite Secret Service man was Walter Busby. Speaking of the feared kidnapping attempt to the head of the Secret Service, Kissinger said in his ripe German accent: "I love Valter. I asked Valter vat he vould do in the event they tried to kidnap me. And Valter said, 'Don't vorry, Mr. Secretary, ve von't let them take you alive.'"

Nixon's detractors often found food for mockery in his frequent invocations of his wife, Pat. There was something unctuous and manipulative in his cloying proclamations on her virtue and loyalty and the perennial pluralizing of the president ("Pat and I are happy to be here in Cleveland," for example). Alluding to the president's apparent waffling on a certain issue, one comic said, "They say Nixon is vacillating. It's not true. Nixon doesn't vacillate. He has been standing pat . . . There's the children to consider." Referring to Nixon's propensity for trumpeting the achievements of his administration, one McGovern aide cracked, "Pat Nixon doesn't want any more children. With Nixon around, she can always hear the patter of little feats." And comedy writer George Foster said, "Nixon has hedged against defeat in 1972. He just put the White House in Pat's name." Reflecting on Mrs. Nixon's contribution to her husband's success, one political observer wrote, "Pat Nixon proves the truth of the old saying that behind every successful man is a very surprised woman."

Nixon made his wife the object of some of his awkward attempts at spontaneous humor. When a crowd of supporters at the GOP convention began to chant, "We want Pat!" Nixon grinned and said, "You can't have her. I've got to keep her." Keep her he did, and often he used her in a uxorious fashion that set one's teeth on edge. In greeting the convention in Miami that was more like a coronation, he said, "Mr. President and Pat—because she is the First Lady of the land, but I think in the hearts of all of us she is 'Pat,' and we are just going to take advantage of it and keep it that way." In a speech at San Diego airport, Nixon thanked Art Linkletter, who was campaigning with him, and made Pat Nixon the subject of some atypical ribald humor. Said Nixon: "When Art Linkletter talks about having breakfast . . . with Pat, I just want to keep the record straight. He has slept in the White House. He slept in the Queen's Room. When Pat's room is being painted, she sleeps in there, so you could say that Art Linkletter has slept in Pat's bed."

The campaign of 1972 also saw a healthy outpouring of humor at the expense of Nixon's running mate, Vice President Spiro Agnew. If there was talk of a "new Nixon" and an "old Nixon," almost as dramatic was the political restyling of Spiro Agnew for the 1972 campaign. The new, refurbished Agnew had undergone a dramatic transformation. Gone were the alliterations and personal epithets that had brought rage from the media and the liberals at whom they were directed all through the first Nixon-Agnew term. Jeff MacNelly, the witty editorial cartoonist of the *Richmond News-Leader*, mocked the Agnew metamorphosis by picturing the Veep's tombstone. On it were some of the scathing words with which he had excoriated his enemies: EFFETE SNOBS, NATTERING NABOBS OF NEGATIVISM, VICARS OF VACILLATION, RADICLIBS, TROGLODYTE LEFTISTS, HOPELESS, HYSTERICAL HYPOCHONDRIACS OF HISTORY. That was the preelection year wit of Spiro Agnew, entombed for the duration of the campaign.

Agnew still drew his share of gibes from the press he had so often wounded. One reporter reflected on the way Nixon had chosen Agnew as his running mate. "I don't know exactly how Nixon chose Agnew, but it certainly cured him of making decisions during a total eclipse." A reporter for the *Miami Herald* reflected wryly that Agnew had a dedicated following in the southern and western states. "If something happens to Agnew, Georgia and Arizona light up." One TV network adviser, musing on Agnew's use of invective, remarked that the candidate's televised speeches should be followed by a half hour of tetanus shots. A Manhattan cabaret comedian took a swipe at Agnew by declaring, fictitiously of course, that First Lady Pat Nixon had led a committee to beautify America. "She went about Washington planting tulips and hollyhocks. And Agnew provided the fertilizer." Some of the Veep's detractors focused on his modest intellectual gifts. Said one member of the press corps, paying sarcastic tribute to the onetime Maryland governor: "Agnew has a quick mind. He can seize the nub of a complex problem immediately. He recently attended a Cabinet meeting where a thorny problem of defense planning was being discussed. It took Agnew only thirty seconds to see a solution, and three hours to find his way back to his office."

If Agnew abandoned his inflammatory rhetoric during the 1972 campaign, he did not abandon his corrosive wit altogether. The more restrained Agnew twitted Sargent Shriver, the Democratic candidate in the Veepstakes, on his personal wealth. Shriver was Jack Kennedy's brother-in-law, and between his own wealth and that of his wife, Eunice Kennedy Shriver, his affluence was considerable. Said Agnew: "My opponent says he knows what it means to be poor. He says 'When I was a kid, my father had eight hungry mouths to feed. My mother and me and six polo ponies.'" Agnew returned to the theme of Shriver's wealth with a fictional story of Agnew and Shriver growing up together in Maryland. "I have vivid memories," said Agnew, "of little Sarge when we'd play hide-and-seek. I'd hide and he'd put a private detective on retainer to go out and find me." There has been a long-standing argument between those who favor finding our presidents among the rich and those who would look for them among the poor. Say the cynics: "Why let the rich run the country? It's enough that they *own* the country." The activism of wealthy presidents like Franklin Roosevelt and John F. Kennedy argues for the virtue of wealth. Richard Nixon's and Spiro Agnew's histories do not support the values of a humble boyhood; one resigned in disgrace, and the other stood accused of accepting bribes in the vice presidential office.

On occasion, the combative Agnew wit would surface under the provocation of the campaign trail. In Tampa hecklers interrupted his standard stump speech. "I'll wait a minute," said Agnew acidly, "to see whether some sort of catatonic reaction will set in—or a freezing of the vocal cords."

Editorial cartoonists had a field day with the pompous, posturing Agnew. Chief among his tormentors was Pat Oliphant, one of America's premier political artists, who came to America from Australia in 1964 to replace Paul Conrad at the *Denver Post*, when Conrad moved on to the *Los Angeles Times*. Art Buchwald called Oliphant "a threat to the American political system. His irreverent cartoons . . . are dangerous because they make people think while they make them laugh." Buchwald's praise was a splendid definition of all the best of America's political writers and cartoonists, preeminently Buchwald himself.

When Richard Nixon announced that Agnew was his choice for vice president, Oliphant pictured Agnew as a complacent lap dog being stroked by Richard Nixon. In his portrayal, the dog's neck is circled by a spiked collar, and on its face reflects obedience and adoration for its master. (The lap dog metaphor seemed felicitous for a vice president. Fifteen years later, in a scathing column excoriating Vice President George Bush's cheerleader image, George Will compared him to a lap dog. Bush confirmed the metaphor by praising George Will as a man whose opinion he respected!) Seizing on the campaign conversion of Agnew from vitriol to gentility, Pat Oliphant showed him in flowing robes, a dove in his hand, a halo atop his head. A disturbed Nixon is watching "the New Agnew" and saying, "Are you trying to make me look shabby?" And Oliphant's ubiquitous duck in a corner of the strip, is saying, "Saint Spiro??"

One of the chief targets of mockery that Nixon endured in 1972 had little to do with him but with the antics of his attorney general's wife, the inimitable Martha Mitchell. Martha was a garrulous, ebullient lady who brought the Nixon administration some of its most spontaneous moments. ("Is Richard Nixon outspoken?" asked one beltway wit. "Only by Martha Mitchell.") Martha's eccentric pronouncements, and her habit of secretly phoning Helen Thomas of the Associated Press from the seclusion of her bathroom, captured the attention and the funny bone of the public. Her declarations were quoted throughout the 1972 campaign for their humor, intentional and otherwise. Here are some of Martha Mitchell's spontaneities:

I'm little Martha Mitchell. . . . No rhyme or reason why I have to withhold my thoughts.

Man has been given his freedom to a greater extent than ever, and that's quite wrong.

Dignity and formality have completely gone from New York.

Margaret Mead caused a lot of the trouble. She advocates taking drugs and early marriage. She and those other spooks just want to get their names in the paper.

My family worked for everything we had. We even have a deed from the King of England for property in South Carolina. Now these jerks come along and try to give it to the Communists.

I have a wonderful concept of President Nixon. He'll kill me when I say it, but it's almost a fatherly love, that's how I think of him.

I love to do devilish things.

I don't think the average American realizes how desperate it is when a group of demonstrators, not peaceful demonstrators, but the very liberal Communists, move into Washington.

I can't get over saying "colored." I said it all my life. All the Negroes seem to resent it and I don't know why.

I'm calling from the bathroom upstairs so John won't hear me. . . .

Had the Democratic party or the American people realized the significance and implications of the Watergate break-in when it occurred in the midst of the 1972 presidential campaign, Nixon might not have made mincemeat of challenger George McGovern. With the virtue of 20-20 hindsight it seems manifest that when five men with electronic equipment, paid by the Republicans, were arrested at gunpoint in the dead of night in the Democratic national headquarters, it was not a matter to be dismissed with a joke and a shrug. Nonetheless, that is very nearly all that the party was able to make of it.

President Nixon dismissed it as "a bizarre incident," press secretary Ron Ziegler called it "a third-rate burglary," and America's comics laughed it away. Perhaps the Vietnam War had created a moral exhaustion with its slaughter of naked peasants, so that a break-in and a bugging met with an ethical vacuum, an attitude of "Well, that's politics." It was only after the Democratic debacle of November 7, in which Nixon received 60.7 percent of the popular votes and swept forty-nine states, that the disintegration of the Nixon landslide began. First, Spiro Agnew resigned in disgrace, under attack for income tax evasion; then came Sam Ervin, Howard Baker, Woodward & Bernstein, and reports of bribery, perjury, forgery, and dirty tricks.

In the midst of Nixon's Watergate shame, Al Franken and Tom Davis of "Saturday Night Live" pilloried Nixon unmercifully. They found his sins sensational fodder for their burn-and-slash wit. They had hammered away at Nixon all through the 1972 campaign, and now, with Nixon on the ropes, they delivered a satiric knockout punch. It was a sketch based on the Woodward & Bernstein bestseller, *The Final Days.* "Saturday Night's" producer, Lorne Michaels, had written an introduction to the Franken-Davis sketch that he himself would deliver. The preface ultimately remained undelivered, but it reflects the show's distaste for Nixon so well that it deserves to be reproduced, at least in part. Some will find it malicious, others amusing, but for better or worse, it reflected the counterculture's animus for Richard Nixon. Said the producer in his undelivered introduction:

Hi. I'm Lorne Michaels. As producer of this show, I make weighty decisions every day. Today I had to make the toughest decision of my career: whether or not to ridicule Richard Nixon one more time. . . . It would be too easy to make light of a man who hasn't slept with his wife for fourteen years . . . and [to suggest] that Nixon and Bebe Rebozo are having a homosexual affair has no place on network television.

The Franken-Davis sketch was presented in the form of a Pat Nixon diary recalling the highlights of her husband's presidential career. Dan Ackroyd played Nixon, and John Belushi did a gutteral impression of Henry Kissinger. When the skit opened, Pat Nixon, played by guest host Madeline Kahn, has been nipping at the cooking sherry and is recalling the final days of her husband's presidency. In these Final Days of "Saturday's Night's" invention, Nixon is talking bitterly to a portrait of Lincoln, complaining, "Well, Abe, you were lucky. They *shot* you." Chevy Chase played the chuckleheaded David Eisenhower, and Gilda Radnor played his wife, Julie. Nixon remarks acidly to an aide that his son-in-law "looks like Howdy Doody." Nixon is obsessed with the other men who had lived in the White House. Later in the sketch he turns to a painting of Jack Kennedy and shouts, "You! Kennedy. You looked so good all the time. They're gonna find out about you too. The president having sex with women within these very walls!" says Nixon with distaste. "That's never happened when Dick Nixon was in the White House. Never! Never! Never!" It will be noted that the "Saturday Night" comic perception of Richard Nixon tended to a preoccupation with the genitals, but, in the year 1972, and the year of Nixon's disgrace that followed, the show and its youthful creators were at the center of a ribald revolution in a cynical and divided country.

Out of the unsavory revelations of Watergate, Bantam published a book which for a brief period threatened to outsell the Bible. It was called *The Watergate Follies* and served to chronicle the scandal in a more frivolous manner than did the Woodward and Bernstein books. *The Watergate Follies* consisted of a group of news photos of the felonious participants in the Watergate fiasco, with dialogic balloons putting words in the mouths of the miscreants. Here are some of them:

Nixon to the public in a televised address: "Political espionage, burglaries, wiretapping, campaigning disruption, illegal use of funds—okay, so we made a mistake."

H. R. Haldeman sits beside Nixon on Air Force One, pointing to a map in the President's lap. Says Haldeman: "This would be a good place to jump."

Nixon addresses a group of aides on the break-in: "Now, let's get our stories straight. Henry, you were in Paris—"

Nixon to the White House press corps: "Are you going to believe me or the facts?"

A stunned Frank Sinatra to Richard Nixon: "You want me to sing at the Impeachment?"

President Nixon to his economic advisers as they sit in a semicircle about his Oval Office desk: "That's very interesting, Arthur, would you mind repeating it into this inkwell?"

Queen Elizabeth to the Shah of Iran in her opulent carriage: "Yes, Mr. Nixon once visited me. He took a spoon."

Nixon to his military chiefs: "The public is clamoring for the truth about Watergate. There's only one thing to do. Start a war."

Pat Nixon to Martha Mitchell: "My husband gives his all for the people and what does he get?" Martha: "Ten to twenty."

An apparently tranquil Nixon at a state dinner, to the woman on his left: "Try the Impeach Melba."

Nixon writing solemnly in his diary: "My seventh crisis began slowly . . ."

Nixon taking the presidential oath of office: "And defend most of the Constitution . . . ."

Nixon to Israeli prime minister, Golda Meir: "I've resigned in disgrace, my friends ignore me, my aides are in prison. What should I do?" Golda Meir: "Have a piece of fruit."

There was a delicious subtlety to the humor of cartoonist Garry Trudeau. When it was learned that Nixon had ordered the secret, unlawful bombing of Cambodia, Trudeau pictured a conversation between the president and White House chief of staff Al Haig:

NIXON. What is it, Haig?

HAIG. Sir, it's about the House hearings on the recent Cambodian bombings. We need to know more about the raids, sir. They say nobody but you knows about them.

NIXON. It's not true. I told everybody who had a need or a right to know.

HAIG. Yes, sir, but who? You've got to be more specific.

NIXON. Well, let me see . . . The pilots, of course.

In another fictional exchange between Nixon and Haig, the president is about to make a TV address to the nation.

NIXON. Call props and tell them to bring over some more Lincoln visuals—a bust, etchings, anything.

HAIG. Mr. President, with all due respect, sir, I think you've just about gone the limit on comparisons of yourself with Lincoln.

NIXON. You think so? Hmm. Maybe you're right, Al.

HAIG. It *would* be the fifth time, sir . . .

NIXON. It's just that I can't *get over* all the parallels.

HAIG. It *is* eerie, sir.

Like Trudeau, Jules Feiffer exposed for us the political vagaries and vulgarities of our time, and he seemed at his best during the Nixon years. "He was a turd, a wonderful turd for a cartoonist," said Feiffer. "From his Checkers speech to his 'You won't have Nixon to kick around anymore' speech to his farewell to the White House staff speech, he was a genius of the second-rate. The Mozart of mediocrity." Feiffer found Nixon a wonderful subject for his satiric pen. "His unintegrated parts invited endless comment," wrote Feiffer. "Uneasy head atop wind-up toy body. Nothing on Nixon fit right."

Feiffer observed that during the 1972 campaign Nixon never quite relaxed: "There were no shirtsleeve photos, even his strolls on the beach were in full dress. I am sure that, naked, he wore knee socks; in the shower, boxer shorts . . . He was our favorite Dick joke, but the joke was on us."

Certainly, the joke was on Nixon when Jules Feiffer put his talented pen to paper to illuminate Nixon's character flaws. As the election year of 1972 began, Feiffer pictured the president on Christmas Eve in a nightgown, holding a candle aloft, speaking to Santa.

NIXON. What did you buy me for '72?

SANTA. More inflation . . . Higher unemployment . . . A stagnant economy . . . The same old war . . . And a disastrous election campaign.

[Nixon bursts into tears.]

NIXON. And you call yourself Santa Claus?

SANTA. And you call yourself President?

Chapter 13
Campaign 1972
The 1000 Percent Populist

It's as if McGovern had a death wish. He makes so
many mistakes that it's hard for us to get a mistake in
edgewise.
                                   —NIXON AIDE

When the debacle of the 1972 presidential campaign
was behind him, Senator George S. McGovern of South Da-
kota whispered in the ear of a Senate colleague: "Three things
beat me. Dirty tricks, tapped phones, and I lost forty-nine
states." At any rate, those were the words one satirist attributed to the populist campaigner.

McGovern's critical problem was reviving his eroded
reputation for honesty after the opening events of his hapless
campaign. He had chosen Senator Tom Eagleton of Missouri
as his running mate without realizing that Eagleton had undergone electric shock treatment for mental depression on numerous occasions. When the revelations came, as they inevitably did, McGovern announced that he backed his running
mate "1000 percent," which made the candidate's subsequent
turnabout doubly embarrassing. Eagleton's distress was the
subject of numberless satiric barbs, not all of them tasteless.
Said one comic: "Tom Eagleton has a lot of troubles in his
head but there's nothing in it." Said another: "A shock treatment is what Eagleton is giving McGovern." At least one Dem-

ocratic leader, Julian Bond, tried feebly to laugh the matter away. Casting a sardonic eye on Nixon's running mate, the bombastic Spiro Agnew, Bond said, "At least we know ours had *treatment*." But the issue would not go away. *Esquire* magazine, in its 1972 annual "Dubious Achievement Awards," pictured a glowing Tom Eagleton for its major award, which traditionally mocks egregious excess. The headline read: WE SUPPORT TOM EAGLETON ONE THOUSAND PERCENT, WE THINK. *Esquire* pointed out that Eagleton had purchased five thousand McGovern-Eagleton buttons, two thousand bumper stickers, and two thousand lapel pins, a fact to which *Esquire* responded, "Awwww." McGovern's aides came in for their share of comedic abuse for not scrupulously examining Eagleton's past. Said one Nixon aide in ridiculing McGovern's staff work: "They weren't thorough. They were the sort of guys who, if they were putting together a TV special with Ted Knight and Doris Day, would call it 'The Ted and Doris Show.'"

When Eagleton withdrew under pressure from media and party, McGovern cast about for a replacement. He settled on Sargent Shriver, who had headed the Kennedy Peace Corps and carried some of the charisma of the New Frontier. Like his presidential brother-in-law, Shriver knew the value of humor in campaigning. He launched a sardonic assault on Richard Nixon, right down to impressions of Nixon's gravelly voice. He startled and amused 1,200 students at a college in Las Vegas by doing an imitation of Nixon's acceptance speech at the GOP's Miami convention. Though the impression did not quite rival Rich Little, it brought laughter to the campus throng. Shriver straightened himself with a mock self-righteousness that was Nixon's trademark, tucked in his chin, and deepened his voice. "I believe in the American system," Shriver growled, and the young audience hooted joyously.

Many were called before Shriver was chosen. Indeed, faced with the likelihood of an ignominious loss, no one was very anxious to take up the cup that Eagleton had laid down. McGovern experienced such difficulty in finding a vice presidential stand-in for Tom Eagleton that one U.S. senator asked him, "George, does the law actually *require* that you have a Vice President?" Shriver promoted himself for the job, over the opposition of the Kennedy family, who disliked seeing the Camelot legacy squandered on a lost cause. The Kennedys are accustomed to winning. Shriver, in fact, was deep on the list of those asked to replace Eagleton, but he made a joke of his discomfort, saying, "I am not embarrassed to be George McGovern's seventh choice for Vice President. Pity Mr. Nixon—his first and only choice was Spiro Agnew." Along the campaign trail, Shriver augmented his Nixon impersonation with jokes that invoked the Kennedy years. He told one group of parents how he had motivated his own children to be more diligent students. "I told them when Lincoln was your age he walked twelve miles to school every day. But my son said, 'That's nothing. When Uncle Jack was your age, he was President.'"

In 1972 numerous democrats were straying from the party. Many saw McGovern as embracing hippies, feminists, and petulant collegians. They blanched at his views on gays, abortions, and amnesty for Vietnam deserters. With the Democratic party painfully split, Shriver tried to laugh away the schism. He quoted Will Rogers, who said, "I am not a member of an organized political party—I am a Democrat."

The great gummy issue of the Watergate caper clung to the Nixon campaign. Each day new information came to light confirming the existence of a well-organized Republican plan to defame the Democratic campaign through espionage and a variety of illegal and immoral devices. But incredibly, McGovern and Shriver were unable to turn the burgeoning scandal into votes. McGovern tried manfully to mock Nixon for the excesses of his election aides. Speaking to one audience he said, "A President who will send saboteurs inside the Democratic ranks is the kind of man who won't hesitate to wiretap your union, your law office, your university, your church or even your home." McGovern tried to turn the Watergate bugging apparatus into strategic humor. At the annual Al Smith charity dinner in New York, McGovern quipped, "I'm sorry President Nixon can't be with us tonight. But I'm sure that somewhere he's listening in."

The fumbles of the McGovern staff seemed to frustrate him more than anything the GOP could produce. Campaign director Gary Hart, who would one day see his own campaign aborted, quipped that the squabbles of the staff were "like reports of Mark Twain's death—greatly exaggerated." But the infighting was real. One of McGovern's key aides, Representative Frank Thomson, returned from a trip to learn that money he had raised for voter registration had been spent by Gary Hart for some other purpose entirely. Cracked Thomson of his diminished status: "If I had wanted to be a linebacker, I would have tried out for the Washington Redskins." There was black humor about the disarray of the hydra-headed McGovern team. "What we need," quipped a bitter campaign aide, "is one man in charge with a big black whip!"

The Miami convention that nominated Richard Nixon and Spiro Agnew had little drama or excitement. Nixon joked defensively about its utter predictability. "Those people," said Nixon, "who said that what took place in Miami was unexciting because we knew how it was going to turn out . . . well, I have never seen a John Wayne movie that was unexciting because you knew he was going to get the bad guy in the end." Yet *Newsweek* magazine called the GOP convention "The Dick & Spiro Show (Rerun)," with an eye to its planning as a scripted extravaganza. PBS covered the event with Bill Moyers, a former adviser to Lyndon Johnson. Moyers supplied a witty moment in discussing the event with *New Yorker* columnist Elizabeth Drew. When a dispute arose over allocation of delegates, Drew said, "Well, they're in power. Did you ever see anyone give up power?" "Once," said Moyers succinctly.

The Nixon nominating convention was laughably unspontaneous. The only moment of unrehearsed humor came when Sammy Davis, Jr. darted forward with a camera. A startled Nixon joshed, "Are you trying to shoot me in the back?" "No," said Davis, "I'm covering the convention for *Jet* magazine." The McGovern convention could have used a little of the Republican's stage management. Joked one party professional about McGovern's free-floating campaign staff: "That crowd could screw up a horseshoe tournament!" When Tom Eagleton refused to resign from the ticket despite revelations of his past shock therapy, it seemed to climax McGovern's opening night troubles. *Washington Post* cartoonist Herblock captured the situation with a drawing of a distraught Democratic donkey behind a desk at McGovern headquarters, head in hand. Strewn across the desk are papers covering the litany of campaign woes: POLLS, DEBTS, CONVENTION BATTLE. The Donkey is on the phone, saying, "Yeah, Tom—sure—uh-huh."

In his acceptance speech, George McGovern tried to put his problems behind him. Referring to the disintegrating Democratic ranks, he cracked, "Never underestimate the power of Richard Nixon to bring harmony to Democratic ranks." His gibe was less than prophetic. McGovern continued his graveyard humor by declaring, "We are going to help Mr. Nixon redeem the pledge he made ten years ago—that you won't have Richard Nixon to kick around anymore." McGovern's speech was in part the product of Frank Mankiewicz, a witty member of the dynastic Mankiewicz family of Hollywood (Joe had written *All About Eve;* Herman wrote *Citizen Kane*). Frank Mankiewicz had been press secretary to Bobby Kennedy during his Senate years and played a major role in the McGovern operation. Rumpled, likable, and low-keyed, Mankiewicz delighted the press with his educated wit. At a meeting of Democrats torn into various warring factions, Mankiewicz cracked, "Every little meaning has a movement all its own." Reporters covering the McGovern campaign would needle Mankiewicz with a parody of "Twinkle, Twinkle Little Star." As the free-form politicians lurched along the campaign trail, the newsmen sang:

Mankiewicz, Mankiewicz, super star,
You're not as smart as you think you are.

Though McGovern captured his party's nomination on the first ballot, thanks to the reforms in the delegate selection process that the Democrats had adopted four years before, the party had strong misgivings about McGovern's constituency. The high visibility of homosexuals, pot-smoking college boys, and black militants formed an aggressive turnoff to many traditional party members. Pat Oliphant dramatized the trauma with a cartoon picturing the Democratic donkey in a Floridian shirt and shorts, hailing a Miami taxi and muttering, "Convention Hall, driver . . . and don't hurry!" When it was learned that Tom Eagleton had a history of psychiatric therapy, Oliphant recalled Spiro Agnew's rise from obscurity as Nixon's vice president. He showed an embarrassed George McGovern addressing his aides on the Eagleton gaffe: "Can we get rid of whatsisname before be becomes a household word?"

McGovern's forays on the campaign trail were less than triumphal. At times his speeches were moving, but he was unable to inject the leavening of wit that might have won him points. On those occasions when he ventured into the field of humor, he produced more animus than zeal. Before a gathering of aggressive feminists, McGovern was lauded by the jovial Liz Carpenter, former resident humorist at the Johnson White House. Acknowledging McGovern's recognition of women's rights, Liz praised the candidate by saying, "We are all here because of George McGovern." The candidate smiled and said, "The credit should go to Adam." Instead of bemused laughter, the line produced angry hisses from the feminists. McGovern gasped, "Can I recover by saying Adam and Eve?"

George McGovern's chaotic campaign and catastrophic loss in the election of 1972 were largely the result of the disaffection created by the Democratic party's noisy newcomers. Speaking before Washington's Gridiron Club, when his struggle had passed into history, McGovern looked back in laughter at his electoral debacle.

"Last year," he said, "we opened the doors of the Democratic party as we promised we would, and twenty million Democrats stalked out."

Chapter 14
Campaign 1968
The Pagliacci of Politics

I can still remember the first time I ever heard Hubert Humphrey speak. He was in the second hour of a five minute talk.
—GERALD R. FORD

There was something unalterably humorous about Hubert Horatio Humphrey, even his name. He was a warm-hearted fellow, witty, spontaneous, garrulous, ebullient, and immensely likable. He wore his black hair drawn across his bulging forehead like Paul Simon playing "The Mikado." He was loquacious to a fault. Said the *New Republic*, "He is like a mad vending machine: insert dime and you get a peanut bar, and then another, and another. There is no stopping it. It rains peanut bars." Humphrey was the prototype of the Washington bureaucrat whose son asks him about Portugal. The man brings home a ton of government pamphlets about the country and his son sighs, "Dad, that's more than I want to know about Portugal." Hubert Humphrey told you more than you wanted to know about Portugal. Or anything. He was a magnet that attracted the gibes of his peers with his bombastic speech and nonstop prolixity.

For four years he had had the unenviable task, for a man so fond of words, of keeping his mouth shut and listening to the lengthy monologues of his boss, the overbearing President Lyndon Johnson. For four long years the fragrance of Lyndon's shoe polish was fresh in Humphrey's nostrils. Humphrey was probably the most maligned of vice presidents since Alexander Throttlebottom, the ineffectual Veep in *Of Thee I Sing*. In that George S. Kaufman–George Gershwin musical comedy, the president tells his vice president to stay out of sight. "Well," says Throttlebottom, "I guess I could go back to my old job." "What was that?" asks the president. "I was a hermit," says Throttlebottom.

Humphrey would have made a poor hermit. He was too gregarious. Said Mark Russell: "When the TV camera was on Hubert, he would never be caught alone. He was always shaking hands with someone. If need be he would shake hands with a plant." It often seemed that even Humphrey's most ardent admirers would end up mocking him unintentionally. When Jimmy Carter accepted the Democratic presidential nomination in 1976, he said, "We must all pay tribute to Hubert Horatio Hornblower . . . uh, Humphrey."

Humphrey was a man of considerable ability, but in the burgeoning age of television, when the electorate sought a man who was larger than life—a Kennedy, a Johnson, or a Reagan—Humphrey was no master of majesty. Ironically, Humphrey seized the presidential nomination in the very year when a TV show called "Laugh-In" seized the public fancy. They were at opposite ends of the communicative spectrum. "Laugh-In" spoke in quick, frenetic news bites, sharp and crisp, acknowledging the public's shortened attention span. Humphrey spoke in voluminous sentences that taxed the patience of the most attentive listener.

True, Humphrey's mind was exemplary, with "the retentive capacity of a sponge." Men with less imagination and liberal instincts would appropriate his ideas and assume the credit for them. Food stamps and the Peace Corps were two of the great ideas of the mid-century. Both were Humphrey's conceptions, and both were executed by other men who received the credit for their creation. Humphrey recalled to mind the hapless screenwriter in Budd Schulberg's Hollywood novel of mendacity, *What Makes Sammy Run?* Sammy Glick has the aggression and chutzpah to seize better men's ideas and ride the cyclone of success to the top. Humphrey was the vic-

tim of the political Sammy Glicks. A Washington comic remarked that Humphrey was the sort of man who would "buy a
pumpkin farm the year they cancelled Halloween." Then he
added, "Hubert visited the Grand Canyon, but it was closed."

This dust bowl liberal was a plain and humble soul. He
would never yield to pomposity and take himself too seriously.
He was able to join the throngs in laughing at himself. When
he sought the presidency in 1960, running head-to-head with
the moneyed aristocracy of Jack Kennedy in the primaries,
Hubert was clearly outmatched—in dollars, staff and kin. As
Stephen Sondheim wrote in his Broadway musical, *Merrily We
Roll Along*, a takeoff on the Kennedy assault on the presidency:

> There's Bobby and Jackie and Jack
> And myriads more in the back—
> There's Ethel and Teddy and Pat alone
> Plus Eunice and Peter and Jean and Joan

Humphrey had the wit and self-deprecating humor to laugh at
his travail, that being the only thing he could to do about it.
With the Kennedy battalions arrayed against him, Hubert
said,

> The whole Kennedy family had talent in depth. No newspaper
> publishers knew my father. Sargent Shriver was the head of the
> Merchandise Mart; I was head of Humphrey's Drug Store . . .
> And what's glamorous about the name Humphrey? I'm not
> glamorous per se. I'm not young. I'm not old. I'm like the girl
> next door—always available but you don't think about mar-
> riage.

Humphrey was a compulsive talker. The way an alcoholic drinks, Humphrey talked. There was not a subject on
which Humphrey did not have a few thousand well-chosen
words. He laughed at his own volubility. "I *like* every subject,"
he laughed. "I can't help it—it's *glands*."

When Lyndon Johnson tormented his Veep, as he did
all his other subordinates in the White House, Humphrey had
the grace to laugh off his own petty humiliations. "Hubert!"
LBJ barked during one legislative breakfast. "I tried to get

hold of you yesterday. Where the hell were you!" Humphrey swiveled his huge head and smiled slyly. "Try the other cheek, Mr. President," he said.

But Humphrey's self-deprecation did little to discourage others from ridiculing him. It is an unfortunate fact of political life that self-deprecation is no guarantee of insulation against the mockery of others. Jerry Ford discovered that when he kidded his own clumsiness the mockery continued. Ford was irrigating the ridicule, not drowning it. Ironically, it was Jerry Ford who was one of the most perennial gagsters with Humphrey as target. At the Gridiron Club, where Washington's newsmen pay self-proclaimed tribute to their own eminence, Humphrey and Ford once attended, representing their respective parties. Ford produced laughter at Humphrey's expense when he said:

> Nat Finney [president of the Gridiron] told me how it would go tonight. He said first he'd give a little talk, and next I'd give a little talk, and then Humphrey would follow. I said, "Who follows Humphrey?" He said, "Hardly anybody."

On another occasion, when Ford and Humphrey shared the same podium, Ford confessed to the audience, "I couldn't find my program, so I leaned over to the man sitting next to me and asked, "What follows Hubert Humphrey?" He looked at his watch, then he looked at me and said, "Christmas."

Hubert Humphrey was one of the few public figures who was so vulnerable to comic reproach that a fellow politician could devote a five-minute routine to his eccentricities and never be disappointed in the response. He was that reliable a target. At one press banquet where Ford was the guest speaker and Humphrey was not present, Ford's address was interrupted by the ringing of a telephone. Public figures rarely do "prop jokes," it being considered beneath the dignity of their office. But in this case Gerald Ford thought the subject justified the prop. A telephone had been placed by the microphone. Ford picked up the receiver. "Hello? . . . Hubert! . . . Uh-huh . . . uh-huh . . . uh-huh." Ford picked up his pipe, loaded it with tobacco, and retrieved the receiver. "Uh-huh. . . ." He lit the pipe, puffed it contentedly, and returned to the phone. "Uh-huh . . . uh-huh . . . Goodbye, Hubert . . . Goodbye, Hubert . . . Goodbye, Hubert." Ford finally hung up the receiver with a sigh and turned to the audience, which by now was convulsed with laughter. "That was Hubert," said Ford. "He just wanted to say hello."

Much of Ford's good-natured raillery at Humphrey's expense was the product of Bob Orben, Ford's resident humorist who found Humphrey's loquacity a constant source of humor. Just as novelist Herman Wouk, in his early days as a gag writer for Fred Allen, found Jack Benny's thrift a surefire source of comedy for his boss, Humphrey's tendency to gab was a golden target for Ford at the various press dinners he addressed. Speaking at the Alfalfa Club, Ford praised his hosts on their wit. "I know you haven't lost your sense of humor," he said, "just by looking at the time schedule they gave me for this dinner . . . '9:50—Candidate's acceptance speech. Hubert Humphrey responds—*briefly*.'"

But Ford recognized Humphrey's wit and acknowledged it on the occasion when he and Hubert were both invited to deliver humorous monologues before a media audience. Said Ford: "Why did I ever say I want to speak here tonight? Matching me against Hubert Humphrey for laughs is like putting Twiggy against Zsa Zsa Gabor."

The writers on "That Was the Week That Was (TW3)," the sixties TV program of political satire, found humor in Humphrey's bombastic sounding name. President Johnson had just announced in his ineffable egoism that any baby who was named after him would be given a steer from the Johnson ranch. Cracked a TW3 writer: "Any baby given the name of Hubert Horatio will also be given a prize—a choice between psychiatric therapy and boxing lessons."

Vice President Hubert Humphrey was surprised to find himself the Democratic nominee in 1968. The nomination should have gone to President Lyndon Baines Johnson, with Humphrey, at best, the loyal running mate. But Johnson's popularity had plunged as the casualty figures rose in Vietnam. Lyndon Johnson and the Democrats had squandered the huge mandate they received four years before. In 1968 the war hung over the election like a thunderclap, ultimately forcing LBJ to make his stunning declaration: "I shall not seek and will not accept the nomination of my party for another term." Johnson's abdication had been long in coming. He had turned the full force of his power, office, and earthy humor on the critics of the war. "I feel like a mongrel bitch assaulted by a pack of males," he gibed. "If I run they chew my tail off. If I hunker down they fuck me to death." Senator William Fulbright, chairman of the Foreign Relations Committee, led the flight of doves in the Congress and in the press, attacking Johnson's escalation. Cracked LBJ: "I wonder if you've seen the latest announcement from the Senate Foreign Relations Committee that it is going to hold hearings on the Viet Cong. . . . They are going to start those hearings in the editorial room of the *New York Times*."

Johnson generated angry taunts wherever he went over the unending war. There were sit-ins, marches, and noisy demonstrations all through the solemn, stormy election year of 1968. The Washington press corps were among Johnson's most strident critics. Johnson often retreated to his church, followed by a pack of newsmen. He needled them by saying, "Come on in. You need this more than I do." Worship offered no escape. LBJ's minister declared in a sermon, as his presidential parishioner squirmed, "There is a general consensus that something is wrong in Vietnam . . . We ask respectfully, why?" Johnson emerged from the church wearing a grim smile that evaporated as the minister saw him to his car. Johnson nodded curtly to the man and said, "Wonderful choir."

The press kept up a drumfire of attack on Johnson all through the election year of 1968. When he attended their Gridiron Dinner and listened to the sardonic sketches and songs aimed at his flaws and foreign policy, the thin-skinned president rose and said, "I have enjoyed the skits—I think." As the projected nominee of his party, he took the occasion to launch some darts at two of the men he thought he might be facing in the upcoming election—Richard Nixon and George Romney, president of American Motors. Said LBJ: "I've been out with the troops for the last two days, and I didn't know until I got in tonight that as a result of the automobile safety regulations, The Rambler had already called in George Romney."

Referring to Romney's auto background and the old gibe about buying a used car from Richard Nixon, LBJ continued: "Ever since I ran off to California when I was a boy, and I washed cars out there for a living, that was before I ever met either Romney or Nixon. It seems like I've always been having trouble with these used car fellers."

It was a traumatic year for LBJ. Dog owners protested when he lifted his daughter's pet beagles by their ears, causing them to yelp with pain. Cracked one Washington wise guy: "Hubert Humphrey doesn't see what all the fuss is about. Johnson's been lifting him that way for years."

1968 was a year when the power of the polls gripped America as never before. A raft of media polls mirrored the public attitude to the war, to Johnson, and to the various candidates. It became a subject of humor when Washington wit Russell Baker wrote sardonically in his *New York Times* column: "Something terrible is happening to the Presidential campaign this year. It is all settled in the press before anybody has had a chance to cast a vote." *New Yorker* cartoonist James Stevenson made an amusing point about the army of polltakers who had marched across the nation. In the cartoon, a stymied poll taker sits with pencil poised over his clipboard. The voter sits on his sofa, smiling agreeably and saying, "Nixon? He's wonderful, too. They're all wonderful—wonderful, warm people, and great great Americans!"

Elliott Reid, on "That Was the Week that Was," played a persistent polltaker who showed the deficiencies of the polling process. An exchange between a polltaker and a New Hampshire voter during that closely watched primary, went like this:

VOTER. I like Rockefeller.

POLLTAKER. What about Nixon?

VOTER. He's okay, but I like Rockefeller.

POLLTAKER. But you do like Nixon.

VOTER. Sure, but I'm for Rockefeller.

POLLTAKER. Let me get this straight. You like Rockefeller but you think Nixon is okay.

VOTER. Sure. Sure. (slams door)

POLLTAKER. (marking form) Undecided.

President Johnson often carried a copy of the latest poll in his breast pocket and would brandish it to show his popularity and that of his unpopular war. But when his ratings declined, he chose to mock them and the idea that one could rule a nation by heeding them. When the press held its Gridiron Dinner at Old Williamsburg, the recreation of the colonial city, Johnson spoke there and said, "The statesmen of Williamsburg were some of our first political analysts, and it was here that a special courier first delivered the advance release which referred to Patrick Henry's private poll from his home district: '46 percent for liberty, 15 percent for death, 15 percent undecided.'" In reading his own plummeting polls and looking ahead to the fall elections, Johnson cracked, "I've been reading a lot about my own polls in the newspapers, and I'm worried it could be I've peaked too soon."

Satirist Mason Williams bent a quizzical eye on the polls in the book, *Pat Paulsen for President*. He wrote,

> The polls show that only three people in the entire country would receive more votes than LBJ if the election were held today. William Jennings Bryan, Wendell Wilkie, and Dizzy Gillespie. . . . You must admit that President Johnson always hits the nail firmly with his head, and after all, it takes 53 cowboys to run the LBJ ranch and we can't expect one cowboy to run the entire country by himself.

So uncertain was the roiling election of 1968, that Russell Baker wrote a slim, amusing volume called *Our Next President*, in which he pictured a humorous and startling scenario for the forthcoming general election. Parodying the familiar style of Theodore White's *Making of the President* series, Baker made *Our Next President* look like *Apocalypse Now*. In his version of the 1968 race, LBJ dumped Humphrey from the ticket in favor of Bobby Kennedy. The Republicans reached a convention deadlock and chose New York City's charismatic young mayor, John Lindsay, as its nominee. The summer riots gave George Wallace's third party sufficient votes to throw the election into the House of Representatives, which was stalemated in choosing a president. Meanwhile, Bobby Kennedy was selected as vice president by the Senate and moved into the Oval Office with no intention of leaving.

Russell Baker's impossible dream was not much more bizarre than the actual scenario that unfolded within the Democratic party. Johnson's popularity and credibility dropped. Martin Luther King was assassinated, triggering riots in Newark, Watts, Washington, and Detroit. Robert Kennedy was murdered after winning the California primary. The Vietnam War divided the country like a knife blade; hawks and doves were at one another's throats. An intellectual senator named Eugene McCarthy campaigned for the Democratic presidential nomination in New Hampshire, and though it seemed a laughable undertaking, it attracted the impassioned support of college students who formed a "children's crusade" that exploited America's bitterness over the war. McCarthy made a powerful showing in New Hampshire that showed Johnson how much his support had corroded.

Mason Williams, the head writer of "The Smothers Comedy Hour," wrote a witty book promoting comic Pat Paulsen's run for the presidency. Said Williams: "So far the only candidate running against President Johnson in the Democratic Party is Senator Eugene McCarthy of Minnesota. I don't believe this man has a chance to win. He has admitted that he is a peace candidate. How can he possibly win on such an anti-American platform?"

Bobby Kennedy was in a turmoil about whether to enter the lists. "To be or not to be?" asked *Newsweek* about his dilemma. As the heir of the Kennedy legacy and the leading opponent to Johnson's war, should he make the bold gamble and challenge LBJ? If he did, he might split his party and hand the election to the GOP. If he failed to act, he would endure five more years of exile in the stuffy U.S. Senate. Bobby's ambivalence was satirized by cartoonist Jules Feiffer in a strip called "THE BOBBY TWINS—EPISODE 2: IN WHICH THE GOOD BOBBY

GOES ON 'FACE THE NATION' AND THE BAD BOBBY RESPONDS." Feiffer showed two Bobbys seated at a microphone. Lamented the first: "We're going in there and we're killing South Vietnamese. We're killing children, we're killing women. We're killing innocent people . . . Do we have that right? . . . I very seriously question whether we have that right. . . ." Whereupon the second Bobby responds: "I will back the Democratic candidate in 1968. I expect that will be President Johnson." The first Bobby turns a troubled face to the second Bobby and says, "I think we're going to have a difficult time explaining this to ourselves."

Bobby Kennedy and Lyndon Johnson had long eyed each other with hostility and distrust. Ever since John Kennedy's death had propelled LBJ into the Oval Office, the Texan had sensed that Bobby led a band of loyalists waiting in the wings to succeed him. Johnson resented Bobby and the New Frontiersmen, suspecting they were cracking cruel jokes about him at their Georgetown dinner tables, as indeed they were. Bobby tried to laugh the feud away. He and Lyndon were the best of friends, he asserted. "The rumors of hostility between us don't square with the facts," he said. "All during my brother's presidency we were the closest of friends. But then one day, as we were leaving the inaugural stands. . . ." Bobby protested that he had no designs on the presidency. "And neither does my wife Ethel Bird." When the 1968 edition of my election-year perennial *Who's in Charge Here?* appeared, on the cover was a photo of LBJ and Bobby that was less than flattering to the president. Bobby said to me with a touch of irony, "That's going to do a lot for my relationship at the White House."

When Gene McCarthy revealed Johnson's feet of clay in the Granite State, Bobby waited a scant four days before he too entered the race, declaring his own candidacy for the presidency in the very spot his brother had declared his own eight years before. Herblock drew a cartoon for the *Washington Post* that showed an unsettled Lyndon Johnson peering into the Oval Office where, eerily, he sees an empty rocking chair— and it is rocking. Such were the shock waves that Bobby's announcement produced. He began his campaign with the Indiana primary. It was the first presidential primary Bobby had ever entered as a candidate. He knew he had to win in Indiana, and he did. His reputation for ruthlessness (Feiffer's "bad Bobby") clung to him like an albatross. He tried to dispel it with humor, speaking modestly, tentatively, and with sardonic humor turned always on himself. He told of encountering a mother superior at a primary stop. "She said she had been praying to St. Jude for me," he declared. "I thanked her, then asked somebody who St. Jude was . . . and then I learned he is the patron saint of lost causes."

At another stop, Bobby asked a sidewalk rally whether their city was going to vote for him. "Otherwise," said Bobby, "Ethel and I and our ten children will have to go on welfare. It'll be less expensive just to send us to the White House. We'll arrange it so all ten kids won't be there at once. And we won't need to expand the place. I'll send some of them away to school—and I'll make one of them Attorney General."

To those who still perceived signs of ruthlessness in Bob Kennedy from his days of fighting racketeering in the American labor movement, he had a comic disclaimer. Feigning indignation, Bobby would say, "People call me ruthless. I am *not* ruthless. And if I find the man who is calling me ruthless, I shall destroy him!"

If the humor of the 1968 campaign seemed to originate mainly in its participants—Johnson's angry jokes, Bobby's self-deprecatory cracks, Humphrey's awkward barbs—it was in part because of the morbidity of the war and the rage of the civil rights struggle, the orgies of anger and rioting. Certainly, television, that marvelous instrument for moving merchandise, offered little political humor in 1968. None of the networks wanted to offend half their audience with political positions in an overheated controversy. A comedic breakthrough called "Laugh-In" was created that year by George Schlatter and Ed Friendly. Friendly had been the NBC executive assigned to "That Was the Week That Was" four years earlier, and he brought to this new show some of the topical humor of TW3. But in place of the sometimes pretentious, heavy-handed content of TW3, the new show was devoted to fun. It was a mosaic of antic bits and pieces. Its slivers of videotape and its spectacular cast, assembled by George Schlatter, revolutionized TV comedy. But "Laugh-In" was only rarely satiric;

it's political insights were skin-deep. The Democrats should have considered themselves fortunate that "Laugh-In" was seldom ideological, since its humor might have been as conservative as TW3's was liberal. Head writer Paul Keyes was a speech writer and friend of Richard Nixon. Indeed, Nixon furthered his appeal to "Laugh-In's" vast audience by appearing on the show and proclaiming the show's trademark line, "Sock it to me." But "Laugh-In's" irreverence was in its pace and its punch lines, not in its politics.

If television comedy ever strayed into the area of political issues during this volcanic period, it was with "The Smothers Brothers Comedy Hour." Here, the subterranean anger of the young, the contempt for Nixon, the subversion of the counterculture, and the antiwar attitudes were all too visible. CBS scheduled the show opposite "Bonanza," a counterprogramming plan similar to putting an animal documentary against "The Cosby Show." To everyone's shock, the Smothers Brothers' show not only survived, it prevailed. It did so with a violent assault of biting humor about Lyndon Johnson and the Vietnam War. One evening the TV audience, accustomed to the gentle inanities of "Gilligan's Island" and "The Beverly Hillbillies," was suddenly confronted by a sketch in which President Johnson transports his ranch to the White House lawn. This was impudent stuff in those days. Several CBS affiliates refused to carry the show.

Young viewers who hated the war—and perhaps felt guilty because their college status was keeping them immune to its dangers—loved the topical bite of "The Smothers Brothers Show." It was an island of satire in the vast wasteland of 1968 television. The Smothers boys, their talented producers, Ernie Chambers and Saul Ilson, and their incisive head writer, Mason Williams, constantly fought with the CBS censors to protect the comedic integrity of the show. One week Williams wrote and performed an attack on TV censorship, wielding an immense pair of scissors. The monologue was censored. A torrent of memos flowed between the apprehensive censors and the Smothers show. One memo from the censors read: "It's okay to satirize the President, as long as you do it with respect." Voltaire and Jonathan Swift take note.

The Smothers show reached an apex of pointed dissent after the Democratic convention in August, which gave Humphrey his nomination along with a hideous public relations problem. Outside the convention hall, thousands of young protesters demonstrated against the war. Mayor Richard Daley ordered his forces into the fray. There were bloody clashes—with tear gas, mace, billy clubs, and beatings. Police savaged the hippies, reporters, and pedestrians with democratic impartiality. The Smothers Brothers assembled a biting production number. Harry Belafonte sang a cheerful calypso tune called "Don't Stop the Carnival" against a background of news film of the Chicago convention riots. The taped images of bloodied youths and avenging policemen filled the screen, as Belafonte sang his cheerful ditty in black humorous counterpoint. The entire number was excised by the censors. A grim joke circulated at the Smother Brothers offices at the time:

"They held a meeting to protest police brutality."
"What happened?"
"The police broke it up with clubs and tear gas."

A wit at *Time* magazine assembled a caustic checklist of useful items to bring to the Democratic convention for the guidance of delegates. "The foresighted Democratic delegate," said *Time*, "would ideally—and intelligently—go equipped with goggles (to protect the eyes from tear gas and Mace), cyclists' crash helmet (from billy clubs, bricks, etc.), flak jacket (from snipers) . . . folding bicycle (there is a cab strike) . . . wire cutters (in case delegate is trapped inside the amphitheatre), all-purpose bail-bond credit card (if arrested) . . . chrysanthemums (for flower power if cornered by militant hippies)." Indeed, the security precautions at the convention were so elaborate, and the special barbed wire fences around the convention hall were so thick that the convention became known as "Stalag 68."

Though Hubert Humphrey—who anomalously proclaimed "the politics of joy"—received his party's prize on the first ballot, the riots, carried into America's livingrooms on national TV, made it a dubious gift. Herblock pictured a worried looking Humphrey holding the trophy that read: WINNER

DEMOCRATIC NOMINATION 1968. The cup was overflowing like a witch's cauldron.

When Humphrey took to the campaign trail with his dubious prize, he was heckled unmercifully. Wherever he went in that troubled autumn, he was met by hostile audiences. Nixon, meanwhile, who had received his nomination amidst comparative tranquility, was waging a calm, televised campaign. Humphrey poured it on, trying to contrast his passion and compassion with Nixon's callous disengagement. Humphrey resorted to sarcastic humor to diminish his opponent. He said:

> You know, every day I read about that cool, that confident, that composed and that smiling Mr. Nixon—the man who campaigns without running, the man who takes it easy and never makes a mistake . . . who either evades or straddles every issue. I'm going to send Mr. Nixon some talcum powder. He must be getting saddle sores, straddling all those issues.

Humphrey sought to give 'em hell, in the well-remembered manner of the feisty Harry Truman, who pulled off an astonishing upset in 1948 over Tom Dewey. Humphrey poured on the coals, giving a courageous, bravura performance, despite the daunting odds and the hostile hecklers. Sometimes the crowds were inspiring. Once a voice in the audience shouted, "Give 'em hell, Hubert!" And Humphrey cracked, "Well, it may be too good for them!" (Nixon remained cool and derisive. Reminded of the current Democratic war cry, Nixon sneered, "It's one thing to give 'em hell. It's another thing to give 'em Humphrey.")

Humphrey seemed unable to cope with the hecklers who taunted him. Few politicians, even those as ebullient and dauntless as Humphrey, could have been expected to maintain his aplomb in the face of such fury. (Al Smith was a memorable exception. When a heckler shouted, "Tell 'em all you know, Al," Smith responded, "I'll tell 'em all we *both* know. That won't take any longer.") When Humphrey sought to slip a punch, he was awkward and uninspired. Once, when his speech was drowned in a sea of boos, he declared that "boo" meant "I'm for you" in the language of the Sioux Indians.

Observing Humphrey's attempts to laugh his way through derision, comedian Pat Paulsen wrote in his book, *How to Wage a
Successful Campaign for the President*, describing his own mock
campaign of 1968, "I challenged my opponents on their home
ground. I challenged Humphrey to a laughing contest during
a war protest demonstration." Then, with nice impartiality,
Paulsen continued, "I pursued George Wallace to debate him
at a small Klan rally in Harlem. Lacking even a decent trade-
in, I offered to buy a used car from Nixon."

Unfortunately for Hubert Humphrey, he was facing
odds that were more formidable than those faced by any presidential candidate in memory. When doves in his audience
hooted their preference for Senator Eugene McCarthy, one
wag on the press bus commented, "Poor Hubert—his public
career has been like one long struggle against McCarthyism."
Humphrey was assailed by the ultraconservative John Birch
Society on one wing, and by Rapp Brown and his activists on
the other. Said Jerry Ford, with mock empathy: "Hubert has
been birched red by the Old Right and rapped brown by the
New Left."

Humphrey's "politics of joy" amidst the sanguinary car-
nage of Vietnam, drew mockery from the intellectual establishment. Wrote poet Marya Mannes, in sardonic doggerel:

Hubert the Happy
Goes yackety, yackety, yackety, yackety, yack.
If anyone tells him for God's sake to knock it,
He cheerfully yacketys back.

As election day neared, there were signs that Humphrey's campaign was escaping from the apathetic quagmire
that engulfed it. He asserted his independence from Lyndon
Johnson's position, declaring that he favored a halt in the
bombing of North Vietnam. Given this hopeful sign, Humphrey's critics began to turn, and money started to flow into
his coffers. A sign appeared in one audience proclaiming
HECKLERS FOR HUMPHREY. A few days before the election, on
the eve of Halloween, Lyndon Johnson called a halt to the
bombing. The move was assailed as cynical politics by the Republicans. Cracked one correspondent: "Mr. Johnson gave

Richard Nixon a trick and Hubert Humphrey a treat for Halloween."

The halt in the bombing helped Humphrey as did his declaration of independence from LBJ—but it was too little too late. Humphrey lost to Nixon by a slight plurality—about 500,000 votes out of the 73 million cast. Humphrey, the Pagliacci of politics, who had been so cruelly maligned during his four years as vice president, fought a tormenting, tumultuous campaign for the presidency, only to come up a buck short.

Chapter 15
Campaign 1968
The Dead Duck

> My own favorite is Richard Nixon . . . This humble
> man has once again offered himself as a candidate on
> the basis of his experience and I think we should ac-
> cept him on that basis. After all, why go to the trou-
> ble of breaking in a new loser?
> —MASON WILLIAMS

Richard Nixon ran in 1968 on the basis of experience, which made many of America's satirists smile. Back in
1960 Nixon had also run on the basis of experience, which
had promoted one observer to quip: "Experience is what he'll
have when this campaign is over." Nixon had still more experience when he lost to Pat Brown for the governorship of California in 1962. Perhaps Nixon agreed with Oscar Wilde that
"experience is the name we give to our mistakes." On that basis, by 1968 Nixon had abundant experience. But he also had
numerous political IOU's from party leaders around the country. For though he had declared after his California defeat,
"This is my last press conference . . . You won't have Nixon to
kick around anymore," he presented himself for the press's
boot in 1968. This was no mere display of masochism. Nixon
had been solidifying his relationship with the GOP brass for
six years. And so, when he entered the presidential primaries
in 1968, the public and the party responded. It seemed to
many that only Nixon could unite the Goldwater right with
the Rockefeller center.

After the debacle of Goldwater's defeat in 1964 and the scorn that Republican moderates had heaped on the Arizonan, the party could stand some unity. Jerry Ford observed that between LBJ and Bobby, Gene McCarthy and George Wallace, the Democrats were a divided party. "But we Republicans are united," quipped Ford. "We'll all rally 'round that great Republican champion, Ronald—Milhaus—Percyfeller."

As the election year began, the GOP did indeed have a number of plausible candidates in the chase. *Newsweek* chuckled that it was like a circus, "the five-count-em-five Republican elephants are lumbering into the big tent. One is showboating to the gallery [Nixon], one has to be prodded to perform at all [Reagan], another has his trunk in his mouth [Romney], the baby pachyderm is bringing up the rear [Scranton], and the scarred old lead elephant [Eisenhower] is counting the house."

Jerry Ford had a quip—sometimes rather close to the bone—about each of the GOP stalwarts. (He had no presidential ambitions himself. The presidency was still six years away for Jerry Ford, and then it would be his without the mess of a primary battle or even an election campaign.) Now Jerry Ford reviewed the Republican contenders from the secure position of House minority leader. George Romney, the Mormon president of American Motors, had dropped out of the race after his gaffe about being brainwashed on a junket to Vietnam. Said Ford: "Our Republican drag race is still exciting even with our Michigan Rambler scratched." (Said one comic of Mormon Romney: "His grandfather had four wives, 36 children, 198 grandchildren, 419 great grandchildren. One more generation and he can stampede the convention.")

Nelson Rockefeller was eyeing the convention, hoping for a draft-producing deadlock. Cracked Ford: "Rockefeller won't volunteer—but last week he installed a hot line to his draft board." Then Ford added, "Nelson is the best man to save the American dollar. It's a family habit . . . Rockefeller is the only taxpayer who can balance the Federal budget with his mad money." Ford had a few jocular remarks about Richard Nixon as well. He said of the man who would one day make him an instant President, "Dick Nixon doesn't have to stay in politics for the money. Only last week the Schick Razor Company offered him two million dollars just to do a shaving commercial . . . for Gillette." Then Ford added, "Dick is the only candidate who gets Five O'Clock Shadow on the Today Show."

Of Ronald Reagan, Ford said: "Governor Reagan says he isn't running for President. I believe him—even if his door chimes do play 'Hail to the Chief.'"

In the election year of 1968, Richard Nixon was the front-runner. He performed well in the primaries he entered that spring, but still he lacked the easy elegance of a Jack Kennedy or even the rustic charm of a Lyndon Johnson. Nixon was, in a word, stiff. He lacked the ability to behave informally, and this drew the gibes of the inveterate Nixon-haters. Reporters chuckled behind their notebooks at his habit of walking on the beach in jacket and tie. Given Nixon's humorless mind-set, even loyalist Lyn Nofziger told a symposium audience, "Every once in a while I lay awake at night trying to think of . . . something funny that Richard Nixon said."

Nixon's trademark was a counterfeit glee, which he used to laugh indiscriminately at anything that was remotely funny. (In this respect he resembled Sammy Davis, Jr., who interestingly enough was one of his most ardent supporters.) Throughout the primaries, Nixon tried to play the good sport in his public appearances. Campaigning in Burbank, he was introduced by comedians Dick Martin and Dan Rowan, whose TV farrago, "Laugh-In," was taped nearby at the NBC studios. "Laugh-In" had immortalized "beautiful downtown Burbank." In his introductory remarks, Dan Rowan cracked to Richard Nixon, "We were going to present you with the key to the city, but Burbank doesn't have any locks." "Yeah" interrupted Dick Martin, "but it does have bagels." This feeble gag produced a paroxysm of uncontrollable laughter from Nixon. The candidate's simulated sense of humor was in full flower.

Not every part of the GOP spectrum embraced Richard Nixon. The far right, which had fueled what Richard Reeves called "the Goldwater caper" four years before, would have preferred Ronald Reagan, the genial governor of California. And so, a scant two days before the convention was ready to give its imprimatur to Nixon, conservative southern legislators prevailed on Reagan to challenge the front-running Nixon. Reagan had come to the convention as a favorite son candidate. Now, at the eleventh hour, he decided to make it clear that he was in and had no intention of pulling out. "As of this moment," Reagan announced, "I am a candidate." With a mere forty-eight hours to go before the balloting would begin, Reagan's formal availability, said one journalistic wag, "was the shortest candidacy in American political history.

Reagan's demeanor was the same warm, appealing one that would win him such adoration once he entered the White House twelve years later. His approach was avuncular and amusing. He spoke of his presidential goals before thirty-five caucuses in two days. To all and sundry he said, "I have mixed emotions—like the man watching his mother-in-law drive off a cliff in his new Cadillac." Reagan's gaggery earned him laughter but few delegate votes. Indeed, his last minute lunge seemed less the product of cunning than desperation. It provoked derisive humor from some party officials. Cracked one governor about Reagan's gambit: "It's like a woman who's eight-and-a-half months pregnant announcing she's going to have a baby." Said another: "Ron's getting the cherry pickers and the flip floppers. He hasn't even got John Wayne."

Along with Reagan's hopes, Nixon buried the ambitions of other fellow Republicans. Herblock, who had been cutting through political cant and bombast for years, pictured Nixon as a grinning grave digger, wringing his hands with glee, as he studies the freshly laid gravestones marked ROMNEY, ROCKEFELLER, and RESPONSIBLE REPUBLICANISM. Herblock had won three Pulitzer Prizes with his witty work. His pen gave the most abstract issues a vivid, human face, and no face reflected more of the political sins than Herblock's Nixon. Throughout the convention and the election campaign that followed, Richard Nixon was a favorite target of much of the media. When he bowed to Pat Brown in the California gubernatorial race six years before, Nixon had been the target of a joke that was less than prophetic. It went:

"Knock-knock."
"Who's there?"
"Nixon."
"Nixon who?"
"You mean you've forgotten already?"

The anti-Nixon line of choice in the 1968 campaign accompanied a photo of a sullen Nixon staring face forward at the camera. The caption read: "Would you buy a used car from this man?"

Nixon had the capacity to engage a deep undercurrent of anger among liberals. When he chose Spiro Agnew as his running mate in 1968, a nasty bit of graffiti began to appear on subway billboards in New York City, which read: DICK AND SPIRO ADD UP TO ZERO. Nixon and Agnew often triggered a scatalogical contempt that said somewhat more about their critics than the candidates. One bit of graffiti read: NIXON IS THE FIRST PRESIDENT TO HAVE AN ASSHOLE FOR A VICE PRESIDENT. Beneath it, in another handwriting, was written: NO, EISENHOWER WAS. Written in a stall in a men's toilet at Rutgers University was the question, "How can anyone hate a President with a name like Dick?" Pat Paulsen, reflecting on the GOP convention, said: "1968 will be remembered as the campaign when the Republicans, torn between old loyalties to Barry Goldwater and the radiant promises of Herbert Hoover, chose Richard Nixon as the compromise candidate." (Alluding to the other party, Paulsen said, "The Democrats, holding a giant convention in Chicago, went through the uncontested formalities of nominating Hubert Humphrey. George Wallace's party chose the former Governor of Alabama, George Wallace. The Yippies, also meeting in Chicago, countered by nominating a pig.")

For his running mate, Nixon had available to him the very cream of the American political system—most of the Republican luminaries who had faltered on the road to the nomination. There was Romney, Rockefeller, Scranton, Percy, plus numerous other notables of the U.S. Senate and House. He chose instead to reach far beyond obscurity to pluck out the bulbous governor of Maryland, a worthy named Spiro T. Agnew. When Richard Nixon lost the presidency in 1960 to a lanky Bostonian named Jack Kennedy, *Esquire* ran a picture of Nixon roaring with laughter. Beneath it was the question: "Why is this man laughing?" In 1968, there was another question hanging in the air. "Spiro who?" Headlines sprang up, reading SPIRO AGNEW—WHO'S HE? One wit volunteered that the name rhymed with "hero," or better yet, "zero." Agnew was "a legend in his own mind," said one wag. Though Agnew was the governor of Maryland, a citizen of that state hooted, "I'm from Maryland and even I have trouble remembering his name." To demonstrate the exquisite obscurity of the man, a reporter for the *Atlanta Constitution* stopped passersby on Peachtree Street, saying: "I'm going to say two words to you. You tell me what they mean." The words were: "Spiro Agnew." Here are some of the replies:

"It's some kind of disease."
"It's some kind of egg."
"He's a Greek who owns that ship-building firm."

Agnew would generate more recognition with his campaign racism, his alliterative attacks on the press, and his resignation from the vice presidency. But at this stage in his political career, he was "Spiro who?"

Still, Agnew did have a definite appeal to border and southern states, and that, combined with his apparent probity, seemed to make him a sound choice as the vice presidential running mate. Nixon started to have second thoughts when, on the campaign trail, Agnew proved himself a loose cannon. He called a Nisei correspondent a "fat Jap" and customarily referred to Polish-Americans as "Polacks." These ethnic slurs produced a pointed bit of satire from cartoonist Pat Oliphant. The Republicans were seeking to woo black votes to the GOP banner, and Oliphant showed Agnew in a series of encounters labeled THE WORLD OF SPIRO AGNEW. The Veep candidate is greeting various offended looking ethnics. "Hi, Polack!" he says. Then, "Hi, Jap!" Then "Hi, Wop!" Then, "Hi, Wetback!" Finally, he meets a dark-skinned man. Says Agnew, "Hi . . . er . . . black Afro-American!"

Some cracked that Agnew was "Nixon's Nixon." The vice presidential candidate had charted a low-road itinerary, and a latent racist was peeking through. No one ever accused Agnew of any intellectual brilliance. One journalist gibed that Agnew's characteristic squint came from overexposure to the Baltimore Colts' football games on Sunday TV. Time after time, Agnew had to backpedal rapidly to escape the repercussions of his off-the-cuff quips. There was a venomous streak to

Agnew's humor that continued to percolate problems for the ticket. There seemed no limit to his eyebrow raisers. He called Hubert Humphrey "squishy soft on Communism," which brought an outcry from Senate Republicans who respected their patriotic colleague. Agnew promptly apologized. Since his campaign odyssey included more suburbs than inner city areas, Agnew airily dismissed his preference by saying, "When you've seen one slum you've seen them all." As Agnew's apologies and explanations piled up, some Americans laughed, while others wept. At one rally he was greeted by a poster that said, APOLOGIZE NOW, SPIRO. IT WILL SAVE TIME.

If Spiro Agnew seemed to cause more trouble than he was worth for Richard Nixon, former Alabama governor George Wallace posed a more serious threat to Nixon's electoral fortunes. He was running as head of a third party, and in the southern states he threatened to siphon votes from the Nixon column. He rivaled and even surpassed Nixon in his vehemence on the subject of law and order, or, as some called it, "lawnorder." Wallace was attacked with scathing sarcasm by the liberals. Said one columnist, "He appeared at the convention in a plain white business sheet." Said a TV satirist, "Wallace has a great deal of respect for the Negro. He feels that every man should own one." Don Wright, editorial cartoonist for the *Miami News*, pictured Wallace holding a large placard containing his party platform. It read:

1. Run over Hippies with yore car.
2. Win war—somehow.
3. Throw bureaucrats' briefcases in Potomac.
4. Run over Yippies with yore car.
5. Throw bureaucrats in Potomac.
6. Wave yore flag
7. Put crooks in jail.
8. Put Supreme Court in jail.
9. Put pink press in jail.
10. Get law and order.
11. Let police run country.

If Wallace competed vigorously with Nixon on the matter of "law and order," it was equally true that Hubert Humphrey gave significant stress to the issue. A few months before, the murder of Martin Luther King had produced outbreaks in many American cities, and all three candidates were running hard against riots. This led Mahood, the acerbic cartoonist for the *Times* of London, to sketch two blacks looking at some posters of Wallace, Nixon, and Humphrey, each placard proclaiming the candidate's devotion to law and order. One of the blacks is saying, "Well, there's the choice—which one would *you* prefer to have hitting you over the head, Alvin?" The inimitable Herblock was sharper still. He showed George Wallace fitting a Ku Klux Klansman for a respectable topcoat over his white robe. The Klansman's topcoat reads LAW AND ORDER, and the white costume beneath is labeled RACISM. Says Wallace to his customer as he pins the hem, "We'll let the overcoat out all the way, and the robe will hardly show at all."

With all the major candidates stressing the law-and-order issue, the mayor of San Francisco was moved to remark: "None of the candidates is running for President. They're all running for Sheriff!"

Whatever the American voters choice for sheriff, they chose Richard Nixon for president by a plurality of half a million voters, with Nixon carrying thirty-one states to Humphrey's fourteen and Wallace's five.

Chapter 16
Campaign 1964
The President of All the People

The stores will soon be marketing the LBJ sweater.
You get such a warm, comfortable feeling as they
pull the wool over your eyes.
—HENRY MORGAN

Every U.S. president and every candidate for the office automatically becomes a target for the witticisms—some whimsical, some cruel—of America's comics, columnists, satirists, and gadflies. And it can be fairly observed that whatever their smiles of counterfeit good fellowship, these public figures are not entirely pleased with the constant ridicule of their flaws, both personal and political. But of all the men who sought or achieved the exalted post of president, none was as sensitive to the mockery of humor as Lyndon Baines Johnson.

President John F. Kennedy used to say: "If you want to stay out of trouble, stay out of sight." And by staying out of sight during his service as Kennedy's vice president—as the constitutional system mandates—Johnson was seldom the target of wounding humor. (He was, of course, the target of beltway humor from his colleagues in the Kennedy White House, but that's another story). But when Lyndon Johnson sought the presidency in his own right, after inheriting it on the black day of Kennedy's death, he became the focus for abundant ridicule. He was an extraordinary man with extraordinary virtues and extraordinary flaws, and the flaws drew most of the humorists' attention.

Johnson was more sensitive to humor and its inherent criticism than any of his predecessors in the Oval Office, primarily because of the immensity of his ego. As his friend, Speaker Sam Rayburn, once observed, "Most politicians have ample egos, but Lyndon is double dipped." Hugh Sidey, of *Time* magazine, observed that Johnson was "incapable of laughing at himself," so it was unsurprising that he would find scant humor in the witty assaults of others. LBJ was especially sensitive to the wit of columnist Art Buchwald, the dean of press humorists. On one occasion Johnson found his aide and confidant, Bill Moyers, sitting at his desk, roaring with laughter at a Buchwald column targeted on LBJ. "You find Buchwald funny?" exploded Johnson. "No sir!" snapped Moyers. On another occasion, Pierre Salinger felt the sting of Johnson's animus over Buchwald's wit. Salinger, whom LBJ inherited as his press secretary from Kennedy, was lunching with the Johnson clan at the LBJ ranch. That morning Pierre had been so imprudent as to mention that Buchwald had written a funny column on Johnson in the *New York Herald Tribune.* There were thunderclaps over the luncheon table when Salinger sat down with the president and his family and staff. "Peer," he said to Salinger with quiet menace. "Ah understand you found Art Buchwald very funny this morning." Salinger admitted he had. "Well," said the president, "will someone bring Peer a copy of this morning's *Herald Tribune.*" A copy was produced as Salinger broke into a gentle sweat. "Peer, why don't you just read the column aloud so we can all enjoy it." Salinger read the 1,250 words of Buchwald's column. When he finished, Johnson swept the table with a monarchal glare. "Well," said the president, "does anybody else find that funny?" There was utter silence.

Johnson's vanity was so thick and his skin so thin that any humor focused upon him was bound to draw blood. His predecessor had had the ability to laugh at himself, but Johnson did not. (I was the beneficiary of Jack Kennedy's taste for humor. It in fact brought me into the Kennedy circle and triggered my career as a political dilettante. In 1962 I had written a little political book called *Who's in Charge Here?* In it, I

floated irreverent speech balloons over the head of President
Kennedy and others in his political family. The target of my
gibes was Kennedy's rocking chair, his speed reading, his
wife's taste in couturier clothes, his daughter, his space program, and his cabinet. When aides brought the book to Kennedy's attention, he invited me to visit him at the White House.
Needless to say, Johnson never contacted me about any of the
book's sequels.)

Lyndon Johnson did not merely grin and bear it when
the wags were at work. He did not bite through the stem of his
pipe as Gerald Ford did when the jokesters were at play. Johnson was vindictive. Even the mildest humor or the gentlest reproach made him irate. This was an abrupt change in sophisti-
cation, taste, and wit from Kennedy. Someone observed that
going from Kennedy to Johnson was like doing a slow dissolve
from Noel Coward to the Dukes of Hazzard. Johnson had no
taste for irony. He rarely listened to other people. His forte
was the self-delivered monologue. He was a long-winded man,
a Potomac Babbit, with few original ideas and little tolerance
for humor at his expense.

Merriman Smith, the late dean of White House correspondents, who wrote for United Press International and who
grew close to LBJ, told me that Johnson was irritated by the
anti-LBJ gibes that regularly appeared on "That Was the
Week That Was," the topical humor show I helped to create
shortly before Johnson inherited the Oval Office. As Campaign 1964 began, the show's writers looked on candidate
Barry Goldwater with skepticism, but they could see Johnson's
deficiencies as well, and their doubts manifested themselves in
cutting humor. For one thing, Johnson's policies were all over
the political spectrum. He assumed a dizzying variety of ideological positions in attempting to lasso members of the right,
left, and center. Said David Frost: "President Johnson has remolded the Democratic Party into the fresh, invigorated, cautious, conservative, liberal, radical force it is today." Johnson
was doubtless not amused.

Another target of the humorists was LBJ's reputation as
a wheeler-dealer. Lyndon favored the ten-gallon hats of his
Texas boyhood, which led TW3 to report: "This week department stores all over America started selling the LBJ ten-gallon

hat. And soon they will be marketing the LBJ Sweater. You get such a warm, comfortable feeling as they pull the wool over your eyes."

Compared to the Ivy League education of the Washington elitists and intellectuals he resented, Johnson had a second-rate education and hadn't read a book in years. He was thus sensitive to humor that mocked his cerebral gifts. Mort Sahl did not endear himself to Johnson when he remarked to one of his overflow campus audiences, "The Democratic party's ad agency also handles the Avis Rent-a-Car account. And they just came up with a new slogan for Johnson. 'He's second best but he tries harder.'"

Johnson's ability to turn the presidency to his own financial gain provoked this cutting remark from one White House correspondent: "I hear they're looking for an alternate route for a channel to replace the Panama Canal. So far, the most promising route goes through downtown Austin."

Jules Feiffer, who shares with Garry Trudeau the mantle of the wittiest cartoonist on the political scene, heaped scorn on Johnson. Said Feiffer in his retrospective of the Ike-to-Reagan years, *Jules Feiffer's America*: "LBJ was not only the first man, he had turned into the first bully, the first thief, the first credibility gap, the first war criminal, the first crack in the system, the first reason to riot in the streets, the first terrorist to the American dream." Feiffer addressed himself to Johnson's conceit, so often expressed during the 1964 campaign, as when he proclaimed that he wanted to be "the President of all the people." Liz Carpenter, who used to write jokes for LBJ's speeches, recalled the genesis of the All-the-People phrase. A roiling crowd in New Orleans had greeted the Johnson campaign train. There were tens of thousands of blacks and whites, "all mixed together," all chanting "We want Lyndon!" Said LBJ, caught up in the frenzy of the moment: "When I walked into the White House that night [after Kennedy's death] to take over the awesome responsibility that was mine, I said—as long as I am President, I am going to be President of all the people." Jules Feiffer, in a pointed series of panels, showed a group of voters looking skyward in awe at LBJ, as he hovers angelically above them.

VOTERS. Oh, what do you see, Mr. President-of-all-the-People?

LBJ. I see a land where love reigns. I see great farms and giant cities. I see men at work, children at play, women at peace.

VOTERS. O, what else do you see, Mr. President-of-all-the-People?

LBJ. I see an end of divisions and controversies. I see small men growing large and closed minds opening wide . . .

VOTERS. O, tell us more Mr. President-of-all-the-People.

LBJ. I see blacks and whites in final harmony. Rich and poor, old and young, big and little, small and large . . .

VOTERS. O, is there nothing more that you see, Mr. President-of-all-the-People?

LBJ. I see a mandate for happiness. I see the determined faces of millions—fat and skinny, tall and short, bold and shy— crying as one, "Onward to the Great Society!"

VOTERS. And how will all these things come about, Mr. President-of-all-the-People?

LBJ. I shall wheel and deal.

The contrast between Johnson's idealistic rhetoric and his manipulative techniques and vindictive rages led even his loyalists to look askance at this president-of-all-the-people. On TV he resembled, said one former Senate colleague, "a cross between Machiavelli and a riverboat gambler."

When David Frost cracked about Johnson's accomplishments in remolding the Democratic party into a variety of contradictory things, he was reflecting a fact that had long been perceived in Washington circles. As *Newsweek* pointed out, "Political parties, like house pets, have a way of coming to resemble their masters." It was certainly true that the Democratic party had been remolded in the image of Lyndon Johnson. And Lyndon Johnson was all things to all people. As the 1964 campaign began, LBJ had replicated the broadly based, widely supported party that Franklin Roosevelt had assembled thirty years before. It was a gargantuan creation, and it took a larger-than-life man to create it. It also took a man who was larger than life to manage its deterioration in four short years.

Johnson's ambitions for America and his own grand ego generated scathing humor. At a San Francisco cabaret, the actor portraying LBJ holds aloft a new book and drawls, "It's a new book all about me. It's called *LBJ: The Greatest President*. It's a fantasy." A biting, satirical play opened off-Broadway in New York and captured the public's attention. It was called *MacBird*, a Johnsonian parody of the Shakespearian tragedy, *Macbeth*. The show played to capacity houses and sold well in paperback. The Second City paid dubious tribute to Johnson's manipulations with a sketch in which LBJ is consulting with an aide:

LBJ. Goldwater's charges about my conflict of interest are getting embarrassing.

AIDE. What do you plan to do, sir?

LBJ. Well, first I'll put the White House in Lady Bird's name. . . .

Johnson's humble beginnings in the hill country of Texas sparked a gag in an early edition of a photo-cartoon book called *News Reals*. In it, Lyndon is hosting a barbecue, spreading goodwill among his guests, as the spare ribs simmer. Says Johnson: "This party on the White House lawn was a good idea. Help yourself to the food, everybody. It's out beyond the oil rig."

LBJ brought such a distinctive style to the White House, with his bullying, his manipulation, his Lincolnesque size, and his P. T. Barnum hokum, that TW3 created an entertaining fiction. Johnson, we said, had remodeled the White House from top to bottom. Said the narrator:

Johnsons's new White House bears little resemblance to the old. Gone is the imposing formality, the august dignity. In its place we have a real folksy, down-to-earth residence in the cozy Ranch House style.

The lawns surrounding the White House have been relandscaped in the picturesque Southwest mood, with live cattle grazing among the oil derricks.

Upon entering the front door of the Executive Mansion, visitors are asked to wipe their feet on the William E. Miller Memorial Welcome Mat [Miller was Goldwater's running mate]; coats are hung in the adjacent closet, which has just been enlarged to make room for various political skeletons.

Entering the Main Gallery, we see paintings depicting great moments in American history: "Lyndon Crossing the Rio Grande," and "Lyndon Signing the Declaration of Independence."

As we enter the President's office, we see the Chief Executive's desk, with its white telephone, red telephone, "hot line" telephone, intercom and—here's something new—a switch for turning on and off the United States of America.

The White House swimming pool, incidentally, is being used to store 14,000 gallons of barbecue sauce left over from the LBJ campaign picnics.

The new Game Room on the second floor . . . includes stuffed heads of Clare Boothe Luce, Strom Thurmond, and William F. Buckley.

The remodeled White House has great popular appeal; a number of families have expressed a desire to move in at any time— the Goldwaters, the Nixons, the Romneys, the Scrantons, and many others.

Sex and scandal raise eyebrows in politics, as Gary Hart discovered to his grief. Often the sexual dalliances of our past presidents remain well hidden with the help of the Secret Service and compliant journalists during the president's lifetime, but leap into print a few years after his demise. Roosevelt's mistress, Eisenhower's driver, and Kennedy's bedroom prodigies are never mentioned in their election campaigns. (Or at least that was the rule B. H., before Hart.) But the sexual proclivities of Johnson's chief protégé were an active element of the 1964 campaign.

Bobby Baker was LBJ's young man in the U.S. Senate. So great was his influence in the social and sexual life of some of the members of that distinguished club that many called Bobby Baker "the 101st Senator." Baker was extremely well connected with a tawdry minority of senators who liked their liquor straight and their women bent. (Merriman Smith once told me: "Summers are hot in Washington, so senators' wives go to Europe and the senators are left to enjoy their secretaries.") Bobby Baker helped this natural process. He was part owner of twenty-two corporations, a vending machine company, and a Washington establishment called the Carousel Motel. Senators knew that Bobby could always be depended on to provide a girl for the night, and should things go badly, an equitable solution. Johnson embraced Bobby Baker, perhaps seeing traces of his own ambitious youth. The records revealed that Bobby Baker had sent his patron an expensive gift—a Magnavox stereo set. When this gamy narrative was leaked to the press, it provoked an eruption of blue humor.

Phyllis Newman reported how often members of the U.S. Senate and their female aides had accepted Bobby Baker's hospitality at the Carousel Motel. Recalling the stereo gift to the Johnsons, Phyllis said, "The Carousel Motel is a place where senators can enjoy low fidelity with high frequency." *Newsweek* picked up the line, and Americans were laughing at it for quite a while.

The Johnson Family tried to keep Bobby Baker at arm's length throughout the campaign. In *News Reals*, Lady Bird Johnson is shown accepting a handsomely framed painting. Says the First Lady: "Oh my, it's another lovely gift from Bobby Baker. I'd better hang it in a nice place. . . . Under the rug."

Bobby Baker was Lyndon's Watergate and Iranscam, though on a lesser scale. Baker was the center of a scandal that had about it the aroma of congressional corruption and sexual promiscuity—journalistically speaking, an unbeatable combination. The scandal spawned humor that showed Johnson without his imperial clothes. As LBJ tried to put maximum distance between himself and his tainted protégé, Alan Alda said: "Clearly, Mr. Johnson is the President of *all* the people—the butcher, the baker, the candlestick maker. Oh, sorry! . . . The butcher, the candlestick maker. . . ." Said David Frost: "According to a Washington rumor, Bobby Baker will receive a telegram from President Johnson on New Year's Eve reading: 'MAY OLD ACQUAINTANCE BE FORGOT.'" Said Elliot Reid: "They still haven't pinned anything on Bobby Baker. The chief witness against him is too busy to testify. He's running the country." When Senator Thomas Dodd issued a report decrying all the sex and violence on television, the *Harvard Lampoon* did a satiric report on sex and violence in the U.S. Senate:

And now for a review of the top shows of recent Senate seasons. THE BOBBY BAKER REVIEW or POTOMAC PLACE . . . sponsored by Johnson & Johnson, it features ex–Senate employee Robert G. Baker, with . . . a supporting cast of lobbyists in the Senate and Senators in the lobby. Your critic found this show tended to glorify sex and corruption. Furthermore, the evildoers were never punished. They were re-elected.

During the summer months of 1964, when TW3 did its annual predictions of things to come and concluded that it would be off the air, the staff's summary included the following prophecies:

July 26th. Bobby Baker makes a big attempt to stop Goldwater. He offers him a stereo set.

July 27th. Goldwater refuses to accept the stereo set. Nixon says, "I'll take it."

Bobby Baker had started as a lowly Senate page, and with the guidance and friendship of Lyndon Johnson, his assets had grown to a cool two million dollars; he was the Democratic party's Horatio Alger. Nancy Ames, the voluptuous blonde TW3 girl, sang a parody of "When I Was a Boy," from Gilbert & Sullivan's *H.M.S. Pinafore,* that needled Baker and his boss. The lyrics ran in part:

> When I was a lad at an early age
> I had a position as a Senate page.
> I ran so fast on the Senate floors
> I attracted the attention of the Senators.
> I ran so fast and I did so well
> That now I am the owner of the Carousel . . .
> I schemed by night and I worked by day
> And I aimed to ingratiate Lyndon J.
> I would always please and never annoy
> And the eyes of Texas were upon me, boy . . .
> Now with what I know, if I care to try,
> I could blow the U.S. Senate seventeen miles high.

With his firsthand knowledge of the workings of the Congress, President Johnson had been able to force through more progressive legislation—Civil Rights and Medicare, for example—than his charismatic predecessor had dreamed of. Johnson's demands on the Congress brought the often lethargic legislators their share of ridicule. Said Henry Morgan: "Mr. Johnson has called on Congress to put in a six-day workweek until his 'must' legislation is passed. A lot of the congressmen resent being asked to work the extra six days."

Though Johnson's poverty program was laudable and compassionate, it too attracted its share of gibes. Said one Washington wise guy: "Next year President Johnson will announce his War on Poverty has been won, and turn his attention to a War on the Middle Class." When deep cuts in procurement by the Department of Defense idled 80,000 workers, reporters called it "Johnson's Poverty on War Campaign." And when Nelson Rockefeller sought the 1964 nomination, one wit suggested that Rockefeller could never comprehend the War on Poverty. "He's never seen the enemy." A monologist in a cabaret on Capitol Hill kidded Johnson's poverty program with a satiric song called "Poverty Pockets." Said the performer:

The President asked me to write this song about the pockets of poverty. I'm not a singer, of course. You'll have to picture this as it will be sung by Sargent Shriver. He's going to be standing on this big hill looking down on this poverty pocket where all these people are standing around starving. He'll look up and sing . . . [in rock tempo]

I'm gonna roll it
I'm gonna rock it
I'm gonna clear up each poverty pocket.
I'm gonna move on this program
And move on it fast
At least until the November
Election is past
And if there is no significant change
Won't you give it a chance?
'Cause Lyndon's War on Poverty's
Doin' all right at the ranch.

It must have been particularly galling to LBJ that despite his prodigious achievements in the interests of social justice, he was looked on with such distrust by the press and the satiric community. To reporters it was dangerous to trust anything he said. When Johnson mounted the stump on the campaign trail in 1964, surrounded by "his people," his most comfortable posture was that of the country preacher, brimming over with gospel admonitions and anecdotes about men of the cloth in the Texas hill country.

One of Johnson's favorite preacher stories concerned a clergyman who drops his sermon notes while heading for church, and before he can retrieve them his hound has chewed them to bits. In apologizing to his congregation, the preacher says, "I am very sorry. Today I have no sermon. I will have to speak as the Lord directs. But I will try to do better tomorrow." Another preacher story that embellished LBJ's 1964 campaign concerned a minister who is enraged to see a man sleeping in the front row of his congregation:

So he whispered to the congregation [said Lyndon], "All those who want to go to the Kingdom of Heaven stand up." They all got to their feet except the man sleeping in the front row.

Then the preacher shouted, "ALL THOSE WHO WANT TO WALK WITH THE DEVIL, STAND UP!" The sleeper came awake with a start and jumped to his feet. He saw the preacher standing tall and angry in the pulpit, and he said, "Well, preacher, I don't know what it is we're votin' on, but it looks like you and I are the only ones for it."

Johnson's corn-fed brand of idealism contrasted strangely with the horny-handed operator who knew that force was the ultimate persuader. Johnson, after all, was the one who didn't trust a man unless "I've got his pecker in my pocket." This cross of the softhearted and the hard-boiled made for an irreconcilable mix. As the campaign unfolded, some cynical bystanders cracked that the difference between Johnson and Goldwater was that "Goldwater preaches what Johnson practices." One journalist predicted that the Arizonan would lose because "he's more honest and less clever." But there is a limit to how far cleverness can take you. Lyndon was impeded by his impatience with anything short of genuflection from the Congress and the press. When he attended his first caucus on Capitol Hill as president and did not receive the degree of deference he thought appropriate, he smirked to an aide, "Now I know the difference between a caucus and a cactus. With a cactus the pricks are on the *outside*."

Despite the alarm generated by some of Barry Goldwater's irresponsible campaign statements and fanned by Johnson's exaggerations, LBJ was finding his own critics unwilling to be seduced by his preacher anecdotes and windy homilies. For some, the LBJ sweet talk could decay the teeth at twenty paces. The press was dismayed at his inability to accept even the mildest reproach and appalled at his attempts to suppress independent reporting. When the *Wall Street Journal* ran a story asserting that the public was losing some of its fondness for Lyndon, the president sneered, "I think everyone knows how the *Wall Street Journal* reflects the views of the man on the street—*Wall Street.* Somebody told me that the writer of that article was free-lancing for *True Romances.*" When he learned that a critical reporter for a New York daily had arrived in Texas, Johnson cracked, "the price of whores is going up in Austin." And when he heard that another unfriendly newsman had been seen in town, Johnson gibed, "See him! I can *smell* him."

In Theodore White's observant report on the election campaign, *The Making of the President 1964*, he points out: "When Johnson thought of America, he thought of it either in primitive terms of Fourth of July patriotism or else as groups of people, forces, leaders, lobbies, pressures . . . he was ill at ease with the broad purposes and meaning of civilization." This was, as I. F. Stone wrote, "the portrait of an intellectually quite limited man. It raises the question of whether the kind of man most likely to become President is really best qualified for the job."

Johnson's own family could recognize his character flaws better than anyone. They had been exposed to them longer. Said daughter Luci: "Daddy, speaking as an outsider, what do you think of the human race?" When it was revealed that Luci Baines Johnson was taking instructions in the Roman Catholic faith because a boy whose school pin she wore was a Catholic, one sardonic reporter said: "Considering Johnson's skill at drawing support from all the divergent groups of our society, it's been rumored that his daughter Lynda Bird is dating a rabbinical student, and Mrs. Johnson is reading up on Zen Buddhism." Johnson was not so much a conversationalist as a monologist. When he was quieted for a time by surgery to remove a throat polyp, his wife said of his imposed silence, "We're going to have to make the most of it."

Lady Bird's plan to beautify America drew its share of mockery. Said one stand-up comic: "Lady Bird Johnson has asked the public for suggestions on ways to beautify America. A flood of mail came in. One of the first letters read: 'Stop hanging your stockings on the shower rod. Lyndon.'" Both of Lyndon's daughters were attractive young women who did not warrant the witticism of one Hollywood wag, who said, "President Johnson has issued the first Executive Order in his plan to beautify America. He has forbidden his daughters to drive in a convertible." Said Larry Blyden: "President Johnson has issued a statement protesting that America's countryside is begin vulgarized by billboards. He issued an order banning highway signs, and the order will be posted on a sign every one hundred yards." On TW3, Nancy Ames sang a parodic hymn to Lady Bird to the tune of "The Yellow Rose of Texas":

She's the Lady Bird of Texas
With initials L. B. J.
And she named her charming daughters
In the same delightful way.
There is L. B. this and L. B. that
And isn't it absurd?
When dear old Lyndon's angry
Why they call him Thunderbird. . . .

She's the Lady Bird of Texas
And she gives a Texas yell.
In the battle of the sexes
She comes out mighty well.
You could never ever fool 'er,
It's a certain law of life
That behind each nation's ruler
Is a most astonished wife.

It was ironic that the often egomaniacal president who would droop his head in sleep when the conversation passed to someone else, would have as his favorite motto: "You ain't learnin' nothing when you're talkin'." Perhaps it was an aphorism he urged on others.

As he campaigned across the country in what would ultimately produce one of the most overwhelming electoral mandates of the century, Johnson gave a bravura performance before massive crowds that were often as frenzied as those that greeted Jack Kennedy in 1960. But if LBJ displayed a manipulative charm of sorts, the ingredient that seemed to be missing was magnanimity. Some protested that Johnson was not a very nice person. He inflicted a gratuitous cruelty on those closest to him—the loyal aides who were serving him. Some of the humor that characterized the 1964 campaign focused on LBJ as a very tough boss. A New York cabaret presented a skit in which Johnson is meeting with a member of his subcabinet, Mennen "Soapy" Williams:

LBJ. Soapy, I've figured out a way to effect a real economy in your department.

SOAPY. What's that, sir?

LBJ. You're fired.

When Johnson called an aide early one morning and learned that he was in the shower, the president pointedly remained on the phone till the flustered fellow was out of the shower, then asked him sarcastically, "Are you all dry? I wouldn't want you to catch cold." When Johnson noticed that an assistant press secretary's desk was a sea of paper, he rasped, "I hope yore mind isn't as messed up as yore desk!" The aide promptly cleared the mess, and the next day Johnson noticed the desk's immaculate condition. Snapped the president: "I sure hope yore mind isn't as empty as yore desk." There was latent savagery to Johnson that made some congressmen fear to oppose him. Quipped Dick Shawn: "President Johnson used the money he saved by budgetary cuts to hold an enormous barbecue to which he invited all the Congressmen who are supporting him. The Congressmen who are *opposing* him were already *at* the barbecue."

Even when Johnson was being avuncular and anecdotal, his humor could carry a threat. On one occasion, he was hectoring his agency heads to reduce their departmental budgets in an attempt to reduce the deficit. Johnson told a story of a railroad that is being built right by the front door of a Texas youth. The boy has applied for a job on the line, and the foreman poses a question to test his intelligence. If the boy can answer it, he will have a job. "Suppose," says the foreman, "you're standing by the switch, you look to the east and you see a locomotive heading west at 60 miles an hour. Then you look to the west and you see another locomotive on the same track heading east at 60 miles an hour. What do you do?" The boy ponders a moment and then says, "I run into the house and get my brother." "Why on earth would you get your brother?" asks the foreman. "Because he's never *seen* a train wreck," says the boy. The anecdote held a cautionary caveat: cut your budget or you are going to be in one hell of a train wreck!

The contrast between Johnson's public warmth and private chilliness inevitably brings to mind the word "hypocrisy." Johnson certainly displayed this quality to a disturbing extent in the most controversial TV commercial ever produced in a presidential campaign. The thirty-second spot was aimed at Barry Goldwater and his verbal excesses. When Campaign 1964 began, Goldwater tried to backpedal his way to respectability. The Johnson commercial sought to remind voters of the irresponsible things Goldwater had said in the past: that the eastern seaboard should be chopped off, that Social Security should be eliminated, that we should lob a nuclear bomb into the Kremlin. The controversial TV spot addressed the latter suggestion. It showed a little girl in a sylvan setting, plucking petals from a daisy. As she counts the petals from one to ten, a more menacing voice is counting downward from ten to one—a nuclear countdown. When the deeper voice reaches zero, we see a nuclear explosion destroy our planet. The commercial ran only once but it triggered a massive reaction, mainly among Republicans injured by the fallout. They claimed it was hitting below the belt. An apparently exercised President Johnson promptly phoned Bill Moyers who had created the ad. Said Moyers in recollection:

> Johnson called me . . . And said he'd been swamped with calls . . . I could tell the moment I answered the phone that he was having a wonderful time putting on an act. He said, "What in the hell do you mean putting on that ad? I've been swamped with calls and the Goldwater people are calling it a low blow."

Johnson summoned Moyers to his office and demanded an explanation. Moyers explained that they were just reminding people that they had better put an experienced hand at the nuclear button. Besides, added Moyers, the commercial was only to be run that single time. As Moyers headed for the door, Johnson stopped him. "Bill! Bill! Just a minute. Are you sure we ought to run it just *once*?"

Said David Frost of the TV commercial flap: "The Republicans protested against the campaign commercial that showed the little girl counting the petals on the daisy." When she reached ten, declared Frost, a nuclear explosion blew up the world. "So far," said Frost dryly, "the commercial has not won a single vote for Mr. Johnson, but it has been responsible for a drastic reduction in the number of little girls picking daisies."

Some of the humor at Johnson's expense during that tumultuous campaign year flowered from the Bugs Bunny grin of Robert Kennedy, and I must confess I played a small part in it. When John F. Kennedy sat in the Oval Office, I had met with him to propose a group of books called "The New Frontier Series." Each book would deal with a different subject of what JFK called "the unfinished business of our society," and the respective editors of the books were to be the relevant members of the Kennedy cabinet. The book on Civil Rights, edited by Attorney General Robert Kennedy, was spearheading the administration's drive for civil rights—thus, my meeting with Bobby in his cavernous justice department office. Four years later, in 1964, there was much media speculation about the possibility of Bobby Kennedy as Lyndon Johnson's running mate in the presidential contest. Bobby was ambivalent. He recalled my work on "That Was the Week That Was" and my *Who's in Charge Here?* books whose irreverence his brother had enjoyed. Bobby called to ask if I had any ideas how he might respond when reporters asked him about the chance of his running with Johnson. Given the bad blood between the two, it seemed an unlikely marriage; still, Bobby did not yet want to close the door. Better to turn the matter aside with humor. I suggested two replies, which Bobby employed:

Q. How do you feel about a Johnson-Kennedy ticket?
A. I'd be willing, but I'm not sure that Mr. Johnson would accept the vice presidency.

Q. Do you think that a Johnson-Kennedy ticket is feasible?
A. I've said that a coalition government is possible in Saigon, but not in Washington.

The acrimony between LBJ and RFK had been of long standing, dating back to Bobby's attempts to persuade his brother against selecting Lyndon as his running mate in 1960. In *The Kennedy Legacy*, Ted Sorensen, the brilliant aide and speech writer who brought the glory of words to the Kennedy years, tries to explain the antagonism that sprang up between Bobby and Lyndon. Sorensen attributes it to Johnson's sense of insecurity. "Johnson had a feeling that the Kennedys were against him," writes Sorensen, "that the Kennedys were condescending to him. He wanted to emulate their graceful wit and intellectual elegance . . . but he seemed at the same time to resent the Kennedys' Eastern polish."

All through the election year of 1964, America's humorists focused on Bobby Kennedy. Predicted one press corps wag: "Bobby Kennedy is going to announce that he'll soon have another mouth to feed. I hear Arthur Schlesinger is joining his staff." When a tenth child was born to Bobby and Ethel, UPI took cognizance of the Kennedy dynasty and printed a mock story that read: "The 49th President of the United States was born yesterday to Robert and Ethel Kennedy—an eight-pound son. The baby's father will be the 38th President of the United States, the baby's brothers, the 43rd, 44th, 45th, 46th, 47th and 48th Presidents of the United States." When former presidents Eisenhower and Truman announced they had finally found a point on which they could agree—they both supported birth control—a capital wag said, "I hear Bobby Kennedy feels he's being smeared."

The perennial showman, LBJ feared that the convention that announced his nomination would be a terrible bore, and he tried to add a modicum of excitement by building suspense into the identity of his running mate. This guessing game produced its share of fun. Given the enormous popular appeal of Bobby Kennedy, there were some who anticipated a Johnson-Kennedy ticket. Said Henry Morgan: "The big question in Washington is 'Will Bobby be asked to run for Vice President?' Insiders point out that since Lyndon became President, he and Bobby have not been as close as one would expect. It seems now that the only conspicuous Democrat definitely out of the running *is* Bobby. There has been no comment on this from Mr. Baker himself."

"That Was the Week That Was" offered a summary of Johnson's possible running mates in the form of a baseball report, with actor David Doyle playing the hyperactive sportscaster:

Hello there, politics fans. This is Buzzy Krankheit reporting once again on the national picture. Tonight lets recap the Democratic League. The big question is, which hurlers will Manager Johnson pick from his bullpen to face the Republicans in the all-important series in November. He may go with his Number One mound ace, Bobby "Fireball" Kennedy . . . Another possible choice for Johnson is the cagey veteran twirler Adlai "Pops" Stevenson, who has been improving his control working in the International League [at the U.N.]. You'll recall Stevenson lost two World Series by pitching over the heads of the American people. And as another possible starter don't count out Lefty Hubey Humphrey. . . ." [The lefty ultimately got the nod.]

As the possible candidates twisted slowly in the wind and Lyndon Johnson enjoyed the attention he was generating among the possible nominees, TW3 offered a sketch called "Choosing a Vice President," in which Henry Morgan and Elliot Read played two Democratic officials weighing the important decision:

REID. Let's see, Johnson is a Southerner so our V.P. should be from the North.

MORGAN. Right. And Johnson has a conservative image, so he'll have to run with a liberal.

REID. Check, and Johnson's known to be a religious man, so we'll need an atheist.

MORGAN. Johnson's for foreign aid so we need an isolationist.

REID. He's married—we need a bachelor.

MORGAN. He's a temperate man, so we need a drunk.

REID. Good. Let's add it up. What does that give us?

MORGAN. Well, what we need for Vice President is a Northern liberal isolationist who's an unmarried, atheistic alcoholic.

[There is a moment of thought.]

REID. Right. Now which one?

[Blackout]

During the 1964 campaign, Lyndon Johnson favored the humor of tall Texas tales. It was therefore most fitting that the election returns, when they came pouring in, resembled nothing so much as a tall tale of Bunyonesque proportions. Was it not a tall Texas tale that a southerner would walk off with 97 percent of the black vote? Or that a Protestant candidate would gather more Catholic votes than the Catholic president who preceded him? Perhaps the tallest tale of all was still to come—that three years later, this incredible man, who rolled up the biggest plurality in presidential history, would "abdicate" his office and retire to his Texas ranch to lick his wounds and write his memoirs.

Chapter 17
Campaign 1964
Mister Malaprop

Time magazine has just named Barry Goldwater Man
of the Year. 1682.
— GOODMAN ACE

A huge plurality of American voters felt that Barry
Goldwater would not make the ideal president. But the small
army of humorists, satirists, and journalistic wits who make
their living from making light of national elections found him
a wonderful source of amusement. Presidents have been chosen for various irrelevant reasons—their presidential look
(Warren Harding), their successes in war (Dwight Eisenhower), their telegenic appeal (Ronald Reagan)—but to select a
chief executive because he makes a good target for lampoonery would be a trifle frivolous. Thus, though Barry Goldwater generated some of the most searching humor in the history
of American politics, he generated few votes.

The Arizonan's words, in or out of context, were so bizarre that they lent themselves to spoofery in all the media of
the humorist—print, cartoon, sketch, blackout, song, and anecdote. And if liberals, Democrats, blacks, and moderates of
his own party did not find Goldwater very funny—he more often produced grimaces and shrugs—he did produce a good
deal of humor during his doomed campaign for the presidency.

Goldwater said he offered "a choice, not an echo," and as he stood at the podium of the GOP convention in San Francisco, his hands aloft in the traditional pose of triumph, his handsome face ruddy with the waves of cheers washing over him, Goldwater had effectively split the rock of the Republican party.

The bellicosity of the ultraconservative Goldwater was so fearsome and his pugnacity in foreign affairs so pronounced that reporters began chanting a nuclear countdown: "Ten, nine, eight, seven, six——." When Goldwater declared his controversial line, "I would remind you that extremism in the defense of freedom is no vice," one correspondent cracked incredulously, "Good Lord! He's going to run as Barry Goldwater!" The candidate's shoot-from-the-hip belligerence was so unsettling that one aide pleaded with the press: "Don't quote what he says—quote what he means."

As Goldwater started tremors running through the nation with his extremist views, moderate members of the Republican party became a source and a subject of his gallows humor. The moderates who had been trampled by Goldwater and his zealous supporters on the road to the 1964 convention included New York governor Nelson Rockefeller, Pennsylvania governor William Scranton, Senator Margaret Chase Smith, Ambassador Henry Cabot Lodge, Governor George Romney, and former Vice President Richard Nixon. The moderates tried to exercise good breeding as Goldwater's hoards crumbled them underfoot. On TW3 we simulated a tennis match between the moderate Governor Scranton, who was loathe to enter the fray, and the combative Goldwater. David Frost did the play-by-play from courtside as follows:

Good afternoon. Sixth game, second set, Mr. Goldwater leading five games to love, due mainly to the fact that during the entire set Mr. Scranton remained in the grandstand.

In the last game, Mr. Goldwater missed the first service but explained he is an Episcopalian. Ah, they're ready to begin. Mr. Goldwater is in the far court, all in white including his stand on civil rights. A great favorite in the Wightman Cup. Mr. Goldwater's serve . . .

Mr. Scranton takes it on his backhand. What's this? Someone has grabbed Mr. Scranton's racket and won't let him start. Now they're showing Mr. Eisenhower from the court. Fifteen love. Mr. Goldwater serving . . .

It's an ace! A palpable ace! Thirty love. Mr. Scranton is not doing too well. This racket doesn't seem to suit him. He's losing his grip and he's busted a gut. Here comes Mr. Goldwater's cannonball service again. . . . Another ace! And now Mr. Scranton is employing a strategy that Mr. Nixon uses whenever he's behind. He's starting to cry.

Mr. Goldwater serves . . . Scranton returns . . . Rockefeller returns . . . Romney returns . . . Nixon returns . . . Margaret Chase Smith returns . . . and now that's incredible—Lodge returns. [He chose to remain in Vietnam throughout the convention.] But there's no doubt that the biggest returns this year will *still* be Lyndon Johnson's. Good afternoon.

All the moderate Republicans were reluctant to oppose Goldwater explicitly, not wanting to antagonize his vocal backers on the far right. Even former president Eisenhower held his tongue. Said one Washington newsman of Ike, who was famed for his strangled syntax: "Eisenhower denied that his anti-Goldwater statement was an anti-Goldwater statement. But he didn't say it was a *pro*-Goldwater statement either. One thing was clear. It was obviously an Eisenhower statement."

It required no special gifts of prophecy to foresee a Goldwater debacle. Johnson had generated a broad base of support by driving Kennedy's New Frontier legislation through Congress, and Goldwater provoked trepidation with both his foreign and domestic policies. It was a case of double casino for LBJ—the affluent applauded the strength of the economy and the needy welcomed Johnson's War on Poverty. Cracked one editorialist: "We can't recall a time when a President had prosperity and poverty going for him at the same time!" Polls foreshadowed an overwhelming triumph for Johnson in November. The possibility of a Goldwater victory seemed remote. Said the *Seattle Post-Intelligencer*: "It may be that Barry Goldwater will be elected. It may also be that Chase

Manhattan will go broke . . . and that Mickey Spillane will win the Nobel Prize for literature." Chase Manhattan continued strong, and Mickey Spillane won nothing but a contract from Miller Lite and the company of John Madden.

Once the Goldwater Caper passed into history, GOP moderates looked ahead to the next election, trying to put the electoral calamity behind them. Said one Washington wit: "It has been revealed that moderate Republicans have formed an organization called The Committee of Sixty-Eight, to study ways to win the next election. It is still unclear whether The Committee of Sixty-Eight is named for the year of the next election or the number of Republicans who could be found."

The demolished moderates displayed little sympathy for their fallen candidate. Both Governor Rockefeller and Ambassador Lodge, who did little to help Goldwater during the campaign, even refused to say which presidential candidate they had voted for, on the grounds that every citizen is entitled to keep his vote a secret. Said Steve Allen: "Goldwater supporters are saying that they have nothing against the secret ballot, but this the first time they've heard of a secret campaign."

The moderates could see catastrophe coming from the day they left town after their convention. Said one GOP politician: "I'm going to have to spend the rest of the campaign explaining what Goldwater means every time he opens his mouth." Gibed another: "He's a cross between the Lone Ranger and Mr. Malaprop." This depressed moderate suggested that Goldwater suffered from foot-in-mouth disease. Observing the narrow ideological appeal of their candidate, one GOP pollster joked, "If this were China, we'd call it The Year of the Underdog." Bumper stickers sprouted that read: JOHNSON FOR PRESIDENT, GOLDWATER FOR HALLOWEEN. America's newspaper publishers have traditionally supported GOP presidential candidates, but Goldwater seemed unsupportable. Wrote *Editor and Publisher*, the weekly journal of the newspaper industry: "What [Senator Goldwater] must bear in mind when he open his mouth is that clarity begins at home."

Goldwater was no fanatic, but fanatics flew to him like filings to a magnet, extolling and embracing him. The most strident of these were members of the John Birch Society, an ultraconservative group whose views may be judged by their perception of Dwight Eisenhower as a tool of communism. The Birch Society sorely tested the capacity for humor of 1964's satirists, but they did not altogether fail. Said Henry Morgan of the society's obsession with communism: "The financial statement of the John Birch Society shows that for the fourth consecutive year, they have ended up losing money. They can't seem to stay out of the red." Said one Potomac observer: "I think the reason the John Birch Society doesn't like Communism is they feel it smacks of Socialism." And one journalist said, "Robert Welch [founder of the society] says the biggest Communist Front in America is the Communist Party. He says a Communist is just a Communist in disguise."

In my 1964 edition of *Who's In Charge Here?* I pictured a ruminative Barry Goldwater saying, "Last night I had a dream that was like a prophecy. I saw myself at the helm of the Ship of State . . . Or was it a Birch canoe?" In 1964 a bevy of groups was springing up in support of Goldwater's candidacy. They employed high-sounding, patriotic names. In my election year book, I showed Goldwater responding to a reporter who has asked what kind of organizations support him. "Well," says the candidate, "take the Christian Minuteman Crusade for Brotherhood and Americanism . . . They're a hate group." In still another photo, the Arizonan is displaying indignation as he studies a newspaper. "I wish the *New York Times* would at least get my *name* straight," he complains. "It's Goldwater. Not Backwater."

Some liberal college students regarded Goldwater as an amiable buffoon, while others took him as a danger to their survival. Goldwater's statements about nuclear weapons (for example, "I'd like to lob an A-bomb into the men's room at the Kremlin") invited ridicule or terror. California collegians greeted the candidate with signs replicating a new black comedy film: DR. STRANGELOVE, or HOW HE BECAME A CONSERVATIVE AND LEARNED TO LOVE THE BOMB.

Goldwater's domination of the GOP convention provoked the startled question, Are there enough zealots in America to put this man in the White House? Common sense said no, the polls said no, Lyndon Johnson said no, but the ferocity of his supporters gave one some doubt. After all, the people who insisted he could never be elected were the same ones who had said he could never get the nomination. But how could one take him seriously? Many did not. They laughed at his assaults on big government and his wish to dismantle the whole damn business. In a cabaret skit, the actor playing Goldwater angrily declares, "This is just one more case of the federal government intruding in an area that should be left to individual initiative." And a reporter replies, "But Senator, the government has *always* run the navy." Goldwater's affection for the simplicities of an earlier age led one humorist to crack, "*Time* magazine has just named Barry Goldwater Man of the Year. 1682." Said another: "You know his favorite TV show, don't you? 'That Was the Century That Was.'" Jonas Salk had recently discovered his famous vaccine, and since Goldwater preached the merits of individual initiative, one wag remarked, "I understand Goldwater opposes the use of the Salk Vaccine. He feels a man should have the right to decide for himself whether he wants polio or not." The candidate's apparent unconcern for the poor and his generally retrogressive attitude toward social issues, led one comic to say: "For any of you who want Mr. Goldwater's views on social welfare, he'll be speaking on television tonight, from 11:00 P.M. to 10:45."

The Goldwater family owned Phoenix's largest department store, and the senator was a strong advocate of the entrepreneurial spirit. Perhaps this led him to question the motivation of the needy. Consequently, Goldwater called for an investigation of the poor. He said that such an inquiry might reveal that their indigence was the result of "low intelligence and low ambition." This led Goodman Ace to say: "I guess Mr. Goldwater figures why should the lazy loafers be supported by people like him who have had the ambition and intelligence to inherit a department store."

The family's retailing establishment came under the comic scrutiny of a Los Angeles improvisational group. Ridiculing Goldwater's position on various social issues, the performer portraying the candidate snapped, "The government should be run like we run Goldwater's Department Store. If there's something you need and we don't have it—you're a Socialist."

Goldwater had proposed giving battlefield commanders in Vietnam the authority to employ nuclear weapons. Wrote TRB in the *New Republic,* "Can you take seriously a man . . . who would delegate the incinerating nuclear weapon to bomb-rattling generals?" When former general Eisenhower gave Goldwater his grudging support, saying that he could live with a Goldwater administration, one satirist gibed: "Maybe Mr. Eisenhower could live with a Goldwater Administration. I guess he'd have as good a chance as anyone else." "With that kind of nuclear policy," said one humorist, "in this election Barry Goldwater has a good chance of losing New York . . . Twice." Said David Frost: "What are the principles of Goldwater's new-style conservatism? He's in favor of the United Nations in principle, but against it in practice. He's in favor of foreign aid in principle, but against it in practice. And of course, *everybody's* against the A-bomb in principle. But he's in favor of it in practice."

Goldwater made a striking figure with a bold, youthful charisma. True, there was none of the Kennedy rhetoric or the Johnson folksiness, but his audiences cheered his dashing pronouncements and sweeping condemnations. He infuriated those who disagreed with his simplistic views and sent them scurrying for humor with which to laugh him away, proving Oscar Wilde's epigram that the world laughs at its tragedies— that being the only thing it can do about them.

Whether it was recklessness or mere carelessness, Goldwater's campaign speeches seemed sublimely indifferent to the special interests of his audience. In ignoring this time-honored political practice, Goldwater seemed to display an unconscious death wish. Aides cringed when he attacked the Employment Opportunity Act in an impoverished area in West Virginia. Supporters winced when he assaulted public power in Knoxville, Tennessee, the home of the TVA. Detractors chortled when he proposed that Social Security be made voluntary, addressing this suggestion to the elderly of St. Petersburg. Cracked a headline in the *St. Petersburg Times:* RIGHT CITY, WRONG SPEECH.

In a satiric cartoon of the period, Goldwater is shown addressing a black tie fund-raising dinner. Says the candidate:

"I am touched by this ovation. And I am touched by this turn-out." A member of the audience responds: "I think he's touched." This sort of ridicule was triggered by Goldwater's bizarre views on a variety of subjects. Here are some of the more extreme of his utterances; they are not without their unintentional humor:

"I would turn to my Joint Chiefs of Staff and say, 'Fellows, we made the decision to win [in Vietnam], now it's your problem.'" —Goldwater in *Der Spiegel.*

"It's their baby." —Goldwater referring to segregation in the Southern states—as quoted in the *New York Herald Tribune.*

"We are told, however, that many people lack skills and cannot get jobs because they did not have an education. That's like saying that people have big feet because they wear big shoes."

"Like a three dollar bill—it's a phony." —Goldwater, on the Civil Rights Act, as quoted in *Time.*

"One Eisenhower in a generation is enough." —Goldwater, as quoted in *Time.*

"I have always favored withdrawing recognition from Russia." —Goldwater, in an interview with *U.S. News & World Report.*

"Where fraternities are not allowed, communism flourishes." —Goldwater, in a speech before The National Interfraternity Conference in Los Angeles.

"There is no way to enforce civil rights." —Goldwater, as quoted in the *Boston Globe.*

Goldwater's comments about the "phony" Civil Rights Act which, in his judgment, could not be enforced, led many black voters to feel threatened by his candidacy. One black delegate at the GOP convention slumped dolefully in his seat, intimidated by the bobbing sea of Goldwater posters. A reporter asked him what he had against Goldwater. "Nothing," grimaced the black man. "Ask him what he has against me." Said a columnist for the *New Republic*: "A foreigner traveling with Barry Goldwater in the south wouldn't know there were any blacks in it. They seem to have withdrawn from the main streets. . . . He tells reporters that 'states' rights have superceded civil rights' so there is no use bothering with them. . . . The issue is everywhere, it intrudes on everybody's thoughts, but it's like sex—it isn't mentioned."

Marvin Kitman, whose delicious satire enlivened many publications from *Harper's* to the *Saturday Evening Post*, wrote a memoir about his own mock campaign for the presidency in 1964 in a book called *The Number-One Best Seller*. Viewing the sorry state of GOP moderates in general and Goldwater's position on civil rights in particular, Kitman issued a press release, which said in part:

Leonia, N.J.—Marvin Kitman, a 34-year-old gagwriter, announced today he is planning to enter the New Hampshire Presidential primary. "I would rather be President than write," Mr. Kitman said. . . .

Mr. Kitman said he had decided to come to the aid of his party at this time to give the Republican voters a choice instead of an echo. "Rockefeller, Romney, Lodge, Stassen, Nixon, Scranton and Mrs. Smith are Franklin Roosevelt Republicans. Goldwater is a McKinley Republican. As a Lincoln Republican, I am the only reactionary in the race."

"My branch of conservatism really goes back 100 years," he added. "I will be running on the Republican Party's platform of 1864, so many of whose promises to the voters have yet to be fulfilled. I'm in favor of abolishing slavery."

Barry Goldwater ran a campaign aimed at reducing government spending, and this produced such sardonic lines as: "Goldwater in '64, Hot Water in '65, Bread and Water in '66." His slogan, which called to America from billboards and TV screens, was: "In your heart you know he's right." This produced antic variations such as: "In your heart you know he's *far* right," and the more abrasive, "In your guts you know he's nuts." Other allusions to Goldwater's position on the political spectrum were, "He'd rather be far right than President," and "He's slightly to the right of Atilla the Hun."

Despite Goldwater's extreme utterances—or because of them—he could on occasion be quite amusing. During the Los Angeles primary, as he watched the returns pouring in to give him a resounding victory, he pointed at liberal CBS correspondent Eric Sevareid. "Look at that," he shouted. "Sevareid's thinking of seven hundred reasons why this can't be happening. Eric's womb is dropping."

Goldwater's choice of a running mate produced its own peculiar levity. The unusual selection was Republican congressman William Miller, a hack politician and graduate of the House Un-American Activities Committee. Skeptics observed that in fourteen years in Congress, Miller had never managed to get a major bill named after him. His principal legislative achievement was a bill to incorporate the "Moms of America." But now it was Miller Time. Asked the reason for his improbable selection, Barry Goldwater said, "One of the reasons I chose Miller is that he drives Johnson nuts."

William Miller's vice presidential candidacy brought the sour smell of sarcasm to Goldwater's campaign (as Bob Dole had done for Gerald Ford and Richard Nixon for Dwight Eisenhower). Miller gleefully mocked the middle name of his Democratic counterpart, referring to him as "Hubert Hor-ay-ti-o Humphrey." Humphrey put the obscure congressman in his place by responding: "He thinks he has a real issue in my middle name . . . I must warn him of the hidden-middle-name vote—all those youngsters blessed with a middle name they choose to convert to an initial—may rise against him." Then, with a mischievous grin, Humphrey added, "Miller should beware of the midlash."

As the campaign progressed, allegations of corruption thickened around William Miller. Accusations of conflicts of interest covered a wide area. Said a TW3 correspondent:

> Perhaps some people don't realize how fully and convincingly Mr. Miller has answered these charges. The first allegation revealed that Miller has been serving as a director and counsel of the Lockport Felt Company at an annual retainer of $7500. During the period, the Congressional Record reveals that twice on the floor of the House he spoke against legislation that would have hurt his firm, without revealing his interest. Mr.

Miller conceded that he had collected the annual retainer. Then Mr. Miller gave us a very full and complete explanation. These are his words:

MILLER. I will not be diverted into a waste of time required to answer sleazy unsubstantiated smears.

TW3. Uh-huh.

MILLER. These are left-handed attempts to embarrass me.

TW3. Yes, yes, go on.

MILLER. I will waste no further time in the rebuttal.

Herblock, who has been called "the best of our political cartoonists, not excluding Thomas Nast," brought his biting wit to bear on the Goldwater campaign. In dismissing the black vote, Goldwater had said, "We're not going to get the Negro vote as a bloc . . . so we ought to go hunting where the ducks are." Herblock responded by picturing a dismayed GOP elephant, wearing a necklace of dead albatrosses labeled: WHITE SUPREMACY VOTES—LOUISIANA, MISSISSIPPI, ALABAMA, GEORGIA, SOUTH CAROLINA. The elephant is moaning, "I met a fellow who took me hunting where the albatrosses were." When former president Eisenhower suppressed his doubts about Goldwater long enough to televise a thiry-minute conversation with the candidate for TV use, Herblock pictured the two men leaning on a fence at Ike's Gettysburg ranch. Ike is saying: "Criticism of you is tommyrot, Barry! Naturally you don't mean all those dopey things you've said." On the twentieth anniversary of D-day, Herblock needled Ike for his cautious posture in the Goldwater affair. The former president had declared he would not take part in any effort to deny Goldwater the nomination, whatever his misgivings. Herblock pictured Ike as an apprehensive old man seated before a poster showing a beaming young Ike reviewing his D-day troops. The enfeebled Ike is on the phone, saying "On second thought, forget it. I won't be a part of a cabal to stop anybody." Asked Herblock: "Is this the man who launched 1000 ships?"

Eisenhower's unwillingness to condemn Goldwater was roundly ridiculed by the nation's wits. When his cordial colloquy with Goldwater was broadcast on NBC, preempting TW3, a viewer wrote the show: "What an inspired idea, for TW3 to present those two aging comedians." When it was reported that Ike would serve as a news analyst for ABC at the Republican convention, a reporter cracked, "The only limitation Ike placed on the deal is he won't endorse any candidate, he won't criticize any candidate, and he won't identify the network." A pair of early morning radio cutups in San Francisco produced this exchange:

> "I hear Ike can't involve himself in the campaign because he's working on a book."
> "Oh? What's he reading?"

Goldwater's critics could not understand the zealots who heaped praise and adulation on the candidate. The positions taken in his writings seemed too extreme, too extraordinary. Goldwater seemed wedded to another century; he was too far right. He questioned the need for Social Security. He refused to recognize Red China. He labeled liberals "socialists" and worse. He accepted the endorsement of the John Birch Society. Yet, surprisingly, Goldwater's supporters were numerous and vocal.

Goldwater had even captured the support of various groups on American campuses, and this phenomenon produced one of the wittier attacks on Goldwater and his philosophy. Julius Monk was the elegant creator of a series of topical entertainments at Plaza 9, a little theater at New York's Plaza Hotel. In 1964 Monk produced a review called "Dime a Dozen" that featured a song dedicated to the college students who embraced Goldwater's views. The song was called "Barry's Boys" and was written by June Reizner. In the space of three minutes and two choruses, Ms. Reizner managed to enumerate and comically demolish most of Goldwater's excesses. Here is a sampling of the coruscating lyrics:

We're the bright young men
Who wanta go back to 1910
We're Barry's Boys.
We're the kids with a cause
A government like grandmama's
We're Barry's boys . . .

We're the kids who agree
To be social without security
We're Barry's Boys.
Because his hat's in the ring
Where Westbrook Pegler once was king—
Now he's too left wing—
So if you don't recognize any old Red China
Or Canada, or Britain
Or South Carolina . . .
Back to Barry—back to cash and carry—
Back with Barry's Boys . . .

Roses are red, violets are blue
Walter Lippmann's a pinko too . . .
Barry Barry make your bid,
I love John Birch but oh you kid . . .
Mother mother wear a grin
And don't complain or we'll turn you in . . .

And really what's so wrong with being young and wealthy
And really when you're aged must you all be healthy?

So let's go back to the days when men were men
And start the First World War all over again . . .
Back with Barry's Boys.

Goldwater's ability to draw to his conservative colors large numbers of collegians is less surprising than the large number of senior citizens who were attracted to his credos, since Goldwater's position on Medicare and Social Security was clearly hostile to their self-interest. I addressed the irony of this seeming contradiction in a sketch written for the pilot of "That Was the Week That Was." (Broadway producer Leland Hayward had imported the audacious show from Britain where a group of precocious young Brits had created the impudent series. Hayward was producing the American counterpart on NBC.) In my Goldwater sketch, a talented comedienne named Doro Morande played an aged scrubwoman working in the Senate Office Building. We see her scrubbing the floors of Barry Goldwater's office, and she tells us of her reverence for the man—how she lovingly polished his rolltop desk and quill pen. The enfeebled old girl proudly declares that she has just resigned from Social Security. "Those social welfare programs destroy individual initiative," she says. Sketches like this led the GOP to preempt TW3 frequently through the fall election campaign, though it is my recollection that we were equally rough on the Johnson persona and policies.

One of the men who wrote with elegance of the Goldwater campaign was Richard Rovere, author of the "Letters from Washington" in the *New Yorker*. Rovere wrote with such clarity that to read a page of his prose was like examining a tray of diamonds. Rovere composed a slim volume about the campaign which he called *The Goldwater Caper*, capturing in the title the quirky qualities of the candidate's campaign. Rovere set the tone of the book by reproducing in its preface an ad whose copy exemplified the mind-set of Goldwater's supporters. The advertisement read:

BE THE FIRST IN YOUR PRECINCT TO OWN
A BARRY GOLDWATER SWEATSHIRT

You'll delight in watching liberals recoil in terror when they see you in your BARRY GOLDWATER SWEATSHIRT. You'll find your BGSS imbues you with renewed courage to suffer the slings and arrows of the extremist lunatic fringes of the ultra-left.

The Barry Goldwater Sweatshirt displays a nearly lifelike head of Barry Goldwater, with his name below to identify him to uninitiated liberals. . . .

The frequent preemption of TW3 freed me to travel as aide and resident humorist for Bobby Kennedy, who was seeking a seat in the U.S. Senate. I observed that Bobby, like many other Democrats that year, was running not so much against his opponent (a benign moderate Republican named Kenneth

Keating) but against Barry Goldwater. Bobby employed humor to mock Goldwater, winning him laughter and votes. In Syracuse Bobby invoked the name of Washington Irving, whose classic "The Legend of Sleepy Hollow" was well known to the populace. Quipped Bobby: "This community produced Rip Van Winkle, who went to sleep and woke up in another century. The only other city that can make such a claim is Phoenix, Arizona." When Bobby's airport speech in Buffalo was interrupted by the roar of a jet screaming off overhead, Bobby looked skyward and deadpanned, "He's heading back to Arizona to report."

Goldwater was soundly defeated, and the *New Republic's* TRB observed wryly that "Lyndon Johnson is the first man in history to be elected for defending the twentieth century." Goldwater's repudiation at the polls reflected the public's inability to accept his primitive political views. After his election defeat, the exhausted candidate vacationed on a Caribbean island. One comic quipped: "I understand that a TV company is filming a new 'Tarzan' series on the same island. So this week the air was filled with the cries of a man swinging from the trees on vines. However, this did not interfere with the work of the film company."

Goldwater's defeat was so stunning—he carried down with him a battalion of candidates for the Senate and state Houses—that many feared for the future of the Republican party. This question was pondered by all the leading members of the GOP. But the question of how to rebuild the Republican party in Goldwater's wake seemed too important a matter to leave to politicians alone. For this reason, TW3 conducted a poll—fictitious, of course—of leaders in other fields on the question: "What is the best way to rebuild the Republican party?"

Said Sammy Davis, Jr.: "If the Republican Party's going to start making it again, they'll have to get back on good terms with my people. And the blacks, too."

Said Leonid Brezhnev: "Of course, coming to power in the Soviet union is a little different. In the Soviet Union we have only one party . . . Well, maybe it's not so different."

Said Roy Cohn: "If the Republican Party is to become a major force again, it will need some tough hard-hitting issues. Now, I hold in my hand the names of 157 Communists . . ."

Said Max Factor: "What the cause of Republicanism needs is a creamy, more liberal complexion, with just a touch of pink."

Said Tennessee Williams: "What the Republican party needs is the sort of things I write about—alcoholism, dope addiction, and sexual promiscuity."
Q. "Will that help the party?"
A. "It usually does."

Chapter 18
Campaign 1960
The Return to Humor

I don't think that either candidate will win.
—MORT SAHL

In 1963 there would be "That Was the Week That Was" to comment satirically on the nation's politicians. In 1965 "Laugh-In" would appear with its frenetic barbs on the social and political scene. In 1967 "The Smothers Brothers Comedy Hour" would arrive with its rebellious gibes at the White House, politicians, and Pentagon. In 1975 "Saturday Night Live" would carry the comic invasion of politics further inland, making it almost subversive. But in the election year of 1960, political humor was sorely limited in the mass media. Curious to report, the most sparkling source of humor in that tumultuous, hard-fought election was one of the candidates, a lean Bostonian named John F. Kennedy.

Mort Sahl had long observed that politicians are a more reliable source of political humor "than the people we pay to amuse us." He cited Adlai Stevenson's witty way with words. Sahl quoted many of Stevenson's mots in his campus appearances, and he also cited those of John F. Kennedy, whose wit has since become legendary.

As Kennedy and Nixon joined in electoral battle that fall of 1960, there was a dearth of political humor to add leavening and perspective to the political scene. Playwrights, journalists, and social critics had lamented the paucity of wit during the Eisenhower years. *Time* magazine called the fifties "the silent generation," and it was most certainly silent of laughter. T. S. Eliot said our legacy would be "a thousand golf balls." And Eric Goldman gave the fifties decade a chilly farewell kiss when he wrote, "Goodbye to the fifties—and good riddance." The comics and historians alike lamented the absence of humor. It was, said Goldman, "a heavy, humorless, sanctimonious, stultifying atmosphere, singularly lacking in the self-mockery that is self-criticism." When someone challenged Mort Sahl to say something funny, he replied, "John Foster Dulles." If Ike's dour secretary of state was a sample of fifties fun, it reflected badly on the level of humor. The Eisenhower years had produced a morose self-satisfaction that was the very antithesis of humor. "Where are the guffaws in this country?" asked Eric Goldman. "Where is the purifying wit and humor? The catharsis of caricature? The outcries against all this nonsense? Sometimes I think we are just boring ourselves to death."

The boredom would cease with the arrival on the national scene of Senator John F. Kennedy and his race for the presidency. For reasons based on both personality and strategy, Kennedy injected a healthy dose of humor into his public statements. He liked the company of witty people ("he's careful to keep his wits about him," said one wag), and his chief speech writer kept him supplied with a stream of dry, subtle, pertinent wit, for those occasions when the bubbling Kennedy spontaneity failed him. Such moments were rare. Kennedy's campaign humor was ubiquitous and a part of his personality —it was wry, laconic, and germane. Kennedy told no rambling anecdotes like the presidential candidates who preceded and followed him. There were no pregnant pauses before a punch line, like a political clone of Bob Hope. There was no "I am reminded of the story . . ." to usher in a tiresome plagiarism from some ancient issue of *Reader's Digest*. Kennedy's wit was as educated as he was, and it supplied America with its most cogent humor of the 1960s campaign.

It was a campaign much in need of levity—a solemn procession to an uncertain conclusion with much at stake—for the candidates and the nation. The 1960s struggle was feral in its ferocity. Both Kennedy and Nixon were able campaigners with considerable stamina. Each had a staff of adroit professionals to chart his strategy. The Kennedy-Nixon matchup was the most fascinating presidential campaign in years and triggered the first of a series of provocative histories by Theodore H. White called *The Making of the President*. (In the comedic arena it triggered a series of humorous books called *Who's in Charge Here?* which, like White's histories, continued quadrennially for many years.

Before Jack Kennedy could undertake the bruising campaign against Richard Nixon, he first had to win the nomination from a field of Democrats who also sought the prize. It was a formidable struggle, and political observers could see in it the first signs of the emerging Kennedy wit.

"A primary fight," said Teddy White, "is America's most original contribution to the art of democracy." It is also the process that politicians most despise for its desperation, obsequity, and panic. (In the 1988 campaign, six Republicans and seven Democrats slogged through the quagmires of the primaries, each to the sound of his own uncertain trumpet.) Kennedy moved through this preconvention period with dexterity and humor. One example is particularly illuminating. In the midst of the crucial West Virginia primary, in which Kennedy faced the robust garrulity of Hubert Humphrey, he dispatched a crisis message to his brother Ted, age twenty-eight. Jack's regimen of twenty speeches a day had ravaged his throat; his vocal cords were gone, and he needed a surrogate. Teddy reached his brother's side and dutifully read Jack's speech to a large audience of miners. Here is how Ted recalled it:

> I was saying to the audience, "Do you want a man who will give the country leadership? Do you want a man who has vigor and vision?" when Jack took the microphone and said in a hoarse whisper, "I would just like to tell my brother that you cannot be selected President until you are 35 years of age."

Two of JFK's most formidable opponents in the 1960 primaries were fellow Senator Stuart Symington and Senate

Minority Leader Lyndon Johnson. The latter was particularly daunting, given his long legislative history and messianic ambition to rule. (Said one reporter who covered Johnson's doings in the Senate: "I once passed him on the Capitol steps and said, 'Lovely morning,' and Lyndon said, 'Thank you.'") Kennedy employed humor to puncture Johnson's pomposities. He told a press audience:

> I dreamed about the 1960 campaign the other night, and I told Stuart Symington and Lyndon Johnson about it in the cloakroom yesterday. I told them how the Lord came into my bedroom, anointed my head and said, "John Kennedy, I hereby anoint you President of the United States." Stu Symington said, "That's strange, Jack, because I too had a similar dream last night, in which the Lord anointed me and declared me President of the United States." And Lyndon Johnson said, "That's very interesting, gentlemen, because I *too* had a similar dream last night—and I don't remember anointing either one of you."

A less confident public man might have felt intimidated by the assembly of rivals for the Democratic nomination. Kennedy merely joked at their great number. Said JFK: "I understand there was a survey in which they asked each U.S. Senator about his preference for the Presidency—and ninety-six Senators each received one vote."

Reflecting on the internal battles being waged for power and leadership in the Democratic party, Kennedy remarked that all the infighting had "succeeded in splitting our party right down the middle—and that gives us more unity than we've had in twenty years."

When Kennedy took to the primary trail, he left behind a pregnant wife and a toddler daughter, Caroline. His schedule was so demanding that his days at home were few. Caroline was caught up in her father's pursuit of the nomination. Cracked Kennedy: "Caroline's first words were 'plane,' 'goodbye,' and 'New Hampshire.' And she recently learned to say 'Wisconsin' and 'West Virginia.' Any day now she is expected to come out with 'Oregon.'" (With the proliferation of primaries since 1960, the young daughter of one of today's candidates would develop a splendid sense of geography.)

At a primary stop in Oregon, two young women presented Kennedy with a toy donkey for his daughter. Kennedy cracked: "Caroline has the greatest collection of donkeys. She doesn't even know what an elephant looks like. We are going to protect her from that knowledge."

When the Kennedy family plane—"The Caroline"—set down in Wisconsin during Kennedy's primary imbroglio with Hubert Humphrey, JFK kidded the whole frantic primary process: "I am the first of an advancing army," he said. "By next spring the state will look like a college campus telephone booth."

Kennedy mocked the tension that he and Humphrey felt as the primaries ground down to their conclusion. At a New York gathering at which various party notables studded the podium, JFK began his address by saying:

> Senator Humphrey, Mrs. Roosevelt, Senator Lehman, Mayor Wagner, Governor Harriman, Senator Morse . . . You can tell who isn't running for office by that relaxed posture they assume up here. Hubert and I are the only ones on edge.

Kennedy's primary wit was augmented by that of the reporters who covered his efforts. One reporter penned a parody of Cole Porter's "My Heart Belongs to Daddy," in which he ridiculed the wealth of Kennedy's father, which was financing his son's campaign—purchasing a comfortable aircraft for Jack's travels so he need not depend on the vagaries of commercial airlines. The lyrics also paid dubious tribute to Bobby Kennedy, Jack's feisty kid brother, who was acting as his campaign manager. The lyrics went:

> I'll have a ball and votes this fall
> Will crown this Bostonian laddy.
> Then I will run for the top-most gun—
> And I learned it all from daddy.
> Now some hob-nob with Brother Bob,
> The boy who drove old Dave Beck batty.
> But Bob will chime that it ain't no crime
> For to take our cue from daddy . . .
> So don't try to beat this laddy,

Though your aim be perfectly swell.
For I send the bill to daddy,
'Cause my daddy he pays it so well.

Kennedy laughed away the healthy infusion of funds that Ambassador Kennedy pumped into his primary campaign —for advertising, staff, salaries, and transportation. He even managed to make light of the underground slurs to the effect that Old Joe Kennedy was actually purchasing votes. Kennedy produced a telegram that he always carried as a prop, waved it in the air, and said, "I have just received this wire from my father. It says 'Don't buy one vote more than is necessary—I'll be damned if I'll pay for a landslide.'"

Once the presidential conventions do their work—with their heroes and fools, their chaos and revelries, their climactic triumphs and humbling failures—then the people must choose. The campaign that follows, from Labor Day to Election Day, is a primitive and barbaric rite. Given the pressures at work on the candidate (and on the staff and media that surround him), it is impossible to sustain the sleepless pace without the saving grace of humor.

So many things must be done within that limited time frame, with not enough hours or money or people to do them. Tens of thousands must be provoked to register; voters must be pushed from apathy to commitment; television must be employed with cunning; rallies must be staged, and speeches written and delivered with conviction.

"To chronicle these campaigns is like packaging fog," wrote Teddy White. But some men try to package it anyway, and they are the polltakers whose measurements and projections often produce as much levity as light. In retrospect, the pronouncements of the 1960 pollsters seem funnier than those of Will Rogers. Ernest Dichter, oracular president of the Institute of Motivational Research, conducted a survey on the image of the two candidates to determine which of them projected the image of a winner. Proclaimed Dichter, "People have been fooled by the father image. Roosevelt died, Ike got dimmer. . . . As a result voters are settling for a brother and son image." [Kennedy was forty-three, Nixon forty-seven.]

"Kennedy is the smoother of the two and that will undo him. He is slick, too perfect, too good-looking. . . ." (One remembers the exchange in an early Neil Simon comedy where a wife rages at her husband: "You dress right, you talk right, you're practically perfect!" and he replies, "That's a rotten thing to say.") As for Richard Nixon, Dichter declared, "He is hard angles, like a triangle." Faced with this sweeping deprecation of both candidates, Mort Sahl dourly predicted, "Neither of the candidates is going to win."

One network commentator observed that "neither candidate has a sense of humor." This reflected a startling degree of opacity. Nixon was certainly a humorless man; his mind-set was bitter and his Quaker parents had not raised him to take the world lightly. But Kennedy was the wittiest man to seek the presidency since, well, Adlai Stevenson four years before. But where Stevenson's humor had about it a whiff of arrogance—"he did not suffer fools gladly," said Hugh Sidey— Kennedy's humor reflected a sparkling personality that propelled him like a comet to the zenith of political authority and public affection.

The network expert who saw no sense of humor in either Nixon or Kennedy was not alone. Many jaded observers in 1960 saw the duo as two peas in a pod—two cool, calculating young politicians deserving neither allegiance nor power.

The matter that was most menacing to Jack Kennedy in the 1960 campaign and which, paradoxically, provided much of its humor, was neatly labeled "the religious issue." That innocent sounding appelation covered an ugly undercurrent of bias. The last time a Roman Catholic had sought the presidency—Governor Al Smith of New York in the twenties—it had produced a mocking joke in which Smith was supposed to have sent a one-word telegram to the Pope saying: "Pack!" Kennedy faced a numbing assault from the forces of the Protestant clergy. The Reverend Dr. Norman Vincent Peale joined 150 Protestant ministers and laymen in issuing a statement: "It is inconceivable that a Roman Catholic President would not be under extreme pressure by the hierarchy of his church to accede to its policies."

Kennedy responded with exquisite humor to slip the punch. He said that reporters were constantly asking him about the Pope's infallibility, and he said, he had gone to his friend Cardinal Spellman to ask how he should respond when newsmen asked him if this were true. Spellman's answer: "I don't know what to tell you, Senator. All I know is he keeps calling me Spillman."

Kennedy's Catholicism was a telling issue. It was difficult for the candidate, so skilled in the quantitative arts, to compute the emotional factor into his plans. It seemed to defy logic and analysis. Kennedy had once reflected that there were only three things that were real—God, human folly, and laughter. "Since the first two are beyond our comprehension," he said, "we will have to make the most of the third." Since the question of religion was beyond the comprehension of his pollsters, Kennedy would have to deal with it with laughter.

Norman Vincent Peale was JFK's chief adversary on the religious issue. He was best known as the author of an inspirational best-seller. So, on the heels of Dr. Peale's attack, Kennedy gibed: "We had an interesting convention in Los Angeles and ended with a strong Democratic platform which we called 'The Rights of Man.' The Republican platform has also been presented. I do not know its title but it has been referred to as 'The Power of Positive Thinking.'"

Responding to another Peale attack, Kennedy wryly declared: "Last week a noted clergyman was quoted as saying that our society may survive in the event of my election, but it certainly won't be what it was. I would like to think he was complimenting me, but I'm not sure he was."

When the drumfire of questions about Kennedy's allegiance to the Vatican continued, the candidate cracked to the press: "Now I understand why Henry the Eighth set up his own church." Campaigning in Iowa, he found himself on a ticket that bore the names O'Brien, McManus, and Kennedy. Said the candidate: "You really run a well-balanced ticket out here." Then, when the laughter subsided, JFK said, "Well, I hope you elect Congressman O'Brien, and I don't hold his name against him."

The "dirty tricks" that were a part of the Watergate scandal and that replicated similar flummery during the Johnson years, made their appearance, albeit in a more subtle form, when John Kennedy was invited to attend the Alfred E. Smith Dinner, a tribute to the late New York governor whose religion denied him the White House. The dinner, which was presided over by the senior prelate of the Catholic church in New York, Cardinal Spellman, seemed calculated to focus attention on Kennedy's religion just when the issue seemed to be in remission. Kennedy was at first wary about accepting the invitation to this strictly religious affair, fearing it would accentuate the Catholic issue. But then, at the eleventh hour, he decided to do what the Kennedys do so well—turn lemons into lemonade. Kennedy accepted the loaded invitation and delivered the wittiest, most sparkling speech of his campaign. As an example of campaign humor, crafted to ridicule an opponent, defuse an issue, and thoroughly entertain, Kennedy's Al Smith speech was an exemplar of the breed. He said:

> I am glad to be here at this notable dinner once again, and I am glad that Mr. Nixon is here also. Now that Cardinal Spellman has demonstrated the proper spirit, I assume that shortly I will be invited to a Quakers dinner honoring Herbert Hoover. [Laughter]
>
> Cardinal Spellman is the only man so widely respected in American politics that he could bring together amicably at the same banquet table, for the first time in this campaign, two political leaders who are increasingly apprehensive about the November election—who have long eyed each other suspiciously and who have disagreed so strongly both publicly and privately—Vice President Nixon and Governor Rockefeller. [Laughter]
>
> But I think the worst news for the Republicans this week was that Casey Stengel has been fired. It must show that perhaps experience does not count. [Laughter and applause]
>
> On this matter of experience, I had announced earlier this year that if successful I would not consider campaign contributions as a substitute for experience in appointing ambassadors. Ever since I made that statement, I have not received one single cent from my father.
>
> One of the inspiring notes that was struck in the last TV debate was struck by Mr. Nixon in his very moving warning to the children of the nation and the candidates against the use of profanity by presidents and ex-presidents when they are on the stump. And I know after fourteen years in the Congress with

the Vice President that he was very sincere in his views about the use of profanity.But I am told that a prominent Republican said to him yesterday in Jacksonville, Florida, "Mr. Vice President, that was a damn fine speech," and the Vice President said, "I appreciate the compliment but not the language." And the Republican went on, "Yessir, I liked it so much that I contributed a thousand dollars to your campaign." And Mr. Nixon replied, "The hell you say." [Laughter and applause]

However, I would not want to give the impression that I am taking former President Truman's use of language lightly. I have just sent him the following note: "Dear Mr. President: I have noted with interest your suggestion as to where those who vote for my opponent should go. While I understand and sympathize with your deep motivation, I think it is important that our side try to refrain from raising the religious issue. [Laughter and applause]

Reporters are a witty, rowdy bunch. Their humor can be ribald, piercing, wounding, iconoclastic, and uproarious. This may account for the relish with which journalists accepted assignment to the Kennedy campaign trail, and the stoicism of those who were assigned to travel with Nixon. The contrast between the jollity of the former and solemnity of the latter cannot be exaggerated. Kennedy, as a former reporter himself, felt a kinship with the newsmen who covered him. He often asked their advice on campaign tactics and respected their acumen. His regard for their sense of humor was also reciprocated. One of the central reasons reporters enjoyed the turmoil, wolfed sandwiches, and truncated sleep of the Kennedy campaign over similar indignities in Nixon's was that Kennedy was a vastly amusing man. His speeches were encrusted with gems of humor. The humor was topical, tasteful, and relevant. It was pointed, irreverent, and original, and it was generally subtle and self-belittling, a reflection of Kennedy's personality and private wit.

Two of the most prolific sources of humor in the Kennedy-Nixon race were not Mort Sahl and Mark Russell. They were two lesser known men—Joseph Kraft and John Bartlow Martin, a pair of journalists who handled "editorial advance" for Kennedy. That esoteric phrase meant the pair would precede Kennedy on the stump, scour the local scene, and, on his arrival, provide the candidate with humorous lines for his numberless speeches. Ted Sorensen and Dick Goodwin were Kennedy's master speech writers, the source of "the glory of words" that swept the candidate into the White House on a surge of political poetry. But Kraft and Martin supplied the relevant local humor that established an immediate rapport between JFK and his audiences. For a political rally in Rochester, New York, Kraft had given the candidate a pertinent story with which to preface his regular campaign speech. Said JFK:

> I am informed by someone with a long memory that when another presidential candidate, Mr. Thomas Dewey, came here to Rochester in 1948, he said, "It is good to be back in Syracuse." He didn't know where he was going or where he was—and I don't think the Republicans do today.

In Modesto, California, the candidate had a witty opening for his remarks provided him by the Kraft-Martin team. He said to the crowd that greeted his campaign train,

> Today we celebrate the one hundred and tenth anniversary of the admission of the State of California to the union. It seems to me that the great story of California has come about because people were not satisfied with things as they were. They liked Massachusetts and they liked Ohio and they liked Oklahoma, but they thought they could do better in California. [a pause] I don't know why they felt that way about Massachusetts.

Kraft and Martin supplied Kennedy with a repertoire of relevant jokes for his travels through the state of Texas. One of these, which had the effect of tickling the Texas vanity in a self-deprecating mode, was this:

> You remember the old story about a citizen of Boston who is visiting the Alamo and hears a Texan talking about the glories of Bowie, Davy Crocket, and the rest, and finally said, "Haven't you heard of Paul Revere?" to which the Texan replied, "Well, he's the man who ran for help."

Some of the wittiest—if scathing—humor in an election campaign is produced by the voters themselves. *Newsweek* opened a floodgate of wit and malice when it invited readers to write their views on the two candidates and printed them in a special part of its Letters section, called "Taking Sides." Here are some of the caustic comments they elicited:

From Phoenix: "While Nixon talks to us about God, Kennedy talks to God about us."

From Seattle: "Thank heavens we are not electing a president for warmth, personality or charm. Kennedy should run for President of Charm, Inc."

From Akron: "Kennedy's New Frontier is just a socialist baby buggy he wants us to climb into."

From Iowa City, Iowa, came a letter kidding Kennedy's Bostonian accent: "I am quite agreed we need a national leadership with 'vigah.' The last time was with FDR."

From Dracut, Massachusetts: "Why does Mr. Kennedy always refer to the accomplishments of former Democratic Presidents? His campaign motto should be the Lost Frontier, not The New Frontier."

On election night, as the votes poured in from all over the republic, the cool, dry wit of the candidate did not desert him. As Kennedy's aides and family waited apprehensively at the TV sets, JFK took a phone call from his running mate in Texas. When Kennedy hung up the receiver, he turned to his friends and said, "That was Lyndon. He said 'I hear *you're* losing Ohio but *we're* doing fine in Pennsylvania.' "

When the grueling campaign was over and Kennedy knew he had captured the prize, he and his family adjourned to the lawn of his Hyannisport home for a game of touch football. Kennedy quarterbacked one team, his brother Bobby the other. Bobby's ebullient wife Ethel was thrilled at the outcome of the election. Said Bobby slyly: "I couldn't have done it without my brother." The Secret Service men who took up their position on the dune grass, watched uneasily as the president was assailed from all sides and went down under a pile of bodies. When Jack Kennedy dived to catch an overthrown pass and landed on his face, Bobby chuckled, "That's my brother, all guts, no brains."

Now it was over. After the rhetoric and humor, the rallies and jumpers, the hope turning to doubt and then to certainty. "Kennedy had run all the way and brilliantly," as Teddy White said. The margin of votes was razor-thin. The people had made their decision, and Jack Kennedy was the president. Never before in the century had the margin of popular votes been so slim. JFK would joke about it on a visit to Chicago early in his presidency:

> Some years ago, in the city of Fall River, Massachusetts, the Mayor was elected by one vote, and every time he went down the street, everyone would come up to him and say, "Say, Dan, I put you in office." And I feel a little like that in Chicago tonight. If all of you had voted the other way—there's about fifty-five hundred of you here tonight—I wouldn't be President of the United States."

With the coming of JFK to the White House and the arrival of the Kennedy clan in Washington, the political climate for humor changed markedly for the better. Suddenly political humor ended its long hibernation and made its appearance in nightclubs, coffeehouses, books, and record albums. The campaign of 1960 had given us a frankly witty president. Humor and whimsy had risen Phoenix-like, and it was no longer subversive to kid the president of the United States.

Chapter 19
Campaign 1960
The Day the Pony Died

There are no funny stories about Richard Nixon.
—ROSE MARY WOODS

Library shelves groan under the weight of satirical books ridiculing Richard Nixon. Philip Roth abandoned his series of novels on the Jewish-American experience long enough to write *Our Gang*, a send-up of the Nixon crowd. Gore Vidal took a sabbatical from his historical novels and elegant essays to write *An Evening With Richard Nixon*, a sardonic indictment using Nixon's own words. Vidal's political play, "The Best Man," was a thinly veiled satire of a convention battle between Nixon and Adlai Stevenson. My own *Who's In Charge Here?* books would be far duller without the quivering jowls of Richard Nixon. And John Osborne has compiled a series of wise and witty books from his reports for the *New Republic* on the Nixon years. Mockery of Richard Nixon also enriches the collected works of columnist Art Buchwald and cartoonists Herblock and Jules Feiffer.

Why has Nixon seemed such an irresistible target to America's satirists? It is for a reason that was seldom discussed in 1960, when Nixon ran as the odds-on favorite against an obscure Massachusetts senator, and that is the widespread distrust of Richard M. Nixon. In such a narrowly decided race, that amorphous ingredient of distrust was, as much as any other, the decisive one.

Politicians are not notable for their ability to generate trust. Yet, even by this waist-high criterion, Richard Nixon fell well below the mean. There was something in his mien and much in his history to support suspicions of his guile. Though other politicians were attentive to the results of polls, many observers felt that Nixon molded his words and acts more closely to the pollster's findings than was altogether healthy. Students of Nixonian oratory observed a sanctimony that raised hackles. He was heavy-handed in his name-dropping, protesting too much about his contact with world leaders. He was too ready to accuse an opponent of treason. He was uxorious in invoking his wife's name. He misstated an adversary's words and then indicted him for them. All these toxic tendencies provoked distrust; they also provoked humor.

Nixon had been ridiculed before, of course, when he ran for Congress, the Senate, and the Vice Presidency. His famous Checkers speech during the latter race was a favorite target for America's wags, for its maudlin tone and manipulative manner. But it was not until he sought the presidency in 1960 that he really mounted the humorists' bull's-eye.

The *New Republic*, that well-regarded publication whose influence far exceeds its circulation, has always been adroit in its insights and assaults on wayward politicians. During the Nixon-Kennedy campaign, it presented what it called "THE ALL-PURPOSE NIXON SPEECH," portions of which are excerpted below. In it, the magazine twitted most of Nixon's rhetorical excesses, the trivial and the wretched. The *New Republic* began by running a needle through Nixon's devotion to public relations. Said the editors:

NOTE: This universal, all-purpose speech was prepared for Vice President Nixon by a pool of public relations and advertising men who pretested each sentence in a sample of 100 cities between the population of 15,000 and 75,000. The image-meter indicated a favorable response among those Americans between 35 and 70 with an average income of $6,500, and with 1.2 barbecue pits per family.

My fellow Americans, it is good to return to _____, a town that Lincoln loved. In Washington we sometimes forget that in this nation of families, the hearth is in the cities like this, and only the chimney—with a little Democratic smoke—is in the Capital. [Pause for restrained laughter; Charlie will start]

But Chancellor Adenauer does not forget. I last saw the Chancellor shortly after I left Russia, where I had the honor of representing President Eisenhower. . . .

Chancellor Adenauer said to me: "Mr. Vice President, don't ever forget that when you saw Mr. Khrushchev you saw a man who has contempt for the little people. . . .

I am betting that the American people will turn their backs on a party that seems to share Mr. Khrushchev's contempt for little people. The Democrat Party [swallow "ic"] seems to think it can prove Abraham Lincoln wrong in saying you can't fool all the people all the time. But the party that forgot Jefferson, I pray, will not turn the people against the party that remembers Lincoln. [throb in voice]

We've got work to do, Americans! Those that love America . . . they are working day and night. The Democrats, who say they love America but who seem to think we should apologize to the man who hates America worst—they are working hard. Can I count on you to work harder? [Wait for roars of "Yes" to be started by Lew and Eddie]

Another quality that produced abundant humor during the campaign, particularly among the reporters who covered Nixon, was his capacity for self-pity. A campaign stop in Danville, Illinois, demonstrated that quality and the humor it provoked. Nixon was speaking, in a solemn, introspective tone, of his mother. It was a morose rhetoric that was replicated by Nixon on the day he resigned the presidency in disgrace. In Danville he said:

I remember my mother used to get up at five o'clock every morning in our little country grocery store to bake pies so that I and my five brothers could get the education my father didn't have. My father came from Ohio, and his mother died when he was quite young. Consequently, he went to work and he only got a sixth-grade education. . . . So they got up early in the morning and she baked pies, while my dad was going over to the market to get vegetables and put them in the store."

Later that day in Centralia, Illinois, Nixon returned to pick at the scab of nostalgia. He said:

> I remember that when we were growing up, my older brother very desperately wanted a pony. My father could have bought it for about seventy-five dollars and my brother, who died when I was quite young, kept saying, "Oh, I want this pony more than anything in the world. . . ." My mother and my father wanted more than anything else to give him what he wanted. It would have been easy for them to say, "Look, you can have a pony." But, you know what happened? My mother and father had a little family council and they came in and they said, "Now look, if we buy this pony we're not going to have enough money to pay the grocery bill; we're not going to have enough money to pay the clothing bill; we're not going to be able to get the shoes for your younger brother." It was an awful hard decision for my mother and father but it was the right thing.

These two speeches triggered a noisy debate on the press bus. Some reporters wanted to call that day "Maudlin Friday." Others preferred to call it simply, "The Day the Pony Died."

It should be observed that the motto of the reporters who cover presidential candidates is: "If you don't have something nice to say—let's hear it." There is a natural cynicism among correspondents continually exposed to politicians that breeds a corrosive humor. Perhaps it comes from living on the edge of irritability—stumbling off a campaign plane at two in the morning, searching for one's luggage, struggling for a few hours sleep in a strange motel room, loping after the candidate to cover an early morning breakfast. Unless you carry a sense of humor as part of your baggage, it is impossible to survive a presidential campaign. Hence the humor and its abrasive tone.

But if Nixon provoked more than his share of malicious wit from the media, the most pungent anti-Nixon humor originated with his electoral foe, John F. Kennedy. Though Nixon liked and admired Kennedy, the affection was not reciprocal. JFK once cracked to an aide in the privacy of a hotel room: "Do you realize the weight of responsibility I carry? I am the only man standing between Richard Nixon and the White House."

The growing crowds that greeted Kennedy as the campaign wound down acted like a stimulant that supplied a special kind of adrenalin. And the keenest part was the joy of needling Nixon—taunting him with humor. There is a traditional wisdom in politics that says it is reckless to use malice in one's humor. Benign humor is thought to be best. Yet in Campaign 1960, John Kennedy's taunts at Nixon's expense often had about them the whiff of malice. In the era before coffeehouses and satirical TV shows, the most amusing humorous attacks leveled at Nixon were launched from the platform of his adversary. Nixon's attacks on Kennedy were slash-and-hack; Kennedy's attacks on Nixon were more subtle. Nixon used a meat ax, Kennedy a rapier.

With his propensity for overkill, Nixon swung a club at Kennedy, calling him a "barefaced liar." In response, Kennedy pinked Nixon with his rapier. Said JFK:

> Two days ago, Mr. Nixon, in that wonderful choice of words which distinguishes him as a great national leader, asserted that I told a barefaced lie. Having seen him four times close up in this campaign, and made up [in the TV debates], I would not accuse Mr. Nixon of being barefaced.

Kennedy's humor often played off a Nixon insult. When Nixon sneeringly referred to his opponent as "another Truman," he felt the nick of Kennedy's rapier: "I regard that as a high compliment, and I have no hesitation in returning the compliment. I consider Mr. Nixon another Dewey." Nixon's name-calling generally left him with more pain than gain. When Nixon called Kennedy "an economic ignoramus" and "a Pied Piper" (because of the horde of youngsters who followed in his wake), JFK was unfazed. He responded, "Mr. Nixon, in the last seven days, has called me an economic ignoramus, a Pied Piper, and all the rest. I just confine myself to calling him a Republican, but he says that is getting low."

The Republicans had dispatched a "Truth Squad" to follow Kennedy about the country, following each of his speeches with a scathing rebuttal. When the practice was finally abandoned, Kennedy quipped, "I see the Truth Squad has been ditched. They told the truth once and they don't let them travel anymore."

Nixon suffered a lethal blow from an unexpected source, the president he had served so loyally. Asked to what decisions Richard Nixon had contributed during his eight years as vice president, President Eisenhower said he would need a week or so to think of any, and this became fodder for the Kennedy wit. He remarked: "A reporter asked President Eisenhower about a month ago what suggestions and ideas Mr. Nixon has had and the President said, 'Give me a week and I will let you know.'" Nixon protested that Ike was simply joking, but the damage was done.

Kennedy even succeeded in turning hecklers into straight men for his anti-Nixon barbs. When a group of contentious Nixon supporters tried to disrupt a Kennedy rally with a chant of "We want Nixon! We want Nixon!" Kennedy merely smiled and said, "I don't think you're going to get him."

The subtlety of Kennedy's humor at Nixon's expense was such that even when JFK vowed silence about his adversary's flaws, he was able to needle him. Early in the campaign, Nixon was hospitalized, and Kennedy declared a moratorium on criticism while his opponent was out of combat. That produced the following press conference exchange:

Q. Senator, did you say you were not going to discuss the Vice President until he is out of the hospital?

KENNEDY. That's right.

Q. But will you resume?

KENNEDY. Well, we will see what happens. I may discuss some of the Republican shortcomings but not Mr. Nixon's.

Q. You are not going to mention his part in any of them?

KENNEDY. Unless I can praise him.

Q. Do you mean as long as he stays in the hospital he has sanctuary?

KENNEDY. Yes, that's right. [thoughtfully] I may go there myself.

Eight days later Nixon was still in the hospital, and a puckish reporter returned to the subject of Kennedy's restraint in attacking Nixon.

Q. Senator, when does the moratorium end on Nixon's hospitalization and your ability to attack him?

KENNEDY. Well, I said I would not mention him until I could praise him, and I have not mentioned him.

Nixon made much of his meeting with General Secretary Nikita Khrushchev at a kitchen exhibit at a Moscow trade fair. The AP photographer had sent back a picture of Nixon shaking his finger under Khrushchev's nose, and it appeared in newspapers all around the world. Kennedy finessed the photo with a bit of whimsy that suggested Nixon's courage might not have been all it appeared to be. Said JFK:

During my visit to Pittsburgh I had seen pictures of Mr. Khrushchev with Mr. Nixon's finger under his nose. Friday night, after the TV debate, when I went over to shake hands with Mr. Nixon and the photographers appeared, suddenly the finger came up to my nose. I thought, here it comes; he is going to tell me how wrong I am about the plight of America, and do you know what he said? "Senator, I hear you have been getting better crowds than I have in Cleveland."

On another occasion Kennedy said of the Nixon-Khrushchev encounter: "Mr. Nixon may be very experienced in his kitchen debates. So are a great many other married men I know."

But whatever Nixon's success in his debate with the Soviet chairman, his first TV debate with Kennedy left his advocates badly disappointed. The sight of Kennedy and Nixon side by side carried a powerful message. The image conveyed the impression that the experienced Nixon and the upstart Kennedy were actually evenly matched. And the contrast of the cool, calm Kennedy with the tense, haggard Nixon made a telling impression. Kennedy explained the outcome of the first debate with typical grace when he told a Minnesota audience, "This week I had the opportunity to debate with Mr. Nixon. I feel I should reveal that I had a great advantage in that debate. . . . Mr. Nixon had just debated with Khrushchev and I had just debated with Hubert Humphrey, and that gave me the edge."

It is a bit puzzling why Jack Kennedy's witty assaults on Richard Nixon were so much more effective than Adlai Stevenson's witty assaults on Dwight Eisenhower in the previous two elections. Much of the difference lay in the great popular affection for Eisenhower and the latent distrust of Nixon. The latter was *vulnerable* to humor. In addition, the humor that seemed a trifle academic in Stevenson seemed like sparkling personality in Kennedy. Yet, it must be acknowledged that Stevenson made campaign humor respectable, and in the process added an extra string to Kennedy's bow.

Stevenson made a more direct contribution to Kennedy's campaign humor. Given Ike's popularity, JFK was loathe to attack him. And so he attacked the Republican party instead. He tried to show that the two parties had very different goals and, as Theodore White expressed it, "pin the Republican tag on Nixon." Kennedy sought to paint Nixon as the ideological offspring of Harding, Hoover, Coolidge, Landon, and Dewey. In doing this he was offered an effective humorous image by Adlai Stevenson. In the closing days of the Nixon-Kennedy campaign, when a razor-thin plurality separated the two, Nixon came to New York with the heavyweights of the GOP. His campaign was joined by President Eisenhower, Governor Rockefeller, and vice presidential candidate Henry Cabot Lodge. It was then that Stevenson provided Kennedy with an inspired bit of metaphorical humor. In his final series of speeches, JFK tied the GOP label to Nixon as tightly and irrevocably as possible. He said:

> You have seen those elephants in the circus. [laughter] They have their heads of ivory, thick skin, no vision, long memory, and when they move around the ring they grab the tail of the elephant in front of them. [cheers] Well, Dick Nixon grabbed

that tail in 1952 and 1956, but in 1960 he is running, not the President. . . . I stand tonight where Woodrow Wilson stood, and Franklin Roosevelt stood, and Harry Truman stood. [cheers] Dick Nixon stands where McKinley stood and Taft— listen to those candidates [laughter]—Harding [groans] Coolidge [groans] Landon [groans] Dewey [groans]. Where do they get those candidates? [laughter and applause]

Nixon brought a good deal of mockery down on his head with his unctuous celebrations of his wife. A typical invocation of his conjugal mate was delivered to a campaign throng on Long Island. Said Nixon in uxorious excess: "I told you I'd bring Pat out to see you, and here she is. Now I ask you, isn't she wonderful? Wasn't she worth waiting for?" Kennedy, of course, would never think of parading his wife across a political platform. Indeed, it took three weeks of campaigning just to explain Jacqueline's absence, when the candidate said simply, "My wife's home having a baby. We're having a boy in November." When his sister Pat joined him he said shyly, "She is representing my wife who is otherwise committed." Unlike his restrained opponent, Nixon often promoted and praised his wife, triggering a volley of raillery. An impressionist doing the hoarse Nixon basso had the vice president say, "Pat adores me. She always stares at me with those adoring eyes. Frankly, it's giving me the creeps."

In the battle of the 1960 campaign, the humorous front at least was the site of a rout. Kennedy was an elegantly witty man, Nixon a solemn one. Even Nixon's strongest advocates could not claim for him a sense of humor. Said Gerald Warren, Nixon's assistant press secretary: "Nixon's humor was mainly unintentional." In support of this thesis, Warren cited two major events: (1) Nixon attended Charles de Gaulle's funeral in Paris and declared, "This is a great day for France!" (2) Standing astride the Great Wall of China on his epochal China trip, Nixon proclaimed, "This is a great wall."

Books in the Humor in Life and Letters Series